All the
Good Ones
Are Married

All the Good Ones Are Married

Married Men and the Women Who Love Them

By
Marion Zola

Times
BOOKS

To the men and women who
shared their lives in these pages

Special thanks for the permissions to quote the following individuals: Joshua S. Golden, M.D.; Babette Lang, Ph.D.; Jerome Supkoff; Judd Marmor, M.D.; Katherina Marmor, Ph.D.; Alvin Lerner; Paul T. Olsen, Ph.D.; Jorge N. Dubin, M.D.; Deborah Rinzler, Ph.D.; and Sandra Allenberg, M.A.

Second printing, September 1981

Published by TIMES BOOKS, a division
of Quadrangle/The New York Times Book Co., Inc.
Three Park Avenue, New York, N.Y. 10016

Published simultaneously in Canada by
Fitzhenry & Whiteside, Ltd., Toronto

Published in association with Stan Corwin Productions, Ltd.

Library of Congress Cataloging in Publication Data
Zola, Marion.
All the good ones are married.

1. Adultery—United States. 2. Husbands—United
States. 3. Single women—United States. I. Title.
HQ806.Z64 1981   306.7'3   80-5776
        ISBN 0-8129-0967-4   AACR1

Manufactured in the United States of America

Acknowledgments

To Marion Neustadter, Fred Plotkin, and Warren Disraeli, who painstakingly read and commented on the manuscript, I offer my loving appreciation. I also wish to thank Catherine Paura and Helyne Landres for their valuable suggestions. Furthermore, I am grateful to my family for their support and interest and to the professionals who unstintingly gave me their time, counsel and insights: Sandra Allenberg, M.A. Marriage and Family Counselor; George Dubin, M.D.; Jerry Finkel, M.D. Columbia Presbyterian Medical Center; Joshua Golden, M.D. Professor of Psychiatry and Director of the Human Sexuality Program, UCLA; Holly C. Hein, M.S.W.; Babette Lang, Ph.D.; Alvin Lerner; Judd Marmor, M.D. Professor of Psychiatry, U.S.C. (former president of the American Psychoanalytic Association); Katherina Marmor, Ph.D. Co-Director, Group Therapy Program Los Angeles Suicide Prevention Center; Paul Olsen, Ph.D. a Director of the National Institute for the Psychotherapies; Nathan Rickles, M.D.; Deborah Rinzler, Ph.D. and Jerome Supkoff.

More than anyone else, Dr. Katherina Marmor has my particular gratitude for sharing her knowledge with me. The hours during which she read various chapters and explored the subjects in this book in our discussions were an inestimable contribution.

I am also indebted to Stan Corwin (one of the good ones who's not currently married) whose perceptions in shaping this material made the book possible.

Beyond this assistance, I had a devoted editor, Susan Kane, who treated the manuscript as if it were her own.

Contents

Introduction

I WALKED in from a trip to New York, turned on my answering machine, and unpacked. The last message was from Adrienne, a textbook editor, my friend for seven years.

A tiny voice whispered, "Lee is dead." Sobbing followed, and then the click off.

I called Adrienne. She was barely awake. This was the very hour of Lee's funeral. I drove to her apartment. Adrienne's usually clear, expressive eyes were vacant, her face pallid. Still in a nightgown, she had not eaten in two days. We made tea and toast together as she explained, "Lee went home two nights ago to tell his wife he was leaving. Naturally, he was nervous. But I expected that. He kissed me good-bye. I wished him luck. I wanted it to go easily for him."

Adrienne didn't notice that she ripped the side of the wide-sleeved nightgown reaching for the cups and saucers Lee had given her. The tear, and her mechanical movements between cupboards and table, revealed a slack, thin body I remembered as prouder, fuller.

I had known Lee and Adrienne in New York, before any of us had moved west. He was an open-faced, warm man, yet, after being in his presence for one moment, one felt his confidence and command. With Lee's children now in high school and college, he felt the time was right to divorce. His decision followed five years of agonized self-debate.

"I watched him drive away," Adrienne continued, "and had a

strange feeling all night. He was supposed to call me if he left the house immediately and went to a motel. At six-thirty I got a call from Lee's sister. His heart attack came after he started talking to his wife. She called the hospital. By the time they got him there, he was dead."

"Did he actually tell her he was leaving?" I asked.

"Lee was talking about how unhappy they'd both been lately. That was as far as he got." Adrienne's glazed look bespoke her lost dream. For five years, she had struggled against Lee's guilt. She had stayed away when he moved his family west to concentrate on improving life with his wife. For a while, Adrienne dated other men, but finally she had also moved across the country at Lee's request. Happiness, she felt, loomed closer.

Adrienne and Lee met while he was an internist in New York City, specializing in colitis. He had written a medical textbook, which she edited. They both battled their romantic feelings for a year.

Adrienne was Lee's first affair in his eighteen-year marriage. Until they met, his relationship at home had been stagnant; never intimate, but not uncomfortable. An apparently conservative pillar of the community, Lee had spent his scant free time with his children and his work. He buried his loneliness in activity. Adrienne's entrance into his life ignited the usual guilt-versus-happiness conflict married men enmeshed in deep affairs go through.

Lee spent more and more time lecturing away from home. When he moved to the West Coast a few years later, he decided he wanted a divorce. Adrienne moved to Los Angeles and took a lower position and salary. One month after she arrived, Lee's wife became ill. He waited to broach the subject of separation until she was well—another six months. The time to leave miraculously came. Perhaps the emotional strain was too great for him. Maybe another pressure would have produced the same fatal result. Disregarding the advice he gave his own patients, Lee had let his exercise routine slip over the last few years. He was overdue for a physical. An existing heart condition could have gone undetected.

Many factors may have figured into his demise, but that didn't matter much to Adrienne now. Lee was gone.

The day of Lee's funeral came. His best friend phoned Adrienne, asking her not to come: "It would be awkward for everyone." She remained in bed . . . without the consolation of friends or family that Lee's wife had.

Now Adrienne regrets not having had Lee's child. "At least I'd have something of him." Then comes self-recrimination. "If he hadn't decided to get a divorce, maybe he would still be alive. At least I could see him, talk to him."

Adrienne came home with me that night. For the next few days she stayed there, trying but unable to edit manuscripts. I heard her pain every time she spoke.

How many other Adriennes were alone, having gambled years on a married man? I thought of what my friend and Lee's wife had in common—having lost the same man. I wondered how differently that loss would affect their lives.

A week after Lee's funeral, I sat in the steam room in my health club.

"Let's face it. All the good ones are married."

"You said it."

I looked across the wet air at two shapely young women sweating out their frustration. I had used those exact words myself.

"I'd just like to rent him for nights and breakfasts."

"Maybe you could work out a deal with her."

"I'm glad I spent three hours at the gym this week torturing my unused body."

"Yeah, me too. I see Alan for one hour this afternoon and maybe two lunches next week."

"I won't see Brent for ten days. He took his family to Acapulco. I should have asked him if I could use their indoor hot tub while they're away."

"Why is it we get love and the truth from five to seven while the wives get Acapulco and indoor hot tubs?"

I sympathized with my steam-room mates. Underneath that spirited banter disappointed compromise murmured. Those women were potential Adriennes, but attrition in the relationship, rather than death, would probably claim their lovers.

During the next couple of days, Adrienne remained with me and sorted out her future plans. In between our long walks on the beach, I went about my usual routine. It seemed that wherever I went, office, dentist, jogging path, women verbalized variations on the theme "All the good ones are married." I know men say it too, but women say it more . . . and more . . . and more. None of these marvelous guys was born married, but why did it often appear so?

Over the next few months, I began asking around: "Have you ever had an affair with a married man?" Every unmarried woman I knew well enough to ask, excluding five, aged twenty-five to fifty, had at least once dated a married man.

Eventually, *married* "other women" surfaced . . . plenty of them. But wives, unlike single women with extramarital relationships, have found legal mates. Many have reasons, like tiny tots and financial dependence, to stay (however unhappily) married while they seek out part-time lovers. Single women choosing married men were the greater mystery. Other women's husbands are rarely accessible for vacations or weekends. They give you far more pain than pleasure, the old refrain goes, so why were these single women flocking to them? There must be solid attractions. Not every unmarried woman is self-destructive. Most of us were brought up with the idea that having an affair with someone else's husband is a one-down slot, probably immoral, at least foolish. Playing second fiddle once suggested a woman could not get a man of her own. Somewhere the scarlet woman stereotype was changing. My interest grew.

After friends, I tried strangers: "Pardon me, have you ever *known* a married man?" It was fairly easy for one woman to ask another this question after a few minutes of conversation. Wherever women gathered for exercise, business, social interchange, I made my impertinent queries. The reaction surprised me. The women were all eager, after a question or two on my part, to detail the events which were or had been an important part of their identities.

Eventually, I collected a myriad of notes on women leading partially secret lives. After a short time, I stopped every woman I could when she began to talk about such an experience and made an appointment for a session which I could tape. Although most were concerned that their identities and those of their lovers be kept confidential, several women, the angry ones, didn't care if I used their real names. (I didn't.)

More than anything else, their stories stressed the love and hurt they felt. If they had not been lied to about the men's marital status or their intentions to marry them, which usually they hadn't, there was less anger than regret for either love or time lost. The few women I met who married their formerly married lovers seemed quite happy. I am sure there are exceptions, but I didn't meet them.

Those I talked with besieged me with tales of personal pain, exultation, humor, and complications, revealing an emphatic texture woven through our modern lifestyle. In all I interviewed over 150 women who had had or were having some kind of affair with a married man.

After several years of listening, I realized that the other two sides of these triangles should be fit together with the first. I wondered how husbands and wives viewed their lives in all this. Subsequently, I interviewed both groups. Men were not difficult to find; a number of the "other" women I interviewed referred me to their present or former lovers. Also, by the time I reached this stage of research, I had developed a lot of brass about asking very personal questions in a very polite tone, and I never went out without my tape recorder! When I saw a wedding band on the hand of a man sitting next to me on a plane or train, in a lawyer's or doctor's office, I would strike up a conversation for a few moments and then conspiratorially say, "May I ask you a personal question?"

After ascertaining that they were not being propositioned when I asked if they had ever had an affair, all the men answered quite directly. About 25 percent were careful not to give me their names or the names of their businesses, but by the end of the discussions about half of those revealed their identities, sometimes with a business card. My male interviewees also include divorced men who had had affairs during their marriages.

In contrast to women, men were briefer in their description of events and people. They emphasized their philosophies and generally talked about more than one affair. Though they might cite one special lady, only rarely did they get into the details of a specific story, as did the women. Approximately 10 percent of the men I approached to interview had had no sexual encounters outside their marriages. They were faithful not out of lack of opportunity but by choice. Of this 10 percent a few were recently married or remarried, and three of the men told me they had platonic affairs—secret friendships that they felt their wives would never understand. They were all attracted to the women in these arrangements but didn't have sex with them for one reason or another.

The overwhelming majority of men I approached had had some sexual experiences outside their marriages. I interviewed about 100 of them. Fewer of these men, though, allowed themselves to become as deeply emotionally involved in their outside relationships as did the women with their married men. (Approximately 90 percent of the women I spoke to, as compared to 75 percent of the men who had had affairs, became significantly attached to their lovers.) Profound love affairs, lasting over two years, involved roughly 50 percent of the married men as compared to 75 percent of the women who had married lovers.

Finding wives to interview whose husbands were unfaithful proved a more delicate task. One cannot approach a stranger or married friend and say, "Excuse me, has your husband cheated on you lately?" If he has, chances are a wife doesn't know about it. If she does, embarrassment, anger, or both are generally attached to the subject and sometimes she isn't ready to reveal those emotions to an interviewer. A number of wives did eventually talk to me. The only married women who spontaneously discussed this subject were those who thought their husbands were faithful or those who were no longer in love with them and didn't care what they did. All the women in this latter group told me they were involved in affairs themselves.

For most of these approximately fifty interviews I had to rely on referrals or on wives who had divorced and were now willing to talk about failed marriages, especially if they included infidelities on the men's part only. They seemed to want to share their anger and pain. One wife sought me out. She was devastated by her husband's second round of unfaithfulness after the birth of their last child. They separated by mutual consent shortly thereafter.

With our Puritan heritage, we Americans may think the French hold an exclusive option on the *cinq à sept* interludes or that Mediterraneans alone harbor mistresses as part of the marriage bargain, but middle-class America is in there pitching. That is today's big difference. Traditionally it was from the lower and upper crusts of society that the other woman came—a secure Madame de Pompadour or Emma Hamilton at one end of the social spectrum and peasant girls hoping for advancement at the other. One group had opportunity, the other need. And they were "kept." Today's "other woman" rarely expects money for what she is doing. She is as attractive, intelligent, and sympathetic as any woman from the average group you'd like to cross-section. She is the secretary, lawyer, mama, grandma, or sister you invite to dinner parties for the most eligible bachelor you know. Or she is respectably keeping home, husband, and children going.

Though the economic, social, and racial range of my interviewees is broad—including ex-convicts, a baroness, and the wives of a team of football players—the concentration is heavily urban, white, and middle-class. My conclusions were drawn only on the basis of the people I interviewed, and I make no claims to represent accurately the population as a whole.

The middle class seemed a logical, accessible choice. Its members own sufficient property and have achieved enough economic status to be concerned about losing a portion of both in the divorce process, so they might be the likeliest group to accommodate unhappy or unfulfilling marriages with lovers. Those who have nothing material to lose or who would not have to significantly change their lifestyles in order to divorce did not command my major attention.

The focus on the urban and suburban group probably makes my figures for extramarital affairs higher than the national average. I had more contact with men who traveled, lived in business centers, and were likely to ask me and other single women for dates than I did with farmers in Idaho. Rural men doubtless have outside, clandestine relationships, but affairs are less frequent when men spend a lot of time home on the range.

In five years, my travels (meeting and pursuing married men—for interviews, of course) gave me an opportunity to talk to people in Canada and Europe as well as in the United States.

A French wife who had taken her husband's other women in stride for years told me, "French women know a man is never happy except in the first six months of life, when a grown woman gives him her undivided attention. After that, it is impossible to please him so you might as well forget about making him happy and please yourself."

That is what millions of women all over the world are apparently now doing . . . and my research indicates that married men are often the people with whom they are doing it! This has been especially true in the last twenty years. Before that, the only attractive means of regular sexual gratification for women was to be married. But two decades ago something came along which practically eliminated the great social stigma of getting pregnant out of wedlock. The pill and, later, the coil provided women with not only sexual independence but a sense that they could have other things that hitherto had only belonged to men. A great energy that had been inhibited by frustration and fear became available for other pursuits—like economic independence.

Because it is no longer mandatory for women to wed in order to gain economic security or to feel accepted by society, the criteria by which their relationships are increasingly evaluated are emotional and sexual compatibility.

Wives tempted by affairs no longer live with the same fears of shame and economic deprivation they once did if they got caught. They are demonstrating more of the kind of independence within the marital relationship that men have had for a long time, and that means they are having more affairs.

But, common as they are, affairs turn into complicated and profound entanglements. The monetary and social freedoms women continue to attain, and our diminishing faith in the everlastingness of marriage and of love, do not prevent people involved in extramarital affairs from experiencing the deepest kind of pain and forming the closest possible attachments. That is why I wrote this book.

The emotional depth and breadth of what the "other women" experienced moved me so deeply, I was eventually compelled to find out what the married men had to say about their own motives, agonies, and joys in these relationships. Finally, I wondered how wives are affected by, and view their roles in, these triangles, and I was able to speak with a number of them who became aware of their husbands' affairs at some point during or after the marriage.

Ironically, against the present backdrop of feminism and burgeoning emotional and business alliances among women, it appears we sometimes compete destructively with each other for our husbands and boyfriends. That is partially the inevitable outcome of the decreasing availability of heterosexual men that statistics attest to. Several hundred interviews with persons of both sexes clarify other reasons.

I am publishing a good bit of case history in the words of the participants themselves. The intimate reasons behind so many women's attachments to married men come through in these stories of pain, of loneliness, of companionship and love, of drama and even comedy. And the stories of husbands and wives resigned to compromising marital situations and of ex-wives who have "resigned" from them reveal how they too are trying to accommodate frustrations, stresses, and disappointments in their lives.

For good or ill, an affair is a unique relationship and it is often the catalyst for significant change in people's lives. The interviews alone reveal some astonishing patterns in the current state of wedded and unwedded love and in sexual and familial relationships in general. The group of professionals I consulted, whose names appear in the Acknowledgments, helped me clarify some of those patterns.

My book is an attempt to share the profound experiences of the other woman, the man in the middle, and the woman at home. Listening to all three of these voices at a time when the institution of marriage is at its shakiest is vital if we are to evaluate the challenges and solutions available to us. I hope that the wisdom gained by the men and women who speak in these pages provides insight . . . or comfort . . . for many of you.

I
THE OTHER WOMAN

CHAPTER 1

Where Are All the Single Men?

My heart is a lonely hunter that hunts on a lonely hill.
—Fiona MacLeod,
"The Lonely Hunter"

SHEER NUMBERS

WHERE HAVE all the young men gone? How about middle-aged men? Okay, any men? We are living in a time when women spend huge chunks of money and time grooming themselves for men but, according to all statistics and women's claims, there are simply not enough desirable men to go around.

In 1978, there were 7.8 million more females than males living in the United States.* It is projected that this figure will prove to be higher in the 1980s. In areas like the West Coast, the ratio of women to men is even greater. Divorced and widowed men remarry sooner and in larger numbers than their female counterparts. And we all know that men die sooner, so as the age level goes up, the difference grows. Thirteen and three-tenths percent of women in the U.S. are over sixty-five while only 9.2 percent of the male population is in the same age group.

A photographer, recently married for the third time, noted the

---

*These are the latest available statistics from U.S. Statistical Abstract.

dramatic change in the female population between his single and divorced years. "I just couldn't get over the sheer volume of attractive, high-quality women out there. I know few bachelors on the level of these single women. Now that I'm married, I can't figure out whom to introduce our unattached women friends to."

It is *social inflation*: Too many women "chasing" too few men. As the supply diminishes, the demand becomes more obvious.

The idea that a man is supposed to equal or surpass his woman's level of professional or economic achievement still has a strong hold on society. But men no longer overwhelmingly outearn and outlearn the available women. High-achieving women looking for bed and board to share have the narrowest range of choices if they seek this traditional kind of relationship.

Practically all single women work today. Slowly, they are approaching the men's level general level of achievement. Ready to support a man as never before, offering all the endowments she inherited from mother, and in many cases uninhibited sex and monetary independence, the unmarried woman opens her arms to the great bachelor world, and guess who rushes in? . . . Not *every* married man, but lots of them.

The Invisible Man

Some attractive men are certainly single, but a lot of those are not out girl-scouting. Everyone seems to know more gay men than gay women, including gay men and women. According to the latest figures available, the Kinsey Institute claims that 13.95 percent of men and 4.25 percent of women in the United States are gay. That is 9.7 percent more gay men than gay women. These estimates exclude responses from both those with only incidental experience and latent homosexuals.

Single women particularly say the ratio seems much higher. And Dr. Paul Olsen of New York's Institute for the Psychotherapies told me, "Men also complain the nicest women are unavailable, but the complaint of gayness in the opposite sex is strictly a female one." One reason is that as all kinds of sexuality have become more acceptable in general, those men who formerly hid their predilections in obligatory marriages no longer feel the necessity to do so. They swell the numbers of "unavailable" single men. And the well-reputed male ego, challenged beyond any historical precedent by the independent woman, may cause some men to turn for their affection to other men with the same fears and feelings.

Male homosexuality and bisexuality are not exclusively bachelor phenomena. Al Lerner, a private investigator in New York, has followed husbands whose wives suspect them of having affairs. (Al is the nice guy at the next table who gives you a book of matches.) Sometimes the lover turns out to be another man. "Many of the men are AC-DC. Between Fifty-second and Fifty-ninth Streets on Manhattan's East Side, you see boys hustling businessmen. They're making deals. When I tell the wife the 'other woman' is a man, she is stunned. She gets more angry because she can't compete."

Nor can a single woman compete with a man's male lover. Whatever the actual numbers, then, men who are interested in women, even if married, are all the more desirable. The married man's interest is his foremost attraction. He is *there . . .* when he is there.

It would be a gross error to suggest there are no heterosexual bachelors at large. It just seems that they manifest less enthusiasm than they did once upon a time. A hesitancy shades their behavior. Fear of divorce more than of marriage sometimes deters them. The transience of everyone's interest in everyone and everything makes commitment look perilous, the commitor vulnerable. And why should a bachelor commit himself, even to a date?

Then there is the group of men who have always been timid with women. They are frequently called confirmed bachelors. Not gay, widowed, divorced, or living with anyone, they are simply passive or noncommittal. In today's large unmarried population they are less noticeable than they used to be.

Sometimes an aggressive lady manages to win one of these men over, hoping that matrimony will bring out the more ardent side of him. But disappointed brides have learned that the fellow's aggressiveness is likely to stay where it has always been: in business, charity, or other outside interests. With her, the man is usually more passive than she had hoped. These "eligible" heterosexual men are not suitable mates for the majority of women.

The moment teaches men that women, now up-front about their needs, are here for them whether they call them or not. Moving into increasingly visible positions, women are easily accessible. A bachelor need not set up his weekend ahead of time. The office, tennis court, restaurant, or bar is full of friendly, "together" ladies who are free on the spur of the moment. If the lady in view is not his first choice, that's okay, because the noncommittal gent doesn't want to get involved anyway. There's always tomorrow. The right one might call him for a date.

A man used to do as he chose to, later tearing up the woman's number, secure that she would never phone. Today, she *is* likely to phone. That fact alone discourages some men from demonstrating too much interest. "She might get the wrong idea," he thinks. "Then I'll have to deal with getting rid of her."

Of course, numerous men relish the new flexibility and not all women do phone. They relate to men exactly as they used to before they received salary raises or carried their own suitcases. But the situation often becomes a stand-off. No one makes a clear gesture toward anyone. Caught in the dilemma between old role-playing and newly encouraged freedom, men and women interchange games or bounce unceasingly between each other's roles. There is a lot of confusion.

GREAT EXPECTATIONS

Confusion in people's heads frequently registers in their bodies. Doctors and clinics specializing in sexual dysfunction are opening all across the country. Male impotence is a major complaint of both sexes.

Dr. Joshua Golden, head of the UCLA Sexual Dysfunction Clinic, thinks that there has always been a substantial amount of impotence. "In certain age groups it's more likely. Women over twenty-five relate to males thirty-five to forty. They are not the fifteen- to twenty-five-year-olds likely to get an erection under any circumstances. Many men experience some difficulty during the initial contact period. If they're able to maintain the relationship over a period of time, the problem may disappear." Indications are that longer running relationships have better hopes of resolving these syndromes.

A man involved exclusively with one woman on a long-term basis is not available to others for casual dating. Those unattached, of course, appear to be the most eligible; at least they are not married or gay or involved seriously with one woman. But many men who never seem to get seriously involved with one woman, psychiatrists repeatedly tell me, have conflicts arising out of unresolved feelings about women in general—distorted perceptions or unrealistic expectations, which continually nip potential relationships in the bud.

I remember a woman movie director telling me about one man she met while on location in Florida. "You're too uninhibited," he said. "Make believe you're in love with me. Maybe that will help." There was no question among the women I interviewed that as their own sexual expression grows stronger, a lot of men's penises grow weaker. A man may feel that a female partner who goes to bed with him as soon as they meet probably does the same with others. That is not necessarily so. But in order to protect himself from being a small star in her imagined large constellation of conquests—the way it used to be for women—a sensitive man may biologically protect himself by non-performance.

One twenty-four-year-old woman went on a spree, sleeping with eight different men on eight consecutive nights. She found seven of the eight impotent. That type of pressure, to perform upon command with a stranger, sounds like the same kind of "rush" women had so much hassle with up to the sixties. Instead of rejecting sex verbally, as women did, men can do it physically—with impotence.

Women don't have that choice. They habitually used excuses to retreat from sex. The truth might have been, "I don't feel you are sufficiently protective toward me yet to keep me from getting hurt, i.e., by your desertion or sleeping with others." And what man would find it easy to say, "I don't want to make love to you because I'm afraid of getting hurt by your desertion or sexual activities with other men"? It doesn't fit with the "flying fuck" macho image that has been imposed on him. Books like *Male Sexuality* and *The Hazards of Being Male* are everywhere, trying to help men gear up, literally, for women's higher expectations.

Dr. Babette Lang, a Los Angeles psychologist, thinks men are put off by women's aggressiveness. "They say they like it, but they don't realize they're afraid. They slip and make remarks like, 'She wouldn't leave me alone, she kept pawing me all the time.' Their fear of castration is so great. There is something real they can see hanging down."

Dr. Golden holds discussion groups with medical interns. They generally agree that sexual liberation creates pressures on both men and women to perform. Because faking an orgasm is easier than faking an erection, men feel the pressure more overtly.

There is the problem of dominating or feeling "more" than the new higher-achieving female. Adrienne remembered a man who was impotent with her. He only had the problem *after* her business promotion. Even though he understood every psychological component of the problem, reversing the pattern was still impossible.

Many of the women I interviewed still want to "marry up"—find men their intellectual or professional betters, or at least equals. Being more accomplished or earning more money than a man makes some women feel they are outdistancing him. But as the top level of the increasingly smaller heterosexual population gets taken, there are more women unable to match themselves "up." The necessity for newly successful females to select among "lower-achieving" males causes insecurity for the latter. (This is less true for the younger men, brought up in the equal rights climate of the sixties and seventies.) Traditionally taught that he should intellectually and psychologically dominate a woman, a man may think his contemporary mate is playing down to him.

It is difficult to ascertain whether or not impotence is actually on the increase. Maybe women's broader sexual experience these days creates a climate in which impotence is more obvious. People also talk more about their sex lives than they did. We all know you are leading a deprived existence if all systems are not go. In the good old days, you simply avoided what did not work. When it was secret and dirty, sex was not something you had to "pass" for a reasonably comfortable life. Today good sex is like a college education used to be: a wholesome national aspiration.

According to the single women I polled, married men aren't caught in the impotence dilemma. They seem to be in excellent shape! I asked one husband on the make why.

"As long as the women aren't our wives," was his candid reply.

Discussions with wives confirmed the fact that plenty of their husbands had the same impotence troubles with them that bachelors had with single women.

Men, sharing splendiferous sex with other women, often perform poorly at home. *Perform* is the key word here. That is what it feels like to lots of husbands, I hear. The moral: another woman can have sexual advantages over a wife.

People enjoy challenges. As the preorgasmic woman appeals strongly to certain men, an impotent husband attracts specific other women. The man has obviously allured the lady if he has made it to her bedroom. His temporary sexual dysfunction will not necessarily deter her. Maternal instincts may rise to the occasion. Actually, the impotent husband appeals strongly to certain women.

Many rare and touching love affairs I heard about started with conflicted love-making. Rena, an artist in her twenties, found the overweight painter at the next easel an appealing bedmate after getting to know him and the problems he had at home. After he overcame his initial impotence, he formed a new sexual relationship which grew into a weekly situation both were eager for.

> I couldn't resist the challenge of his problems and the fact that he was unhappily married. He was about thirty pounds overweight and I'd never been with an overweight man before. I sort of set out one evening and deliberately pushed Gene into having three orgasms. It left him with a new view, I think. He'd never been sexually raunchy before. It's not the idea of using dirty words so much as being able to be so direct. He's a damn good lay. His wife doesn't think so, but I do.

Many wives with problematic sex lives told me they never expressed dissatisfaction with their husbands. They may be completely supportive and have the same negative results. It comes with the territory. Practical aspects of marriage sometimes intrude on a couple's inward focus. But with enough care and interest, they will not. Marriage can even improve sexually after many years. And if the bond is strong, another person will not permanently interfere. A rule I have learned: if the other woman becomes an important figure, trouble already exists in the marriage.

The other woman enters the scene with psychological advantages: she meets the husband fresh—no humiliating associations, no failed episodes. With family and business responsibilities facing him daily, a man's affair often becomes the only area of his life where he is not impotent. The world is tough. He may not be.

With his other woman, a husband has built-in control. No matter how independent or successful his lover is, he still "dominates" her by means of his status. He calls the shots as to when and for how long they meet. She probably waits for his calls and visits. That alone puts him in control. Additionally, the love-making doesn't follow dishes, children's homework, and three work-related phone calls. Nothing happens outside the bedroom to tell either one, "I'm dissatisfied with how you're running your end of things." There are, at least at the start, no joint ventures except a desire to please each other. That is a big plus. It changes the man's feelings about himself and his relationship to a woman. Therefore, although the impotent husband begins as a sexual challenge, he often becomes the other woman's best bedmate.

CHAPTER 2
Meeting the Married Man

But of all pains, the greatest pain
It is to love, but love in vain.
> —Abraham Cowley,
> *Anacreon VII, Gold*

HER IGNORANCE—HIS BLISS

Had I known he was married, I would never have gone on that first date. I did not want to get mixed up with a married man because my mother's life was destroyed by such an affair. I have an illegitimate sister and I always thought, "No way will I do that." But all I had to do is look at Don once. I couldn't help myself.

SAMANTHA WAS was not lied to by Don. The "friend" who arranged the date merely omitted the vital fact of his marriage. Samantha's discovery did not help her. She rejected the possibility of Don's strong commitment to his wife in favor of an appealing image—the unhappy husband who will come around.

It is astonishing to me how cooperative a victim can be. By the time a woman has learned the facts of a man's connubial state, she has often created defenses to reject them. Wanting him to be single, her trust of his essential worthiness encourages his factual or emotional lying about the true nature of his marital relationship. Logic may indicate that the man has a strong commitment at home, but her heart and her lover insist it is wrong. What happened to a watch repairer who had been dating a tennis instructor for seven months is not as unlikely as it may at first sound.

Laurin's doorbell rang. She opened the door to a tall, angry woman of about thirty who brought a knife to her throat, took her outside, and insisted they both confront the woman's husband.

> That was the first time I ever knew of her. When we reached their house, my boyfriend was feeding their baby and he just kept on feeding it.
>
> His wife said, "Tell him what you told me."
>
> I said, "I just told her you said you weren't married."
>
> He did nothing but kept feeding the baby.

A few minutes later Laurin left their house. Her lover called the next day, all apologies.

"He tried to convince me they weren't really married, and kept on lying. I let him talk me out of it at least three times because I wanted to believe it."

Laurin is not unique.

Women do get hooked into relationships before they know the men are married. Only a small percentage of husbands, I gather, do not indicate their status verbally when there is no wedding band to say otherwise. But unless the woman knows him, the man's honor is her only ally.

Zach, a senior, met Andrea, a freshman, in high school. Six years later, from the audience of an off-Broadway show, he was surprised to see her tall, slender figure onstage in her first supporting role. Zach came backstage, gave her the big rush, proposed on their second date, and convinced Andrea, lonely in New York, at twenty, to marry him.

"He was a knight in shining armor. I was naive. I think he was infatuated with me because I was a virgin."

They were to be married a few weeks later, but Zach had to go home to Washington first. Andrea phoned him one night. A woman answered. Zach grabbed the phone and told Andrea he would take the first train in and explain. He arrived to say he was married, very unhappily, with three children.

Remarkably, Zach got a divorce and married Andrea in a lavish wedding that included an orchestra playing all the songs from the show she'd been in. Shortly thereafter, their fights and his drinking began. They separated while she was pregnant.

Andrea's story was the only one among the people I interviewed in which a man who had deceived a woman about his status later married her.

A man having affairs does a lot of lying. Deceiving his wife is mandatory unless there is an open marriage going on. When the man lies to the other woman, though, he rarely recovers a foothold. She usually drops him pronto.

Men I spoke with expressed the fear of losing women immediately if they "tell." Others assume that as long as the information is transmitted by the end of the first night, it is kosher.

For Don, it worked. Samantha and he were fixed up on a blind date. She only knew that he was a terrific guy coming in from out of town; no mention was made of marital status. By the time she found out that Don, one of America's wealthiest executives, was married, Samantha was sufficiently hooked.

HALF-IN HALF-OUT

The truth can be maddeningly elusive. Sometimes the man himself is not sure whether he is married. Milt was such a man. Maureen thought he was safe.

> Milt was still married but separated, living alone, in the process of divorce. He had been separated for two months. We were fond of each other and eventually lived together. He wanted to marry me and was proceeding on his divorce, but when we'd get involved in personal problems, he'd go back to his wife. If he'd been single in the first place, the whole situation wouldn't have happened. It seems they've always decided to divorce before

they've met you but are indeed not single. You think, oh, that's no problem. He's getting a divorce anyway. I had nothing to do with it.

This was the beginning of a heartbreaking three years. When a husband says he is separated, other women have learned that often it is a wishful rather than a legal state. Maybe he is experimenting before returning home for good or for a few more years. Though divorce proceedings have begun, they can often be halted before completion.

Women of all age groups find themselves caught in that unfortunate gray area in someone else's marriage—divorce still a possibility but not yet a reality. That fact sometimes creates a lot of false hope and, later, suffering.

The man in question is not necessarily lying so much as changing his mind periodically and not expressing his ambivalence. Maybe one week he sincerely intends to divorce. Then something happens the following week to alter the dynamics between him and his wife. These family crises affect his other relationship and determine his reactions to it. The ambiguous separation tune has a lot of variations.

Estelle, a thirty-four-year-old buyer for a department-store chain, lived in the apartment building where a virile-looking Episcopal priest occasionally visited a friend of his. Never had the slim, quiet woman from Cleveland considered in her years of looking for a husband that she would fall for a married priest!

Basically, I consider the whole world married and usually check on any guy I date. But my girlfriend who introduced us didn't know. Who suspects a priest? I didn't want to have affairs with married men, but Vernon was very nice, good-looking, gentle. The first night we went out, he told me he was married and in the process of separation from his wife.

Estelle and Vernon eventually went on a dreamlike trip to Cape Cod, stopping at cozy inns in between Vernon's church business. He took her with him everywhere. I wondered how he explained Estelle's presence.

He said I was his friend. I remember going to church and talking to a lot of fathers. I thought it was a kick. They talked about Father this and Father that and I got in on some of the local gossip. They were the four most perfect days of my life. The most intimate time I've ever had with any man. I don't mean the sex was unusually good. The main event was being together. He listened to me, which most men do not do. He made room for me to come into his life.

Vernon had had his first outside affair with a member of his congregation. His story was that his wife knew all about his past women and knew about Estelle. They continued seeing each other for several months. Estelle resented Vernon's getting up in the middle of the night and returning home. Never had a man left her after making love. She knew he lived at home, but only temporarily, she thought. Vernon assured her the divorce was imminent.

I'm not sure how, but suddenly my perception of him totally changed. He no longer appealed to me. No concrete reason, but I began to see things I didn't like about him, that he was really full of crap.

Something clicked in Estelle's mind that made her self-protective feelings rise to aid her. She sensed Vernon wasn't going to separate. They didn't discuss it. She merely broke it off. All at once, Vernon's sincerity, openness, and priestliness looked phony, hypocritical. Had he been single, she feels, it would have taken much longer to discover his hollowness.

Vernon may once have contemplated, or planned, separation. People change their minds. Even after legal separation or divorce, men sometimes return home or remarry their former spouses. In my own research I met ten men who went back to their wives after separation and one who remarried his after their divorce.

Twelve years of post-college social life convinced Melissa, a literary agent, to try a last resort—a dating agency. She knew how carefully applicants were screened by this most exclusive and expensive service. If nothing else, she reasoned, "One knows the man is single and can afford to pay the fee."

Ralph was a heavyset, clean-cut attorney. His cherubic face and polished manners continued to inspire trust. Three months into their relationship, Melissa was feeling pretty secure, spending Saturday nights through Sunday mornings with him. They saw a great deal of each other. Ralph said he was legally separated and never mentioned children.

One day, Melissa dropped in to the dating agency, right next door to her own office, to meet a friend who worked there. While waiting, she was standing at the manager's desk. Ralph's file was lying open. Reading upside down, Melissa learned of two children. Her stomach churned. Intuition told her more bad surprises lay ahead.

She kept hoping Ralph would tell her about his children. Melissa didn't have the guts to ask him directly. They were supposed to go on a trip together. She would leave it till then. The day before they were to depart, Ralph took her to the most elegant restaurant in town, ordered a ninety-dollar bottle of wine, and confessed. One of the terms of his legal separation was attending reconciliation court. He hadn't bothered telling the dating agency—or Melissa—he was moving back home. The marriage counselor had asked that the trip he had promised Melissa serve as an opportunity for his wife and Ralph to be alone together. He claimed he hadn't brought up the children issue because she would ask about his wife and he didn't want to get into it.

To this "rational" presentation, Melissa responded, "Bullshit."

Ralph said he had very little hope about his marriage, to which she said, "Bullshit," once more.

Hurt for a few months, she never dated him again. Ralph reconciled with his wife.

The more women and men I interviewed, the more familiar Melissa's experience sounded. Husbands go back even after long separations. Men, apparently, are creatures of habit more than are women. When another woman enters a husband's life at the point where he is in transition, she had better be prepared to lose him.

He may do several turnabouts. When a man is half-in half-out, the situation always seems precarious.

IT'S JUST THE NEARNESS

What is a friend? A single soul dwelling in two bodies.
—Aristotle,
Diogenes Laertius

People in urban centers are often isolated. Initiating relationships can be a problem. The ones nearest frequently become dearest. Rather than remain alone, many become involved with those nearest—neighbors, friends, or business associates.

Adrienne, my friend who could not attend her lover's funeral, was editing Lee's medical textbook, discovering during those long meetings together a mutual subtlety of intellect, sense of humor, and ability to extract the essence of experience. It was late afternoon when he arrived for their first long meeting. They remained in the office long after everyone went home. A kind of refinement underscored the talk, the man-woman pull rippling beneath it.

> Neither Lee nor I had ever considered an affair. I knew how dumb it was to be involved with a married man and Lee's marriage had been stable, if not happy, for twenty years.

Medicine had been Lee's mistress, and prominence the balm when life at home irritated. Shortly after Lee and Adrienne met, he told her, "I'm probably the most married man you'll ever meet." He had never had an affair and, outside of work, his family took all his energy.

Adrienne and Lee had some of those long publishing lunches. They were considered a good investment for the firm. Lee had been a big-selling author with his last book on the psychological relationship between doctor and patient.

> We went to our favorite small restaurant. There had always been the joking acknowledgment of our attraction, wishing we'd met before he was married . . . even though I would have been

only six. The restaurant was full. Lee is quite formal and proper—also he's known there—so I was astonished when he leaned over and kissed me on the mouth.

"Thank you," he said, for nothing specific. Even more amazing was the fact that he'd read my mind. I was thinking how much I wanted that kiss, even though it was something I wanted not to want.

A few days later, Lee and Adrienne worked into the night at her office. When they saw it was ten-thirty, Lee called home saying he would stay over at the hospital. He was too tired to drive back to Great Neck. Author and editor went to a restaurant and closed it up. By the time they headed to the garage for Lee's car, it was after one A.M. The garage had closed and rain was falling prodigiously. Under a canopy, they huddled together, Adrienne's eye makeup running, both of them drenched. When they finally reached Adrienne's apartment, they looked at each other, charged with desire.

"I hope you're not going to invite me up," Lee said, knowing she'd understand he couldn't say no.

"I'm not."

"That's my girl."

The couple parted. A few weeks later, they finished proofing galleys together. On a Friday they said good-bye, alone in the office. During the year they had known each other, Adrienne noted that several times Lee had looked almost pained. He had excused himself to lie down for a few moments on her office couch. It never occurred to her that the discomfort was sexual frustration. Lee admitted it only much later. Adrienne told me:

> I realized I was deeply in love with him. No one treated others with more courtesy or had a greater sense of play about him. This bald, undistinguished-looking man attracted me more than anyone I'd ever met.
>
> He was leaving. I yearned to be close to him, to feel his energy and awareness. I decided to tell him my feelings right there, in the office.

"I realize that it won't make a hoot of difference in the direction of our lives, but I want you."

"What you're saying, I hoped for a thousand times, and hoped not."

They returned to Adrienne's apartment, consummating the union that had been mentally forged long ago. Without their actual work together and the rationalization it provided, these two people would never have justified their contact. And the sneakiest way romance wins us is by contact. The strongest feelings between people develop over a period of time, out of friendship. Strange as it may seem, the married man often has more time to elicit romantic feelings from a woman than does the bachelor who dates her. The current atmosphere pressures single people into testing the strength or weakness of their physical attraction toward each other early in the relationship. Very often, it is too early. The appeal that might have grown out of an emotional feeling has been lost.

Married men may have a better chance at friendship. They almost always have to spend more time with a woman, displaying their charms, than bachelors do. They don't expect a woman, especially if she is single, to fall into bed with them. This period of protest, during which the woman is saying no to an affair but yes to seeing him, gives the married man a good opportunity to get close to her. He expects to be rebuffed at first and is not easily discouraged. It is during this *protest period*, which I heard about over and over and which may take days, weeks, months, and even years, that the woman who falls in love with him will do so. When the couple ultimately has sex, the relationship probably has some depth.

Outside of social contact, a woman's easiest access to a man is their mutual place of business. Office romance has long been a staple of the American extramarital scene. Entire books and movies have dealt with it. Working provides opportunities for closeness over long periods of time free of social or sexual pressures. Faults and quirks, as well as the ability to manage success and failure, are exposed to workmates who share common goals and adversities. They are partners of sorts before they are bedmates. The woman need not set herself up for rejection as she might in a blind date, and the discomfort of bars and discotheques is entirely avoided.

When a work peer or superior seeks her out, the woman knows he is interested in her, not in his own professional advancement. The female secretary, nurse, or assistant and her male boss are part of a familiar dominance-compliance or leader-helper paradigm. There is a facile flow toward each other which often fosters romance. Though his marriage might discourage her interest at first, if the woman likes him and has been without any other romance for a while, she may change her mind.

CHAPTER 3

Loving
a Married Man

There is no fury like a woman searching for a new lover.
—Cyril Connolly,
*The Unquiet Grave**

THE PRACTICAL MIND

ONCE A woman determines she isn't meeting or holding bachelors she likes, a decision must be made. Keep looking for the right one? Have an affair with a married man and keep looking? Make no demands and fall in love—(why isn't it "rise in love"?)—with anyone she can? Become a lesbian? Lead a celibate life? Forget marriage and concentrate on her career? This last one, very popular these days, lends itself to the practical mind . . . and a married lover. It isn't fear of marriage or the thrill of secret passion that drives the single woman so much, she tells me, as needs of her own.

Her motives may relate to the price of professional success. Those launching careers or businesses in today's competitive milieu find it distracting to whip up gourmet dinners while their male peers stay in the office until midnight. These women do not avoid marriage for emotional reasons so much as see it as inconvenient. No matter what her salary, a wife's household tasks are mainly hers alone. It is still the rare man willing to share them.

*Cyril Connolly, *The Unquiet Grave* (New York, Harper Bros., 1941) Act I. Reprinted with permission.

Time is a factor. Working women meet men who are colleagues or mentors, both frequently married. The friendship and professional support they proffer on any given evening, doing late work or sharing a business dinner, seem more important than a blind date. With the little free time she has, the professional woman finds married men may provide the essence, if not the continuity, of the warmth she yearns for.

A high-achieving woman need not have a harsh manner or tone; her mere accomplishment may threaten a bachelor's security. To compensate, this type of woman sometimes tries to hide her abilities. A college professor observed, "We women are as afraid of power as men are of love. They think love is feminine, while we see power as masculine."

Unable to find a single lover who wasn't skittish about dating her, this economics professor eventually took up with a married policeman on her college campus.

"It doesn't have to be a knight on a white horse. A motorcycle will do just fine."

Women doctors, pilots, and others in high-level or predominantly male professions lament the fact that men are often reluctant to date them. The majority of males they meet are subordinates. Understandably, there is a built-in resistance to making a pass at one's boss. Good jobs are hard to come by. The remedy for Roberta, an animated attorney in her forties, is the married man.

We are sitting in New York's Sherry Netherland Hotel bar. This is one of the places Roberta occasionally frequents after work. The men she inevitably prefers here are married. Roberta spends mornings in a community legal center and afternoons in private practice.

"I don't have much room for social life. My boys are fifteen and seventeen. I've raised them alone and like to spend my free nights at home with them. I'm most compatible with a hard-working man for whom play is a vital element in his life. In the small free time we have, it counts for a lot."

Roberta finds intimacy develops quickly with a married man. "He can risk being open because he has to be if he wants the best of two worlds."

Women mentioned a capacity for intimacy more than any other quality as a desirable trait married men apparently have. They don't, as bachelors do, have time to constantly form new relationships. If the other woman accepts part-time love, the man usually stays around a while, allowing intimacy to develop. Also, the fact that there usually are no social circumstances to justify their meeting fosters a concentration on the lovers' inner selves.

What becomes of those receiving fractured ecstasy? I asked Roberta if all the closeness does not breed heartbreak. She admitted it did, but no more often than with single men.

"Bachelors with good jobs play for the best deal each day," she says. "'We'll talk soon,' or, 'Let's get together again,' they tell you. There are so many options they need never form a relationship."

Roberta's viewpoint is common. Over and over I heard that bachelors are reluctant to have any demands made on them. Though married men have no time for her on weekends and holidays, Roberta insists, "I'd rather take the risk of eventually getting hurt with a married man than be paranoid about long-range security."

Roberta represents women weighing changing options as they get older. Psychiatrists and psychologists concur that in the present social climate they neither encourage nor discourage women's liaisons with married men. Rather, they explore whether or not the patient suffers within that relationship. Several mentioned that their major work in such instances consists of relieving guilt and self-condemnation. Many a busy woman, it seems, would rather spend her time with someone she knows will be good company and fulfill her needs than search for someone single. The result is compartmentalization.

On a plane last year, I was sitting next to a publicist in her fifties who was going to London for a conference. She told me of a relationship she had been having with a married man for ten years. Luckily his wife worked weekends, teaching seminars for executives.

"I fly from Los Angeles to San Francisco every weekend. What better world could a woman have than to spend Monday through Friday doing the work she loves without the hassle and trouble of having anyone around and then Friday night be able to put it aside and spend a marvelous Saturday and Sunday of intimacy, affection, and lust with the man she loves? Then to put that aside again Sunday night, and return to work."

My flying companion was not the least conflicted about her life. She presumed the wife knew that there was some relationship, but didn't ask about her attitude.

Emotional and sexual requirements may be completely answered by someone married, or they may be partially fulfilled, while a woman still dates single men. Sandra Allenburg, a Los Angeles marriage and family counselor, says, "It's a basic human need to be close, cared for, to touch. If you can't get it anyplace else, you get it from someone married. I guess that part of it is healthy as long as the expectation is no greater than that." Today's expectations may not be.

POWER PLAYS AND WORKS

Power is the greatest aphrodisiac.

—Henry Kissinger[*]

A man's power derives from professional position, money, social standing, achievement, or merely his relationship to a woman. The most blatantly powerful figure in a working woman's life is her mentor. He need not be her boss, but he must be a means to achievement. With or without any other advantages, the mentor figure holds out career advancement as the ultimate incentive. Success for the woman means independence and the ability to obtain power on her own.

Chris's motives for getting to know Frank were strictly professional. A divorced fledgling journalist, the gaminelike Chris met Frank, twice her size and age, at a Fund For Animals benefit. He was a sharp magazine publisher of sophisticated political commentary. He was not handsome or outgoing, but he was extremely important in his field. Chris wanted experience in the business—Frank offered her the

[*] Marvin Kalb and Bernard Kalb, *Kissinger* (Boston: Little Brown, 1977), p. 10.

chance to learn her craft. She had sold only two articles to local Midwestern papers when they met. Frank taught Chris what he could, hired her as an assistant, and ultimately lost her to a prestigious Eastern paper. Though she fell in love with Frank, Chris never lost sight of her original goal.

Chris consciously began this liaison. Others who, like her, want to rise in or start businesses, want professional mentors but end up inextricably embroiled. The sexual component works toward that. The whole mentor-protégé structure fits snugly with traditional heterosexual ego dynamics. Unless she surpasses her mentor, the female protégé is a satisfying partner. Several of these connections I heard about ended in marriage.

Powerful men are usually middle-aged or older. Ambitious in youth, their fortieth or fiftieth birthdays may be truly that—the first day they slow down to catch up on living they have neglected. That is *one* reason why powerful older men so often take on younger girlfriends. They want to know what they feel they have missed during years of hard work and family growth. At a point of emotional security, the forty- to sixty-year-old man can allow his tenderer, more sentimental qualities to develop. He need not be the intractable wall holding up everything in his world.

For the young woman, according to Dr. Olsen, "There is something fascinating about the older man who is going to give her something. It may be an Oedipal wish.* An enormous experimentation is going on by the younger woman. Also, older men are more apt to be at points in their marriages where they are looking for a romance."

The powerful man, women tell me, frequently initiates a liaison without the aid of good looks or sensitivity. Trafficking successfully in the world, he talks effectively to people, convincing them of his viewpoint. He may operate on a superficial level, but by the time the spurious side of him displays itself, the man has already conquered his prey. At that point, the other woman needs a sense of humor. Linda had it . . .

---

* "The Oedipus complex in the girl . . . in my experience . . . seldom goes beyond the wish to take the mother's place, the feminine attitude toward the father." Sigmund Freud, *Collected Papers*, Vol. II (London: Hogarth Press Ltd., 1924), p. 273.

"His bombasity was extraordinary," Linda tells me of the short South American ambassador she met through friends.

> Cocky to waiters, he had no manners I could respect. But I was entertained by Carlos's eccentricities. One morning for breakfast he ordered a large dinner steak, three servings of papaya, and a strawberry milkshake. I had tea. Our bill was thirty-two dollars.

Linda, a witty, short-haired dental hygienist from London, never asked if Carlos was married. For her it was just a night out with sparkling, fun-loving folk. Carlos kept Linda screaming with laughter. He spent money lavishly and "made things happen with the snap of his fingers." One thing led to another, and they spent the weekend together.

Carlos returned to London several weeks later and they repeated the same routine. The couple made ordinary but not unpleasant love. The talk afterward was mostly political. He had headed several international economic councils and had pulled off a few impressive political maneuvers. Linda was eventually invited to Paris, where Carlos had recently taken up his new ambassadorial post. She stayed at a hotel on his account.

The first night Carlos got up from bed and went home at 2 A.M. That's when she began to suspect he was married. "I speculated, on the other hand, that it might not be correct for him to have a lady staying in the official residence with no missus."

The following evening, Linda found herself at the official residence, where a woman was addressed by Carlos's teen-age son as Aunt Consuela. She provided the house tour.

> Upstairs she pointed out the master bedroom saying, "And this is where the Ambassador and I sleep." Snap! I finally deduced that the oldest child was from a former marriage and had been instructed to call Carlos's wife Aunt. What gall! The man brings a woman he's sleeping with to his wife's house—and the woman is me!!

Linda found the whole imbroglio humorous.

Gigantic egos and brazen gestures go together. Men like Carlos get away with both. Though their good fortune may be temporary, from what I hear, the men know they can count on the needs and politeness of those around them, and they understand just how far each person can be bullied.

The next day, Linda found herself at the ambassadorial residence yet again.

> A vision in red silk pajamas, Carlos descended the stairs followed by Consuela in a fur-trimmed peignoir set. We all said, "Good morning" and had breakfast together. I felt ridiculous, but tickled at the same time that this could be happening to me.
>
> Soon Carlos's mother and aunt came. Along with his three children, the whole bloomin' lot of us went on a picnic.

Linda had asked Carlos, after the first night, "What the hell is going on?"

"Don't worry about it. It's my problem," came his assured response.

Linda decided to forget the negatives, stay away from Carlos's family, and enjoy herself. She shopped, went to museums, and had a thoroughly good time (with an embassy car at her disposal). Carlos's chauffeur proved a delightful guide each day, and every evening Carlos took her to fabulous parties.

The last day, Linda stopped at the embassy to say good-bye. Carlos, having a manicure, was already on the phone arranging an air ticket for a girlfriend in Rome.

He looked up at Linda, smiled diabolically, and announced, "Well, you know how it is, duck." He laughed that privileged laugh.

Linda refused to see Carlos the next time he called. She had the maturity and sense of humor to survive him, and kept his limited worth in perspective.

Glamour and dynamism attract women to powerful men. If they are rich, important, famous, and/or accomplished, they can be irresistible. Offering challenge and opportunity for exotic or stimulating experience, the powerhouse magnetizes, especially the lady with nothing more emotionally binding in her life.

Until recently, only extraordinary women possessed money, position, and independence. Others secured luxury and exposure to the world through their husbands or the other men they knew who, aided by a dash of charm, seduced them. A man's power and a woman's need make younger-older, protégé-mentor, student-teacher combinations unavoidable. Likewise, male doctors, lawyers, accountants, anyone privy to confidential information, has a potential liaison on his hands. The woman need not be particularly dependent—we all want what carries us away from the everyday. The pull of the powerful man, to many of the women I interviewed, was what finally relinquished their misgivings about becoming an "other woman."

A Strange Security

He is faithful . . . in his way.

—Many "other women"

Tables turn. Joyce never imagined when her boyfriend, Ben, upset her time after time that fifteen years later she would dictate the rules of their relationship and he would wait by the phone hoping she would call. I met the plain-featured but expressive and confident Joyce on the Metroliner from New York to Washington. Not long ago she received a call from Ben, her first lover. They had spoken a few times during the nine years he had been married, but Joyce rarely thought of him.

Business brought Ben to Washington last year. He contacted Joyce, by then secretary to a Congresswoman. When they met at her apartment, Ben noticed an obvious difference between the girl he had had emotionally wrapped around his finger and the woman now in control of her life. Joyce was someone he wanted to get close to again.

She handed him a drink. They moved to the terrace and talked. Both were a bit shy. Ben seemed softer, the old arrogance gone. Joyce recalls, "He stayed the night. In college, I had thought that he was a fabulous lover, but now both of us are even better."

Ben's wife had become more like a sister to him than a lover (many of the men I interviewed mentioned this when talking about why they had affairs). He was thrilled with the idea of experiencing the woman whose sexuality he had first aroused. Being faithful seemed less important than it used to.

Joyce's expectations had changed since college and during the past few years, when she had become financially independent and free to do as she pleased. She no longer wanted Ben to fulfill her every need.

> If he did, he would become a hazard. I would get too involved with an unavailable man. That first evening he was only staying in town one night. The nostalgic attraction was there, so I thought I should enjoy the benefits of the suffering I had endured when I was younger and less knowing in the ways of men and their potential for exquisite, uninvolved passion.

Ben presently roams the globe as an expert on irrigation, advising governments and agricultural councils. Joyce said, "Being his wife, staying home with his kids and laundry while he is off with women like me, doesn't sound like the good life." She enjoys the best of Ben—the long hours of inventive love-making, the glamorous evenings.

When her emotions start to tinge her lust, Joyce remedies the situation by making sure she has another date and usually some good sex within a week after Ben's departure. She lives much the way some men always have—her focus is her work, the only constant on which she counts. If the right man came along, it would delight Joyce. Meanwhile, she is investing her emotions and time where they can pay off, professionally.

> I used to be unhappy that I hadn't married. Now I'm enjoying the fruits of a great job and a rather eclectic group of friends. I'll never give up my lifestyle for something that isn't as good or better. I'm not interested in a man to support me or make children. If he can't give me at least part of the nourishment and sensitivity I get from a woman friend and the passion I get from a married lover, I will keep to my piecemeal, often luscious life.

Joyce has a "safe" relationship this moment. That may or may not change.

Ask Mr. Average why a single woman like Joyce takes up with a married man. Most of the men I interviewed said, "Simple, she doesn't want a commitment. It's safe." Impossible alliances do defend one against intimacy. But so do bad marriages. Appear to have a relationship, whether with a spouse or married lover, and one is relieved of "needing" another. One who doesn't need, the theory has it, cannot be hurt.

Mariana, whose classical looks suggest a figure in ancient frescoes rather than someone discussing psychological motivations, thinks the single life is the "safer." Her voluptuous form, as she leans forward in her seat, tenses with anger when she speaks of her homeland in Greece.

> Women had to put up with all kinds of garbage. I know lots of them who scrubbed floors while the men sat in cafes in their custom-made suits. I cannot control my fear of that role. I'm afraid to fall in love with any man and ruin my future. I want to be strong, not another dependent mother figure.

Instead of a stultifying marriage, Mariana chose an impossible relationship and safety . . . she thought. In her mind, the married accountant who gave her a lift when she broke her boot heel was not a date. They had dinner and sensed their mutual attraction. "Men always use women," she reasoned. "I'll use him for one night."

An age-old temptation trapped her. The one-night fling stretched into years of agonized, ambivalent love-making. Again and again, women craving physical love seem to get drawn into powerful attachments. Some find the division between sex and love impossible. The ostensible safety of a part-time passionate relationship with a married man can turn out to be dangerous because of the emotional force of sex. Safety or danger is in the groin of the beholder.

The only safety feature consistently noted by the women I spoke with who were involved with married men was protection from unwanted competition. Their lover's time generally permits only one additional woman in his life—a wife. Unless the woman wants to marry her lover, the wife is often not viewed with great trepidation. Even if the woman's goal is marriage, the wife is perceived as competition mainly by virtue of her motherhood, legal status, and prior meeting of the man. A woman more recently chosen, treated as the adored love object, eliciting the passions, attention, and time of her man, generally feels like the first woman in his heart.

In addition to cutting down on competition with unknown women, choosing a married man usually shields the other woman from the pain of rejection. Rarely is a permanent relationship possible, so the question of what will happen between them is moot. When he divorces, it is a bonus for the woman who wants that.

The married lover is most often totally accepting. He makes a woman feel important if only for the danger he risks in seeing her. There's no criticism or disregard of her because he's grateful for her presence; his emotional generosity costs him nothing. The other woman cannot call upon him for commitments because he already has them. As long as she's there, he's trying to please and keep her.

This total acceptance is particularly important to women who have suffered rejection. And fear of rejection by bachelors may not relate to a woman's actual dating experience but start instead with childhood rejection. It does not necessarily refer to cold or harsh treatment.* One way women apparently avoid repeating any such feelings is choosing a married man. The latter's interest and affection are least likely to diminish. He wants her more than the local bachelor who's got all the women he can make time for. Over and over women voiced their disenchantment with bachelors who

---

* "Such rejection may take the form of blunt statements stressing the child's worthlessness or inadequacy, or it may be expressed more subtly through attitudes and actions that indicate a lack of respect, involvement or caring. In some cases the parent has subjected the child to a constant barrage of criticism and humiliation. In other cases there is no frank rejection or depreciation but, rather, a void in the parent-child relationship. The parents may or may not be consciously aware of their behavior." Harold I. Kaplan, M.D., Alfred M. Freedman, M.D., & Benjamin J. Sadock, M.D., *Comprehensive Textbook of Psychiatry*, Vol. 3, 3rd Edition (Baltimore/London: Williams and Wilkins, 1980), p. 2802.

either deserted them after the successful seduction or continued initiating liaisons after they were involved with them.

A similar avoidance of rejection has been cited as one cause of female homosexuality.

> It is at the Oedipal stage, when the child is approximately between three and four years of age, that he normally develops an emotional or sexual reaction toward the parent of the opposite sex. . . . It is also quite possible that, if the girl at the height of the Oedipal phase feels thoroughly frustrated in her attempts to reach out and be accepted by her father and the men she wants approval from, she may relinquish all hope of ever being accepted by any man, and she may seek freedom from unbearable anxiety in a psychosexual relationship with a woman. *

These facts indicate that taking a husband away from a wife might be another way in which a woman attempts to resolve this earlier conflict. A girl rejected by her father at the period of heightened attachment may inadvertently perceive her mother as a wall between them. Taking a husband from a wife is one way to counteract that loss later on. Different dynamics are operative when a woman becomes involved with a friend's husband. She may transfer her competitive feelings toward her own mother to the man's wife.

Various forbidden sexual alliances may be acted out with a married man. He can represent a relative, other than the father, for whom the girl yearns. A psychiatrist is another example of the forbidden sexual partner for whom a married man may substitute. But most psychiatrists I talked with felt that the women who see them and have married lovers are seeking needed intimacy more than a substitute for themselves.

It has become a pat answer that women have affairs to avoid commitment and closeness. While it is true in some cases, I found

---

*May E. Romm, "Sexuality and Homosexuality" in *Sexual Inversion: The Multiple Roots of Homosexuality*, Judd Marmor ed. (New York: Basic Books, 1965) p. 28.

that there are more significant needs that will override these for most of them. Being touched and sharing time, pleasure, and pain with someone who cares or seems to care seem by far to be the commoner motives of the women who choose the shaky security of a married lover.

THE HEALTHY ANIMAL

The ruling passion, be it what it will,
The ruling passion conquers reason still.
—Alexander Pope,
Moral Essays, Epistle III
To Lord Bathurst

The changing attitudes toward women and sexuality in the last two decades have allowed more people to express their sexual needs. Fewer are fervent about religion anymore. Faith in otherworldliness is at an all-time low. Being the second woman in a man's life has to do with wanting something concrete today rather than the debatable security of marriage, if it comes. More practical, frustrated, and free-spirited (*liberated* always sounds like the cages were just opened) than their predecessors, women now admit they are unwilling to live in some mythical "one day," as in "one day you're going to meet . . ." Finish it with your long-standing fantasy . . . even your mother's. It makes no difference.

Add modern conveniences, reliable birth control and her own apartment, and a woman's clandestine meeting turns congenial, snug. And even if she goes to a motel, sex is less serious, if only because it often precedes emotional ties. Commitments used to come first. The whole business was more dangerous.

Many of my women interviewees chose married men for subtler reasons. The innocent female usually wants a first sexual encounter with a confidence-inspiring male, especially if she has waited longer than her peers. An intuitive need to protect herself may move the younger woman toward the tender older man rather than the socially acceptable younger one.

Brian, a sophisticated businessman, told me he actually hoped his daughter would have sex first with an older married man. "He'd be better to her," he said.

Paula, a twenty-four-year-old nubile stewardess, confirms that idea in her first sexual relationship. "He was the high school football coach. I was captain of the cheerleaders. I babysat for him and his wife all during high school." Paula transmitted her desire effectively. The coach eventually fulfilled her fantasies.

"Afterward, I was elated. Someone I had cared for so much for so long had done it. I kept asking myself, 'Am I dreaming?' He was the one I had always thought about it with and suddenly it was true."

Women also view married men as more experienced than single ones, true or not. They are drawn to these men for a heightened physical experience.

"I'll make you feel like a piece of fire. Your whole body will burst into flames," one man promised.

To an inexperienced female, this is a provocative prediction. Chanin, a twenty-two-year-old salesgirl, was traveling in Europe. The married guide on her bus tour spent much of their five days trying, unsuccessfully, to seduce her. Eventually, the soft Florence night air, Italian music, and his promises overwhelmed her. She was not a virgin, but it was the first time she had an orgasm.

"I did turn into a piece of fire. It was the right person to happen with."

Chanin is not the only young woman around wanting a "forbidden" man. Afraid of getting hurt and not anxious to marry yet, she reasons the older man will be a sensitive physical partner, at least temporarily. His solicitude and experience alone argue for him.

Girlhood dreams are part of the picture; calculating though it may sound, a sexual arrangement may actually guard against promiscuity. "If you're not jumping from one bed to another out of need," says thirty-one-year-old Pamela, "it's easier to select an eligible bachelor for his character and intelligence. I hate being dependent on men to feel decent, but the older I get the more I need sex."

So do a lot of women, including those who for years refused the idea of a relationship with a married man.

Pamela originally had come from Chicago to New York with no interest in married men. She had never owned a negligee and makes no effort to conceal her bright freckles beneath makeup.

As we lunch together in the World Trade Center, her tanned country casualness looks almost out of place in this crowded urban setting.

> I met Roger waiting on a movie line eight years ago. He invited me to have a sandwich. In the midst of pastrami, he informed me he was married with five children. He gave me a list of superb reasons to have an affair with him, but I staunchly refused. Not only wasn't I interested in married men, but I felt it was a rotten thing to do to Mrs. Roger. We were both equally confident of convincing the other. Since they were my genitals that were not to be made available, I won the argument.

Enough meaningless dating changes a woman's perspective. Five years later, Pamela overcame her original morality. She wanted a physical relationship and didn't relish sleeping with any man she was dating.

> I called Roger. We met in a crowded restaurant. "I want to apply for the position as your mistress," I whispered.
>
> "What?"
>
> Roger couldn't hear me above the din. Finally I got my message across. To his credit, Roger was honest enough to admit that he had somebody in that capacity at present but would be delighted to change partners. He assured me it would be done pronto.
>
> I thought of the poor other woman. I was now involved in deceiving two women. But I had learned to think in terms of self-preservation. Wasn't that the goal of good mental health? With no guilt and less hope for anything emotional, I plunged into what has now become the best sex I've ever had. Roger is

your standard, multigeared jock with matching lighthearted-ness. Good in bed and just slick enough so that I'll never fall in love with him. His control is so skilled, it's contagious.

I have no illusions. The day I feel I need him more than he thinks he needs me, I'll break it off. Right now I wouldn't trade those wild afternoon hours in front of my fireplace for anything. I feel more relaxed. Everyone says I look better. The bonus is that Roger has had a vasectomy. My hated diaphragm can be locked away. I know this is not a permanent way of life. But from what I see today, I'm not too optimistic about finding anyone single and terrific. I keep giving them a chance to prove I'm wrong. Whatever the future, I know I can always depend on pizza, a good movie, and Roger.

There are many Pamelas. It appears that a growing proportion of women in touch with their needs are not able to fulfill them with one person. When the situation calls for it, they do the same kind of emotional and sexual segregating once thought exclusively a male talent. Some rather original arrangements have been made by women trying to manage married lovers and their work schedules.

"I have an hour between eleven and twelve free," a Los Angeles college teacher said. "We drive to Griffith Park Observatory, jog in the hills, and share a picnic. One windy, rainy day, we stretched out on the ground right there. No one was around, so we made love. Then I went back and taught my class."

For less waterproof women, there is a variation on the French *cinq à sept* refresher. Three to five is the time slot a Boston school teacher sets aside for her lover, every weekday afternoon.

"What else could I do between three and five?" she asked.

According to what I hear, a woman could meet her lover horseback riding, jogging, playing tennis. Lots of people do these instead of or in conjunction with love-making.

One sportsy lady remembers, "We started to make love on the ground when our horses ran away. Another time we canoed over to a big rock and tied the boat up. The rock was our bed."

Someone whose boyfriend sees her only in tennis clothes remarked, "Even though I'm a beginner and he is advanced, we play almost every day because that playing is his courtship, literally."

The more public or uncomfortable the meetings, often the more heightened and rhapsodic they are.

A woman with no athletic proclivities can nonetheless schedule some offbeat amorous activities. My two-hundred-fifty-pound neighbor owns an answering service. One married client, she noticed, used to pick up all his messages in person. The gentleman in question was duly encouraged. When he did call in, he was told, "Your box is empty," or similar double entendres. He got her "message." He began visiting the service until, "One night, he rubbed my feet and another night continued upwards. The next thing I knew, I was on the floor."

These two established a lengthy affair. As the man had no spare cash for hotels and such, they made love right on the desk at her office.

Judging from its information recording, the phone company apparently feels no one is using its directories. Not true. My neighbor found them suitable for heightening her short lover when they stood to make love. The next time you're ready to explode at an inefficient answering service, please consider what you're possibly interrupting.

The new feminine separation of emotional and physical gratification has its surprises. Women of all ages are discovering that spiritual support missing in "arrangements" with men can come from unexpected sources—women friends, for example. Despite the tug of war for men, we women need and get a good deal of sympathetic nourishment from each other today. Many of us are still surprised and delighted by our satisfying evenings out together.

"I have to have my strokes in some way," a teacher told me. "It may be enough on a given day to have a friend put her arm around me or just talk." This division of functions between friends and lovers may be imperfect, but it can be a single woman's best option.

"My chances of having a nice time with a great woman are better than with most men," a middle-aged widow tells me. "We're still groping, some of us get rattled when there's car trouble and a bill is occasionally fussed over, but we're getting there fast."

These women say fulfillment with each other improves women's relationships with men. It lightens the load on the latter.

There used to be a greater reluctance among women to befriend a competitor. Women's dependence upon men led to competition among the dependents. The race was to get near the real power base—men. Increasingly, women are beginning to move and shake the world. It is less necessary, in order to win life's benefits, to outdo a woman friend for a man. Women can fulfill physical and psychological needs with different people—men and women.

A Fine Romance

No, make me mistress to the man I love;
If there be yet another name more free,
more fond than mistress, make me that to thee!
                                        —Alexander Pope,
                                        Eloisa to Abelard

The couple sitting next to me on Flight 3 from New York to Los Angeles refused the stewardess's every offer of food. I knew from that and a few quick sidelong glances that my questions didn't have a chance. They entwined themselves as much as public decorum and physical limitations permitted and took up the arm rest between them. Intensely absorbed in each other's comfort and emotions, the two looked serious, concerned, yet satisfied. He wore a wedding band. She did not. When her hand lingered on his thigh, he curved protectively around her, reading with her the book she had opened. Their bittersweet closeness probably followed a few days they had maneuvered together.

As we landed and got off the plane, I saw the woman turn her plain but inspired face toward the man. He touched her chin as delicately as if he were touching a rose. In the terminal I saw them walking in different directions—he toward a middle-aged woman and children, she to a cab alone. Not another glance between them. I wondered whether they would soon meet again.

Six months later, I was at the St. Regis Hotel Maisonette Room in New York with a married man (interviews can be fun). The music was nostalgic, the lighting soft. An inveterate eater myself, it struck me that no one else in the room was paying much attention to the food before them.

Only one table had more than two people. Almost everyone in the room danced at some point. I sensed that most of these folks were married to others—by the broad smiles, the hands tightly enmeshed, the close dancing. The strained silence sometimes obvious between married couples in restaurants was nowhere to be found here.

I gazed at the dance floor. Moving slowly, there were my two neighbors from the plane flight of six months before. Oblivious to the music's rhythm, they glided around the room to their own beat, hanging in the warm world of each other's arms.

Such pleasure may be halved by the loneliness that follows, but there is no denying the intensity of rhapsodic meetings in short spaces of time. Between those who feel mated is a secret shared—a fusion, one tiny unit poised against the cautious, judicial world. Every sensation is heightened. Men who hardly remember their wives' birthdays begin writing poetry and celebrating self-created anniversaries. They can afford to be impulsive, less guarded. Even the toughies let down some defenses, especially in middle age, after a degree of status is secured.

Romance used to be a verb, as in "He romanced her." Now the word has settled into an old noun groove. But no one who has been "romanced" forgets it: the breathless dates, exotic vacations, their own song.

There are instances in which people want to get married, need to get married, and pick a logical, socially easy choice. They are not "in love." The great amour sometimes comes, inconveniently, later in life, when home and family complexes are smoothly, if not lovingly, humming along. And, simply because the other woman is removed from the man's daily world, she easily becomes a romantic figure to him.

Merry became an expert on romance. A lover of music and sports, she had actively dated all through her twenties. One summer weekend, she visited friends at their house on Fire Island, a well-known New York summer retreat. Walking barefoot along the bay, she watched the sun which hung against the pale sky. It was the quietest hour of the day. Everyone was inside preparing for the evening. In the distance, a man on a bicycle rode toward her. Suddenly, the bike was in front of her. She looked up, her eyes catching the direct gaze of a gray-haired man with a youthful, smooth face and slender body. He rode on with a boyish determination.

Merry walked on . . . something about his face . . . familiar . . . almost Michelangelo's David. Only a second, but something had happened between them. She half turned her head. He was a block away by now, turning around to look at her. She was embarrassed. Twice more they looked at each other with half-turned heads from growing distances. Merry was determined not to peek again. The gray-haired man turned his bike around. He pedaled up next to her.

"Can I have ten minutes of your life to watch the sun go down?"

Merry looked into his guileless eyes, nodded, and walked silently to the pier with him. They sat wordlessly watching the sun set.

Later: "I'm sorry I can't ask you to spend the evening with me, but I have previous plans," he explained.

They parted. He never asked her name. Merry saw him the next day on the beach with his wife and children. They stared at each other across the sand, an understood resignation between them.

Six months later, in the midst of a snowstorm, they met on a bus in Manhattan. Gregory was his name. Merry refused the cup of coffee he offered. Gregory told her that he now knew their meeting was fated.

She said, "No, it was coincidence. We will never see each other again."

Gregory swore she was wrong, but despite his protestations, they parted . . . until three years later, when another *coincidental* meeting precipitated the inevitable passion that Gregory had sensed from the start.

Bonds sometimes seem to form by otherworldly design. One must, of course, be receptive or not consciously resistant. Every day people do fight romance, passion, and friendship—anything which they feel jeopardizes an already valuable relationship. But romance, unopposed by a strong commitment elsewhere, allures us.

We will reject it, succumb to it, remember it, maybe regret it. Each person decides whether he can afford the price tag. Merry took a chance. At the beginning, she only saw Gregory once a week and still maintained an active social life of her own.

> I really didn't want this thing with someone else's husband. Over a period of ten months, Gregory began coming over more and more often. I knew I was in love with him, but I was only thirty-one. I didn't want to spend the rest of my life as someone's mistress.

Though she very much loved him, Merry determined not to have an illicit relationship. She introduced him to her family and friends. He was so obviously in love with Merry—who had never been happier—that her family just accepted this arrangement.

> He promised me that when his youngest son was sixteen (the boy was four when we met), he would divorce and marry me. I never doubted Greg for a moment because I was so convinced we were made for each other. After the first year, we fixed a schedule so that we could make plans. Every Monday and Thursday, he and I would spend the evening together and either all day Saturday or Sunday.
>
> I was surprised that Greg was able to set things up like this. I asked about his wife. "She's pretty bright and I'm sure she knows I don't go to bars or the racetrack." He gave me the definite impression that his wife preferred the security of their marriage to the risks she might incur by insisting he give me up.

Merry and Gregory were an extremely compatible twosome, brightening every gathering they attended. No one who knew them ever questioned the propriety of their relationship, because the match was perfect. A few people asked Gregory why he didn't divorce, but he never had any great answers to give them. "The children" or "I'm weak" were about all he offered. A few times during those twelve years they did run into his wife. She was a stately, refined-looking woman.

We were at an art gallery opening. Gregory calmly said, "My wife has just arrived." He immediately went up to her, before she spotted us, and asked her to come over and meet me. He didn't explain who I was, though I'm sure it was obvious. "Helyne, this is Merry. Merry, my wife." I stood speechless after the formalities. With incredible élan and much grace on his wife's part, we all left. Gregory put me in a cab and whispered he'd meet me at my apartment.

He arrived a half hour later, having taken Helyne to a friend's house. He told me they said very little on the subject. I never heard any more about it. The other few times I saw her we just nodded at each other.

Twelve years went by quite happily for the lovers. The day after Gregory's son's sixteenth birthday, Merry, impatient for his divorce, asked if he had seen his lawyer. He told her it was not something he could do. No matter how much he loved her, it was simply impossible. He was going crazy about the whole thing. Merry left him right there in the restaurant where he had told her the news and went straight to her aunt's apartment.

My aunt and I were very close. She was the wisest woman I knew. I was crying uncontrollably and told her I'd never see him again. She thought I was crazy and that my life had gone along smoothly and with great happiness those twelve years. I knew he was married from the start, we were marvelous together and had managed at least one or two vacations every year we'd been together. By the end of the weekend, she convinced me I would never find anyone else like Gregory. I knew she was right.

But Merry couldn't hide her disappointment. Gregory saw this and hated himself for being so gutless. It was the first promise to Merry he had broken and was sick about it. In fact, he became ill with the guilt toward both women and began moping around the house, developing one psychosomatic ailment after another. He tried provoking arguments with Helyne until he realized how ridiculous he was being.

"After all these years, why don't we have the truth out?" he finally told his wife. He gave her credit for knowing everything and he was right. He didn't ask her if she had had lovers and didn't care. Gregory said he would leave, fuss or not. She didn't fuss. He gave her an extremely generous settlement, and the children seemed to understand and adjust to the divorce quite easily.

Gregory married Merry and they received a congratulatory phone call from Helyne.

> "You were so generous I want to thank you and wish you all the best." He told her how well she'd behaved and suggested that they'd always be friends and see each other.
> "How about Mondays and Thursdays?" she suggested.

Any lady with a sense of humor like that must have been difficult to leave.

Merry and I are sitting and talking in the top floor bar of Hong Kong's Sheraton Hotel, facing the tall buildings of Kowloon. The spectacular harbor, crowded with junks, lies below. Gregory, a tall, slender man in his fifties, joins us. I told him I had just heard the story of his and Merry's romance. "My blood runs cold to think I might have missed this marriage," he tells me. "I never knew people could feel like this year after year."

Like Merry, the women in my interviews did not intend to be other women. But someone else's husband can have more than sexual excitement and romance to recommend him. Women may learn a great deal from them. Sometimes they begin new careers after exposure to worlds they would otherwise have missed. Additionally, people want a supportive figure sharing and following the continuing drama (or comedy) of their lives. One of marriage's chief attractions is knowing someone on your side—you hope—is there to laugh with, to whom you can explain and surrender the masks and burdens of the day. They bear witness to your life's events and affirm your existence.

Close family members or friends of the same sex serve that function for a few. The majority do not have those intimate associations, at least not on a daily basis. Married men frequently became the only dependable figures in the lives of the single women who confided in me. They call often. The affair has no room for disloyalty or criticism.

"In all those years, I never heard one critical word," Martha, a secretary, assures me of her twenty-five-year affair still in progress. She says she never wanted marriage with her lover. "Except for Christmas and holiday loneliness, I've had much the best of life with him. You see, we're always trying to please each other."

Martha and other single people, especially those with no children, often miss having someone else in their lives who remains a long-term confidant. Add this to today's social instability—the frequent changes of jobs, cities, and residences—and a woman's married lover, someone who wants to stay with her, has the enhanced appeal of permanence—ironic as that seems.

To get that kind of dependability many people marry . . . the wrong spouses. They turn out to be adversaries, or people who play victim. The latter want to be seen as weak enough so that their mates feel they have to stick around and care for them. A lot of women seem to feel a better solution than these matches is the compartmentalized existence which includes a married lover. The fulfillment is joyful, if part-time. Not expecting her man to provide everything, as most do in wedlock, disappointment may be kept to a minimum. The many friends or acquaintances we traditionally see less of in marriage are kept up with because our essential pursuits don't change. The eclectic medley of characters we know is not traded in for couples with similar goals and problems. The variety missing in so many marriages is easier to preserve in a love affair.

While the relationship lasts, a woman benefits from a mentor, friend, teacher, traveling companion, guide, enthusiastic lover, or all of these. Simultaneously, she can look for a permanent (whatever that means anymore) companion while alleviating her loneliness and frustration with a lover. If she is establishing a new career, raising children alone, tired of searching for the "right" one, or unhappily married, she may be able to fill the emptiness that would otherwise remain in her life.

If the relationship turns serious, it may work out for marriage or a lifetime of passion. But the odds weigh heavily against it. At least

75 percent of the affairs I heard about died of attrition or frustration; sometimes they were replaced by more viable romances.

A woman surrenders to the affair despite those lousy odds if she feels she needs it enough and believes "It is better to have loved and lost . . ."

WHEN THE MUSIC DIES

For the lips of a strange woman drop as a honeycomb, and her mouth is smoother than oil:
But her end is bitter as wormwood, sharp as a two-edged sword.
—Proverbs 5:3–4

Like swallows to Capistrano, husbands return regularly, post-Labor Day, from the mountains and shores of family vacations to the cities, suburbs, their work . . . and other women. Migration occurs as children settle into school and the family's fall routine begins. The end of summer holidays marks the species' new season of crowded schedules, furtive meetings, and romantic rendezvous.

Though an affair may nourish a woman, especially if it culminates in her lover's divorce, it may be a season of more lows than highs. Women I spoke with said that to protect themselves, they only partake of arrangements—situations they believe are limited to their enjoyment of the moment. Love, they think, will not intrude. Men are generally picked for these set-ups deliberately for some nonlovable qualities. Physical appeal and charm are their dominant, and sometimes only, assets. Successful lust, however, sometimes has a stronger hold than the woman imagines. She becomes too involved, and even when the involvement seems merely sexual or superficial, her plans can backfire. Such was Joanne's experience.

Thirty-two, a divorcee and former stockbroker, Joanne, after divorcing her husband, moved from their large Manhattan West Side condominium to a studio apartment in the East Eighties. We talked in her white Mediterranean-style room, colored floor pillows and native stoneware around us. Except for the pain evident on her face as she talked of her past, Joanne looked young for her age. Her practicality, ready glibness, and ability to laugh at herself made her genial company.

Joanne met Ramón—a dashing Spaniard—at a cocktail party. He was her first sexual partner since her divorce, and too good to be true. A poetic note followed every visit. As soon as the old Continental allure got to Joanne, Ramón suddenly became intermittently attentive, but just attentive enough so that her need festered on. He would call after long intervals, or after she had finally cried herself to sleep at 3 A.M. She hung on until the magnetism wasn't worth the masochism.

Joanne stopped seeing Ramón. One morning several weeks later she became teary-eyed thinking of his rejection and her loneliness. In this mood she went out, on the spring Saturday, to do her chores.

In the drugstore, Ken appeared. For ages he had smiled and flirted, but three or four walks to Gristede's were as far as it had gotten. Originally they had met when she was looking for her dentist's office. Ken is a dentist too and works in the same building. He directed Joanne and for two years they passed each other in their neighborhood.

Occasionally, his wife, a pleasant, plain-looking woman in her forties, was with him. The constant twinkle in Ken's eye and abnormal concern about Joanne when they were alone suggested that he was used to accommodating new players to his seductive game.

"Who was he?" Ken confidentially asked, observing her red-rimmed eyes. Personal questions tumbled easily from him.

"Why do you men always assume it's a man?"

"Because it always is. . . . Was he married?"

"It happens I just lost my job." A perfectly true fact. Joanne was one of eleven stockbrokers in her brokerage house trimmed in recent cutbacks.

"No one cries about that." He was right.

"Okay, but I am worried about a job."

Also, Joanne's separation and her refusal on principle to accept alimony left her receiving nothing but unemployment compensation. She could find no openings in her field at the moment.

"I'm sorry about that, but I'm more sorry that someone hurt you," Ken said, before adding:

"I went through something similar myself eight years ago."

I was all set to say good-bye, but Ken just wouldn't let the subject drop.

"I wasn't in love, thank goodness. But I don't want to go into it."

"Okay, sure. Call if you want to talk."

"Thanks."

Joanne didn't call, or do much of anything else the next two weeks but hunt for jobs and meet a lot of working friends for lunch. They were sympathetic, and they picked up the checks. But she wasn't distracted from the hurt of Ramón.

At 6:40 one Tuesday, Ken called.

"What do you think of White and Rosenfeld?"

"One of the top security houses on the Street. Why?"

"A patient of mine turns out to be a partner and thinks he can do something for you. If you're interested, I'll arrange an interview this week."

Just then they were cut off. Thirty seconds later the phone rang.

"Where are you?" I asked dumbly like a lamb going to slaughter.

"In a phone booth on your corner. I'm on my way home."

I was furiously debating whether or not to invite him up to discuss the job. I'd never given in to the advances of men I didn't morally or emotionally want to sleep with, but I sensed I was very shaky at that moment.

"You want to hear the particulars? I could come up for a couple of minutes. Have to be home at seven though."

Joanne realized later it was cunning of Ken to assure her he would only stay a few minutes. No one could intend to make love that fast. Anyway, flirting was second nature to a woman who worked in a man's business and the only viable survival kit she'd ever found in this world. He came up.

Ken explained, "This guy likes me and owes me a big favor."
"Why?"
"I came in from a vacation to take care of some teeth he had
broken."
"Thank you."
"That's all right." Ken described a job even too good for Joanne's
fantasies. He promised to set up an interview for her.

> "Anytime, anywhere." We went to the door and Ken pretended
> to give me a friendly hug, but he held me against him a
> moment longer than he should have. It was long enough for me
> to know my body was corrupting all my good intentions.

Joanne had the interview and got the job. Ken called to find out
what happened. He insisted on bringing some champagne for a
celebratory drink. By this time it was obvious to her that she had
had an overdose of aloneness and discipline.

> After three sips of champagne and two kisses, I knew I wanted
> him, but wasn't ready to give in yet. Also, I don't like to make
> such decisions when I'm high or turned on. I have to suffer a
> while, weighing the morality, denying myself gratification. This
> way I can never accuse myself of acting only out of need.
> "I've been in love twice in my life," Ken told me in a somber
> tone. "The first time I married her; the second time I wanted to
> but didn't have the guts to leave my wife."
> "How long did it last?"
> "Two years. We were very happy, but I couldn't bust up my
> family. Almost did several times. A horrible thing happened."
> "What?"
> "The woman committed suicide. Nearly killed me too." At
> this time Kenneth's eyes filled.
> "God, how could you live with it?"
> "It wasn't easy. Lots of analysis until I could handle it. I was
> impotent for a while. I'll never let myself get involved again . . .
> never." The fact that even Ken had suffered kind of softened me
> further. I began to sympathize with him.

"I'm surprised you can have affairs altogether now."

"After eight years I finally do it with no remorse. I need sex, that's all. There are just so many variations to fu . . . making love." He was a clever bastard. "Figure, after doing it with your wife each way several thousand times, there's just not much excitement left. That's the way I've felt for years. I can't torture myself over it the rest of my life. I'm a good husband and father."

"Where does your wife think you are now?"

"My club. They always say, 'He's probably in the library. We don't page there.' That alone is worth the yearly fee . . . and they know it." Kenneth had obviously worked all these details out a thousand times. I told myself to watch the ball, figuratively speaking, and forget about the grandstand. I should worry about *my* needs. The one thing that made me consider Ken a good candidate for a lover was that I wouldn't fall in love with him. He was too smooth-talking and egotistical.

My question about logistics obviously signaled him that I was thinking about having sex.

"I like you very much. It could be a lot of fun." He said this in his sincerest sincere tone. Not the most romantic invitation of my life, but then I had all those wonderful reasons to help me: I could function better at work if I were more relaxed; he was very passionate, honest, funny, and wouldn't hurt me because he had only to gain from this relationship. Also, I'd lose weight—a long-standing problem in my life.

Joanne and Ken began making love once or twice a week in her apartment. She was frightened and delighted every time he rang the bell. For the first time in her life, she became sexually aggressive, experiencing more and deeper orgasms than she had had with her husband, Larry, in five years.

Ken always brought wine or some exotic food to munch between rounds . . . with him, there were always at least two. Everything went smoothly. Somehow, though, I never felt I knew him. Of all the men I've now been with, sexually or not, he was the strangest to me because I never knew his thoughts.

Like a good student, I learned ways to please him and tried things I'd never done, what he called "post-graduate work." I was considerably loosened up and felt marvelous. I used to wonder whether I could really be passionate in sex without love. It's so contrived. But I found out I could. I'm not pretending it's like sex with love, but there was a severe shortage of that commodity in my life.

During the next month, Ken kept asking Joanne if she was handling the affair all right. I guess he was surprised, maybe even disappointed, that she was. In retrospect, she thinks, he couldn't believe that she hadn't fallen apart over him yet. She answered him that everything was fine. Little by little Ken's charms were more appealing. Inevitably, they grew closer.

I was amazed how emotional, romantic me could enjoy pure sex . . . until one day.

The whole business began to be a bit cool for my makeup. I didn't expect "I love you," but is "I'm crazy about you" or "You're marvelous" too big a commitment? I don't know if I would have believed him. He smiled too easily and often (except when we made love—a fact I most appreciated), but my insecure soul began to wonder if he really cared for me. Once, coming close to the subject, he said, "If I didn't like you, would I be here?" "Like" was not the kind of assurance policy I needed.

I could have killed myself one night for asking him to stay a little longer. "I always stay as long as I can. I know when I'll be missed. Please don't ask." Even though this answer was so negative, I looked forward every week to the only touching or closeness I had in my life. For once, the refrigerator was not as irresistible as usual.

One day I met Ken's wife in the supermarket. Naturally, I was friendly but felt awful about seeing her. "I'm not going to let her do the marketing anymore," Ken quipped when I told him. If it weren't me it would be someone else, I kept telling myself, but wondered if she was aware of her husband's interests. There was no chance with the way she looked— careless, kind of sloppy—that she'd ever known any outside action herself. I wondered whether or not she could guess. I asked Ken if he thought his wife sensed it. "I don't know. She's never asked about anything."

Joanne and Ken often made love on a sheet spread on her carpet. He was creative, doing inventive things with Mars Bars that never occurred to Joanne. As she began to lose weight, he continually gained! She had lost nine pounds in two months and her new job was splendid. She congratulated herself on finding the right cure for Ramón, her Spanish affliction. To share her sublime state, Joanne decided to do something nice for Ken; she would show her appreciation for her new tranquility.

Ken always arrived around six-thirty. I decided to make us dinner. Cooking for men, to me, is like sex for some women—a commitment, a giving, so I always had to think twice before gaily plunging through a supermarket door. But that Tuesday, James Beard and I whipped up something just this side of two million calories. By nine P.M. and my third phone call to Ken's answering service, I realized something was wrong.

Joanne thought over their recent conversations and found nothing that could have put him off. She told herself that his wife must have, at gunpoint, demanded him to be with her that evening. There were no letters or lipstick marks that could have given him away. In fact, the one time she borrowed his handkerchief, she kept it to wash out her makeup that had gotten on it. What man could find a more cautious mistress? She ate almost nothing that night (for her, the ultimate sign of depression). The next day, she began phoning again:

"The doctor is with a patient" was all I heard. His nurse had obviously been briefed for this. I wondered if this was Ken's usual escape from a tedious affair. But even my past falling self-image had not crashed to a point where the drabness of my soul and body could be sold to me so quickly. Also, the ancient female rationalization of "he's probably lying wounded in a train wreck" was out because he was obviously happily drilling and filling teeth. I thought about barging in for a showdown, but I had too much class to let his nurse witness my hysterics and too much fury to do it quietly. I couldn't believe it. After a week of eating and afternoon movies, my phone was still silent. What happened to the fellow who'd launched a thousand orgasms?

I became a pizza addict for a while and then struggled to get off the fifteen pounds I gained. Something happens to a girl— this girl, anyway—when she's sexually abused: my label for what Ken did. All my little cells shut down. I couldn't be close to another man.

After some time passed they opened again, as cells will. Joanne began going out exclusively with single men, but the only two she liked well enough to sleep with were impotent. When I contacted her a year and half later, she was again involved with a married man. I was surprised.

I know it's incredible that I'd let myself in for the same pain, but I really don't think it will be. Ken is a familiar breed . . . physically irresistible, heartless. I pass him in the neighborhood with his wife sometimes. I have too much pride to show I'm interested in what happened. He probably couldn't handle the closeness that was developing between us.

Stan, my present boyfriend, is another matter. He's very ordinary-looking and has never had an affair. He's at least as vulnerable as I am and has proven his deep feelings in a thousand ways. I tried single men but besides sexual hang-ups, the ones I met didn't want to get close either. It's always a holding back from their real feelings. At least with Stan I have a totally supportive friend there. The sex is wonderful because the love is real. I cannot live in the future when the present needs filling.

Joanne became involved with a man who found even a little bit of closeness threatening. Though she hadn't been demanding marriage from Ken, her minimal needs were too much for him to respond to. The way out he took was easiest for him and painful for her. Though I was initially startled to learn that Joanne was once again involved with a married man, I realized later that amongst my interviewees, the pattern of repeating this experience was typical. People's needs for tenderness and companionship are overwhelming, and that they are willing to suffer predictable consequences to fulfill them is understandable.

Even Samantha, the young lady who met her wealthy lover on a blind date, claims she had her eyes open about the affair and was able to foresee its sad end. On his wife's and Samantha's mutual birthday, Don left them both. He had an aide tell Samantha the news.

Len said, "Samantha, I've got some bad news for you."

I immediately thought Don was sick or in a hospital.

He said, "Don's wife found out about you and threatened to do horrendous things. Don's not going to see you anymore."

"What do you mean? After three years, he's going to just not see me?"

"That's what he promised her."

I couldn't believe Don wouldn't call to tell me that himself. I became completely hysterical, wailing almost. Five hours later, Don called.

He said in a sad little voice, "Someone called my wife. I don't know who, but she filled her in on everything—your name, address, and phone number."

He said, "I love you, I'll always love you. You're my life. As soon as I figure out what I'm doing with her, you and I will get back together. I need to be free now and figure out what I want to do with myself."

Samantha realized Don was leaving both of them. He immediately got a divorce.

The whole experience hurt like hell. I didn't want to live much. I tried to take an overdose of pills, but they were the wrong kind and didn't do the trick.

I tried starving myself to death, not leaving the apartment for six weeks. I slept two hours a night and had what they call spontaneous hysteria. If anything reminded me of him, it was terrible.

I called a young platonic friend of mine. He moved in and stayed for six weeks. He wouldn't let me out of his sight and quit work to take care of me. He was wonderful and knew exactly what I needed at that state of depression. He was gentle, understanding, and compassionate. After six weeks he said, "You're okay now," and he left.

I had another two or three weeks of getting myself together. One night I decided I still had a lot of living to do. I took a new job in a clothing store. With Don, I'd forgotten all about work because he said he'd always take care of me. He didn't.

I will always love Don. Until I die, I'll never take this necklace off.

Samantha fingers a heart of diamonds around her neck.

He gave it to me on our first Valentine's Day. I just can't take it off . . . I've tried. But when I do, I feel like nobody loves me. I have called him dozens of times . . . he won't take my calls. It hurts terribly, but what can I do? I will not let it destroy me anymore. I felt like a jigsaw puzzle somebody had thrown in the air that had to be put back together.

Stories like Samantha's are particularly gloomy because they depict situations which a less needy person would avoid. Samantha lacked self-esteem and security, both psychological and financial. She found the combination of attention, glamour, money, and what affection there was overwhelming.

In the foregoing stories, neither Joanne nor Samantha had control over the time or circumstances of their lovers' departures. The men to whom they had given a significant part of themselves demonstrated a lack of respect for their feelings. The wounds inflicted left them with a sense of degradation.

Joanne belongs to that group of women that intends to keep its affairs strictly physical . . . as many men do. But more of their male counterparts are skilled at maintaining a light, uninvolved arrangement. There are those who believe it is all a matter of cultural training, experience, and learning the craft. Certainly a practiced female has a better chance of controlling her emotions than someone like Joanne, but psychiatrists tell me that women, despite their increased independence and experience, still have greater attachments than do most men. Add a cold departure like Ken's or Don's, and the music involved may not justify the finale.

When the decision to terminate an extramarital relationship is wholly or partially the woman's, she can retain dignity. Still, the mutually emotional affair affects her long-range goals profoundly. Because the man in question is kind, sensitive, attentive, never hurting her except by withholding a commitment, she is unlikely to give him up. At least she will not do so easily. He remains the favorite against which each man she meets is measured—often with good reason. The married lover shares his inner self with her. He wants his girlfriend to make his life complete—to give him what he cannot or will not establish with his wife. The responsiveness he proffers in exchange is difficult to match in the single man, who does not appear to need her as much.

In a few special circumstances—like that of a young woman's knowingly looking for a tender first sexual experience, or a wife wanting to sexually supplement a basically good marriage or get out of a bad one—such "healthy animal" liaisons may be valuable. But when the other woman allows herself vulnerability, even if it is reciprocal, I found some measure of agony inevitably follows . . . if she wants more of a commitment than the man offers.

There are affairs ending in what women view as defeat that they consider worth the intoxication and sense of belonging only found in love. The men I interviewed felt the same way. When the partners have not previously endured similar anguish, you can bet they will opt for taking a chance. If they have known the torment, they still might. When the impractical love affair is relinquished, despite its well-known ache, it is done so reluctantly. Love is difficult to resist. Either way it hurts; more often it hurts the woman.

Though marriage, according to divorce statistics, is increasingly a speculative venture, affairs are gambles too, and the pitfalls are not as well known. The stakes are high. Whether the game is worth playing depends strictly on a woman's goals and how much she is willing to risk for ephemeral joy. If she is not prepared to lose the bet, she had better steer clear of the tables.

The Root of All Evil

Don't thou marry for money,
But go where money is.
—Alfred Tennyson,
"Northern Farmer: New Style"

They say money is the root of all evil. Correctly, the quote reads, "The love of money is the root of all evil."* Or, "The lack of money is the root of all evil."** Either way, it is at the root of some extramarital relationships. Not that these other women get paid, exactly—there is another word for that—but men with money have facility and mobility. Their liaisons go smoothly.

I asked women if their boyfriends had money or if it made a difference to them. About half the men cited had above average incomes. A small percentage were exorbitantly rich. The rest were below average in wealth or middle-class. Some earned less than the women.

"I'd have an affair with a poor guy, but I wouldn't marry one," a fifty-year-old woman told me. To her and about half the women I

---

*I Timothy 6:10.
**George Bernard Shaw, the definitive text of *Man and Superman*, *Maxims for Revolutionists* (London: Penguin Books, 1946). Reprinted by permission of the Society of Authors on behalf of the Bernard Shaw Estate.

interviewed, money was not a factor in the affair. A few of the men were actually broke.

When lovers live in different cities or countries, money becomes a necessity. Taking planes instead of trains, and talking long distance, brings separated lovers together. And all other things being equal, married men with money offer advantages, making a woman's life easier and more enjoyable. (That is true of single men, too.)

Luxuries only money can buy have historically been men's to bestow. Until recently, when women's salaries began climbing toward some equality with men's, few of them could afford travel and elegant entertaining. Wealthy men moving around meet a larger number of women and have more legitimate reasons for so doing than their officebound counterparts.

Psychologically, it is easier for a husband to have an involvement away from his home town. Men say it helps to isolate the experience from their married lives. The man becomes more daring, sexually and emotionally. Nothing between him and his other woman connects with his daily life or its constellation of relatives and business associates.

For very young women, money is particularly dazzling. Clothes and expensive gifts may lure them into relationships which require more sophisticated emotional equipment than they possess. Actresses and models, whose professions are extremely competitive and insecure, are financially more dependent than women with steady incomes. Likewise, it is easier for a young woman with no career commitment to fall into the easy life some wealthy men provide. She believes the wealthy man will not miss the money he spends on her. I met some regular job holders who accepted allowances. The transition from refusal to acceptance can be gradual . . . mentally as well as actually.

Heirs aside, every young man knows he had better establish himself early on, because no one else will care for him. But the vague image of the woman as supportee still has a hold on both sexes. It is fading, but women in their twenties generally earn low salaries. Some of the ones I met, wanting independence from their parents, accept money from married men they date. They may indeed love them. They cannot, on their own money, live the middle-class life they knew at home and may not be willing to struggle the way their parents once did.

Approximately 15 percent of the women I interviewed were at least partially kept by wealthy married men, often in an atmosphere of affection and tenderness.

With Don, Samantha (of the diamond heart necklace) thought she had everything.

> I was twenty-six years old going on fourteen. I'd been through two marriages and two divorces but was the least sophisticated person you'll ever know. I was broke all the time. I discovered the night we met that Don lived both in Texas and Acapulco. He was just my type—sophisticated, beautifully dressed, charming. When we were introduced, bells rang, banjos played, all the stupid fairy tales happened just like that.
>
> After dinner, he took me home and told me, "I'm married, have three kids, and will never get divorced. I promise you nothing but fun and happiness."

Samantha, who held a minimal sales job, was unaware that Don was married when they had their first date. Don told Samantha, at the start of their relationship, she could date anyone she wanted. After six months, he changed his mind.

"You're my woman and I feel very strongly about that," he said.

By this time Samantha was in love with him and leading a fantasy existence.

> The first week we met, he came into my apartment and asked me to call over a friend who was the same size. She came and he had her take my entire wardrobe except what I had on. We immediately went to Bonwit's, where he bought me a complete new wardrobe.

In addition to picking up all of Samantha's bills, Don continually gave her fabulous presents and a $10,000-a-month allowance!

"It's not easy to spend ten thousand dollars a month, especially when I was traveling with him half the time. My friends had three wonderful years of trips and presents too."

I asked Samantha if she thought Don was as materially generous to his family.

> No. Last Christmas, for example, he flew in three five-foot-square wooden crates filled with presents for me. They included a sable coat, a seal coat trimmed in sable, sterling pieces, antique porcelain I collect, and a color television set.

Samantha asked him, "What did you buy your wife?"
"Oh, a Gucci purse."
"And your daughter?"
"A typewriter."
"That's nice. Did you get the automatic return on it?"
"No, they wanted a hundred more for that."

> His wife's birthday and mine were on the same day. He would send his secretary out to buy something for her. But for my birthday I'd get things like a nine-thousand-dollar diamond ring which *he* picked out. Always elaborate, expensive presents, but that was his guilt talking.

When their liaison began, Don told Samantha he was taking over full responsibility for her life, then and always. She must never think about money again. But the bucks ended when the romance did, three years later. By that time, Samantha had amassed over $250,000 in jewels and cash. After a long, depressing emotional bout, during which she tried to commit suicide twice, Samantha pulled herself together, got a job, and learned to live alone. Recently she was married, to another man named Don. Samantha looks back.

> From the start I knew I'd get hurt. My eyes were wide open, but I decided to choose the pain because I wanted him. I also knew Don would eventually leave me, not the other way around. But

I thought I was prepared to handle all this. Don never believed after three years that I genuinely loved *him* and not his money, power, or what he could do for me. He was my life.

Arrangements like Samantha's, I found, often start with simple intentions. They usually change. It is difficult to spend much time with someone you like, who is good to you, and not become attached.

The American kept woman has a British counterpart. London's *Entrepreneur* magazine recently carried an article by Laura Hamilton.* With pension plan, an apartment which would soon be hers, and built-in holidays, her description of her affair sounded like a bona fide job.

> On paper, I became a self-employed marketing consultant, and James's accountant organized my financial affairs. I've often wondered how the Inland Revenue might react to such an unusual deal—but I guessed that James was more than a match for any mealy-mouthed tax inspector. James's solicitor says he handles quite a lot of work of "this nature." In fact, I know the mistresses of several of James's friends—so that's four instances I know about!

After a year or so, Laura's objectivity was obscured. She was attached to James, "even to the point of crying when he had to leave me. When he gave me the pearls on Christmas Eve, I was thrilled and deliriously happy. I hadn't got his present with me because it was too heavy to carry."

Laura expected James to come to her flat for his present, but he explained he couldn't. He had to meet his wife in town and wouldn't see Laura until after Christmas.

> I'd never really imagined what would happen at times like Christmas. The previous year we'd spent together in New York

---

* "The Cost of Living," by Laura Hamilton, from *Entrepreneur*, Winter 1978, p. 20. Reprinted by permission.

while his wife went to the Philippines to see their daughter. I knew I was being selfish and reacting badly, but I felt angry and let down—and very lonely.

Laura's cure for her depression was her own holiday and unexpected affair with a younger man. She returned refreshed and cheerful, delighted to accompany her lover to his business conferences.

"I'm happy because my today is delightfully worry-free, my lover/provider is attentive, quite attractive and very wealthy. My tomorrow is financially secure and the future looks rosy."

A note at the end of the article indicates that this lady was up on her legal precedents. Though her lover was married, it seems that in England "decisions have been made by the courts in favor of mistresses. They are regarded as quasi 'partners' and as such have some claim on assets acquired during the 'partnership'" Michelle Triola Marvin might have been a student of British customs.

The women I interviewed were divided about fifty-fifty on the importance of money in their affairs. This indicates that money is not a significant factor in whether or not a woman takes a married lover. In considering any relationship, money will always matter to some.

Kept is an odd expression, considering very few such women ever seem to become permanent fixtures in their men's lives. Excluding double marriages—a legal wife in one place and an unofficial one in another—none of the money-based relationships I heard of became legal unions. Only two of the hundreds of women I spoke with were kept—completely cared for financially by their lovers. But I heard from many who were accepting partial support or extravagant presents.

Al Lerner, the investigator, followed one man into Tiffany's, where he spent $10,000 on a bracelet for his girlfriend. He assures me that on New York's East Side, charge accounts and expensive apartments are frequently bought by married men for kept women.

Celine, a novice clothing designer, was supporting herself none too grandly. Bob came into her life suggesting she quit her job so she could travel with him. He was fabulously rich, the president of a publicly owned company. Their six years together included for her a lavish allowance, a luxury apartment of her own, and charge accounts at the best stores. Bob's wife never knew of Celine.

That was the scenario until last year. The women had been, until them, only acquainted in gym class, social functions, and so on. They spoke cordially during that time. After his wife found out about Celine, the two were civil but, understandably, not friendly. Both women gave Bob ultimatums. He divorced his wife and ended his affair with his girlfriend immediately afterward. He helped Celine out financially until her career got going again. Bob's wife has just married his former best friend.

I heard about married men who keep women "invisibly," often opulently, for years. Perhaps it is a kind of insurance that the other woman will not contact his wife. She has a financial interest in maintaining calm waters and becomes, at times, a kind of prisoner in diamonds. One sad woman I met wanted to end the affair but no longer had the means, either financial or emotional, to do so.

There used to be a greater incentive to be kept. Most women had no access to independent incomes. This often encouraged the unmarried among them, who were having such affairs, into these financial arrangements. Rejecting families viewed their experience with alarmed condemnation. Until the last few decades, being kept may have seemed one of the more attractive options available to working-class women. Having little hope of marrying well, it was their only avenue to material comfort, often with love.

Overwhelmingly, I found that the need for intimacy, sex, and friendship, more than material comfort, motivates women to form relationships with married men: they are trying to fulfill emotional needs. I also found that the more types of support a woman depends on from another woman's husband, the more devastated she will be if they are withdrawn against her will. As women pay more attention to their own monetary goals and investments, they are less likely to be dazzled by someone else's.

CHAPTER 4
Wives as Other Women

Marriage: **n.** *a community consisting of a master, a mistress, and two slaves, making in all, two.*

—Ambrose Bierce,
The Devil's Dictionary

HER BETTER HALF

HER BETTER half is what a wife's lover might be compared to her husband. Married women can be more lonely than single ones. Their husbands, physically on the scene but often sexually and/or emotionally absent, create tremendous frustration. A number of wives told me they were deeply in love with their husbands but simply felt their own sexuality was on the wax while their mates' was clearly on the wane. Needing more sex or wanting love "before it's too late" some wives solve the dilemma by taking lovers. They may be married men.

Single men are very busy taking care of the unmarried female population. They do not have the time or patience to fit their romantic interludes into a wife's limited schedule. A bachelor need not accommodate the time and emotional availability of a married woman because he is in such demand in the unmarried world. It does occasionally happen that he falls in love with someone else's wife, but this is not typical. So wives often choose their lovers from among the amenable married population. A lot of these men told me they preferred married women because they are less likely to hassle them about marriage. Moreover, they meet and get to know each other socially more easily.

I discovered that a couple's married male friend, half of a pair they see on a regular basis, is often the elected candidate. The wife chooses or acquiesces to her husband's friend, reasoning that this particular man is the least suspect. Another advantage is that both lovers are trying to manage another relationship simultaneously. Their problems are similar. The man and woman who keep their liaison a secret from the other two mates, while continuing to meet socially, can satisfy the needs they have over and above that of intimacy. Sometimes these include winning a competition with their own spouses or their lovers' spouses or a figure from the past.

But these arrangements are not without their liabilities. Women who are unhappily married and fall in love with other men generally prefer to divorce and be with the new lover. That is what I found to be true, and it was confirmed by Jerry Supkoff, a Los Angeles lawyer who sees plenty of divorce action. "Most men would rather stay in bad marriages. But when a woman finds another man to love her, nothing is going to keep her with that first man." If these men are also married, there is another divorce to consider. Convincing her lover to divorce is as difficult for the married woman as it is for the single one. Married men who fall in love divorce less frequently than do women who have the same experience. Thus, the suffering quotient for wives tends to be higher than for their married lovers.

So why do married women roam?

"My husband is simply not interested in sex. Life goes by fast, and I'm starved for it. Now I'm always looking for a good affair," Janine said. She only thought to take a lover after her best friend was killed in an auto accident and, for the first time, her own mortality became palpable.

Consider a group of wives discussing infidelity around the fireplace in a New England ski lodge.

"My husband went on business trips. I was so lonely and full of resentment that I soon got involved with a married man and felt no guilt." Another assured us her motivations were "ego and boredom." On the conflicts of maintaining husband and lover, they agreed, the solution is to have affairs but never fall in love.

Locked into marriages they can't financially or emotionally afford to leave, some bored wives have always turned to other men. Literary figures like Madame Bovary, with her notorious flight to guilt-ridden rapture, still inspire a few otherwise fainthearted women. Society's condemnation no longer holds them back as it did, and its punishments are less severe.

Whichever marital partner has an outside relationship says his or her spouse is not particularly sexy. In fact, each thinks his own gender is probably the more physical of the two. But lust only goes so far. Wives, like everyone else, want the big love affair, a total relationship. Most told me they felt more capable of intimacy than their husbands. When these women find it, they rarely let it go, and may follow it right out of their marriages. While the men I spoke with generally tried to keep their home lives the constant factor and their love relationships the intermittent luxury, the women wanted their existence integrated.

A WAY OUT

It's very easy to get married, but very hard to find your mate.
—Alexia, a wife who thought she *did*.

"He knew I was interested in him and that I'd always be there when he wanted me," says Alexia of the married man she had met horseback riding. She enjoyed having an interest in someone who paid complete attention to her, at least when they were together. As they rode through the woods or made love in her apartment, there was no one else but the two of them.

> It was a beautiful, long affair. I was enjoying a sex life I didn't realize existed. Not in my married life. He made me feel so desirable and gave me a chance to learn, at forty-two, that love-making was a great and marvelous part of life. I was completely happy.

Alexia never considered that her lover would divorce, so her expectations never exceeded her grasp. But when a woman divorces in the hope that her married lover will too, her courage should be based on the knowledge that she might lose him.

A healthy affair never cures a sick marriage; at least, not that I heard of. It might make the one who strays feel better or more sexual. Leaving a marriage takes mettle. The fears of rejection by others or the inability to relate to them hover near. For some, an affair which won't lead to another entanglement makes the transition easier, and a married man's obvious limitations can render him a surprisingly effective partner.

The newly divorced woman needs to have fun and to achieve a sense of her own worth more than she needs immediate remarriage. Knowing the married man cannot be too serious about a relationship is a form of security for this woman. The affair can be a joyous breather between long-term commitments or it can be the catalyst to finishing off a marriage that has run past its healthy course.

"I took a chance because I had someone waiting in the wings," remembers Monica, a white-haired, aristocratic-looking sculptress now in her sixties.

> My generation was raised to think that having dealings with someone else's husband is vile. I actually was so naive the first night I met Ronny as he talked of his dreadful marriage, I was sure he was heading for the divorce courts, or suicide. I certainly would never nag anyone to get divorced. I listened politely and made all the proper noises. If I felt that way about my husband, I would have walked out. In fact, I did.

Twenty years ago, Monica met Ronny through her husband.

> Ronny really did do a complete fall in love job, traveled from Europe, where he lived, to see me all the time—the whole bit. My own marriage was coming to an end and this relationship finished it.

I asked if Ronny had ever promised to divorce. Monica said he had never used those words, but there was, to her, no other course open, given his feelings. Between them were mutual enchantment and an uncanny amount of good luck in their effect on each other's careers. "It would have been splendid, because he had what I lack—absolute brass. There was nothing Ronny wouldn't try or do, whereas I'm very careful."

After four years of high romance, their differences in personality and values gathered importance. Monica is well-educated, refined, and socially adept, whereas Ronny's dynamism and sheer wit have propelled him to limelight success. "The things we liked were identical, but we liked them differently."

Monica gained prestige in her field. On the surface Ronny needed her, but at the precise time she had her first sellout show, he took on another woman. "I realize," Monica said, "that one of my problems is productivity. A famous psychologist said that no man would ever forgive me that."

Times have changed. Men constantly tell me they prefer busy, productive women. But with some, that may be only an idea whose time is over when it affects what he gets for dinner.

Monica broke off with Ronny, simultaneously moving to Mexico for two years. He never did divorce. Monica has not remarried. Now an elite artistic and social circle provides her with a vibrant life. But her spirit is perceptibly tinged with sadness.

Knowing what the end of the relationship with Ronny would be might have prevented Monica's divorce, but a lover's attention naturally gives a wife courage. Unhappy with her husband, she leaves him in the hopes her new man will become exclusively hers. Even when he is, the new match doesn't always work.

Take Sylvia. She thought her first marriage stable for years. Things changed gradually. She and her husband were professors at the same university. Sylvia, an anthropologist, got tenure; her husband, a biologist, didn't. That did his self-image no good.

"At the end he became horrible and drank because his ego was shot. I made a bastard out of him the way men make bitches out of women," Sylvia said.

She began writing a textbook in her field with Kirk, a married man. He was not particularly attractive, but Sylvia's family responsibilities, children, business, and drinking husband contrasted sharply to the fun they began to have together over long lunches.

Prior to any involvement, he told Sylvia that he would never leave his wife.

"At this time, I had only slept with one man in my life—my husband. Being unfaithful was not easy. With all my obligations, I didn't even know how I could manage it." One day, as Kirk said good-bye, Sylvia felt a strong attraction toward him. He paused in the doorway.

Sylvia said, "If I ever get out of this marriage, I'll never marry again. If you ever did, would you?"

"I could never get a divorce. She's been a great mother, doesn't mind what I do. I care about the kids, and she doesn't question me about when I'm not there. We have no sex.* One night several years ago she asked me if I'd like to make love. I said, 'Not tonight, honey.'"

At that moment, Sylvia thought, "We're going to get married. I just knew it intuitively as we talked about how neither of us could get divorced. I'd already decided."

Sylvia did divorce because she could not stand the pressure of sneaking around. After a time, she fell in love with Kirk, but did not push him. "If it doesn't work out, you've broken up a family. So I never pressured him."

A year later, Kirk was still married. Not a believer in self-pity, Sylvia journeyed abroad, trying to get over him.

A short time after Sylvia returned, Kirk filed for divorce. Eventually they did marry, but the bliss wore off within the first few years.

In retrospect, Sylvia realizes, "I wasn't in love with Kirk. I was in love with love. But in those days I thought you had to have a man and be married. I thought you had to be in love to be a whole person. I don't feel that way anymore."

Neither do a lot of women. That is why they're willing to take a

---

*One of the foremost playboys in the U.S. told me that "no sex at home" has been part of the married man's pitch for eons.

piece of a "good" man rather than stay in a legally complete but uninspiring union.

There is no question that women like Monica and Sylvia, divorcing before their lovers do, run the risk that they will remain single. Both women felt that their own divorces were probable. A married man happened to be the inspiration. But "no one takes anyone away from a marriage who doesn't want to be taken," both married lovers and wives tell me.

In the past, when women felt more constrained to marry and stay that way, the love was often minimal compared to other practical necessities the union provided. People expected or accepted less intimacy. Today, we divorce more readily and stay single longer, risking loneliness in the hope of finding a real mate. Sometimes, we never do. But those other times . . .

CHAPTER 5
Indian Summer

You think I couldn't make you a
good lover still?
You're crazy if you don't think so.
I could make you miserable with
anyone else.
You would close your eyes with those
tame tootsies
And dream about me, plead for me . . .
    —Eve Merriam,
    "A Conversation Against Death" *

IF THINGS are tough for women in general, can you imagine what meeting an eligible man is like for those over sixty-five? Even fifty-five?

Let's start with numbers. In 1978, 12.7 percent of the population were women over sixty-five, while only 9.2 percent were men in the same age group.** By the year 2000 the difference is expected to rise. Consider, with these facts, the preference for younger women that men seem to have and you will understand the older woman's plight. Wives are not exempt from problems. Envied by their widowed friends for having spouses, older wives often told me they had impotent husbands but were themselves still avid for sex. The husband in fact might merely be adhering to social expecta-

---

*Excerpts from "A Conversation Against Death" by Eve Merriam. Copyright © 1972 by Eve Merriam. Reprinted by permission of the author.

**These are the latest figures available from the U.S. Statistical Abstract.

tion. His cultural training probably suggested that old men were feeble and nonsexual, and he bought the propaganda.

We are learning that sexuality is a matter of an individual's makeup, much of which is psychologically based. "Loss of sexual vigor should be no greater than loss of other physical capabilities (Rubin, 1965; Masters and Johnson, 1970). Rather, impotency before advanced age, between eighty and ninety years, often appears to be a function of psychological problems rather than physical incapacities. . . . Age does not necessarily alter performance nor does it eliminate the quality of satisfaction and pleasure of sexual gratification (Greenblatt and Leng, 1972)." *

Until this century, when people's lifespans have increased, we had little opportunity to study the physiology and psychology of our senior population. Experts now unanimously acknowledge that sexuality offers significant emotional and physical expressions for older people. There is no reason to give up on sex at any age. Back in 1948 and 1953, Kinsey's documented studies taught us that sexual expressions persist through the ninth decade but it has taken, and continues to take, time for mores and morals to catch up with these facts.

The chance of finding a sexual partner has always been slimmer for the older female than the older male. Media advertising frequently depicts the mature man as glamorous and sophisticated and totally ignores the same qualities in the older woman. The latter considered themselves lucky to find any man to go out with— younger, gay, married, whatever. And there were strong taboos connected with these men. It was easier to stay alone, many thought. A number of unmarried women over sixty-five told me they had interesting friends, enjoyed their own company, and simply couldn't be bothered anymore with the hopeless search for love. It is unfortunate that they are resigned to their aloneness in view of the knowledge we have gained about sexuality and longevity.

Dr. Weg, an associate professor of biology at the University of

---

* "Sexual Inadequacy in the Elderly," by Ruth B. Weg, Ph.D., reprinted from *Physiology and Pathology of Human Aging* (New York: Academic Press, 1975), p. 207.

Southern California, stresses the fact that the differences between younger and older women as sex partners is only a matter of response time (the same holds true for penile excitation in men). This response time does not refer to clitoral excitation, which remains unaltered, but response in lubrication of the vulval and vaginal areas.

> The nipples and the breasts are still very responsive to stimulation even in eighty- and ninety-year-old women. There is no vaginal erogenous tissue; and although noted repeatedly by Kinsey and Masters and Johnson, little attention is given to that fact. With clitoral stimulation the contractions start in the fundus of the uterus, move in both directions and move down to the vaginal area as well. But it is clitoral stimulation that is the sensate focus for orgasm in the female, young or old, and a capacity that does not change.*

Today's mature woman is finding solutions to the challenge of her unfulfilled hungers. Dr. Katherina Marmor, codirector of the group-therapy program at the Los Angeles Suicide Prevention Center, has seen a cross section of older women in her clinical practice.

She confirms the fact that the assets older men have historically relied upon to attract younger members of the opposite sex have begun to work for many of their female counterparts. Professional, accomplished, or monied older women offer younger men advantages. They may open social or professional doors for them or provide them with emotional and financial security in addition, frequently, to love. Particularly men in the arts or on the verge of launching careers need various kinds of bolstering or need protection from personal relationships with more competitive, young women.

The climate at the start of the 1980s is significantly less restrictive

---

* "Physiology and Sexuality in the Aging," by Ruth B. Weg, Ph. D., reprinted from *Sexuality and Aging*, I.M. Burnside, ed. (Los Angeles: Andrus Gerontology Center, 1975), p. 11.

than it was a decade ago. Though the Equal Rights Amendment is still pending as I write this, women are beginning to taste fully the options that men have always known. The falling away of old inhibitions frees women to consider for lovers men they would never have thought of romantically in the past. Among those are other women's husbands.

Take Laura.

That July Tuesday when Laura unlocked the bookshop she had owned and run for two years on Manhattan's West Side, she didn't imagine that one of her least favorite customers would be the vehicle for her renaissance and the kind of love she had only vaguely imagined in her high school days in Milwaukee.

Neither did Laura think, at sixty-eight and not having been to bed with a man since she'd divorced thirteen years before, that a robust, charismatic, thirty-eight-year-old architect would zealously pursue her the way Matthew began to shortly after they met. When he first came into the store, Laura thought she recognized him from the indoor pool where she went for daily swims. Matthew, accompanied by his cheerless wife, began chatting with Laura. She was astonished that the demanding, tight-looking woman who once every few weeks bought the latest nonfiction best seller would be married to such a dashing, affable man.

After she noted the couple's incongruity, Laura ignored Matthew. For a number of years, absorbed in her work, first as an editor and later as a bookstore owner, Laura had given up on men—they often disappointed, and the handsome ones, like Matthew, were all womanizers. Anyway, he was too young for whatever sensual ideas she might still harbor.

Matthew wasn't used to being ignored, and he began to study Laura with interest now at the pool where they both swam. He stopped by the shop every few days and was continually amazed at the kind of detachment Laura displayed toward him as she reordered books or helped other customers. During his increasingly frequent visits, he tried to engage her in conversation but received only polite replies to his questions. He never guessed as he became intrigued with her that she was anywhere near her actual age. Laura told me:

By this time I had bought the idea, and a very wrong one, that
when you got older sex didn't matter . . . one just didn't want it.
When Matthew made a big play for me, I thought he was crazy.

Matthew began bringing gifts of flowers, records, and small
edibles, all suggestive of an atmosphere in which he wished he and
Laura would soon be ensconced. After three months of his
persistence, the bemused Laura could not deny the pull of his
maleness anymore. "I thought, what the hell, I'll go to bed with
him. What have I got to lose?"

She soon found out. At sixty-eight, certain of the affair's futility,
she lost her heart completely to the ardent man who was to be with
her for three years. It took a long time for Laura to believe that he
cared for her. She imagined at first that it was an experiment by a
young man who had some artistic or medical curiosity about the
physiology of older women. But his passion in bed belied any such
interest, even after he knew her age.

For her own protection, Laura never questioned her lover about
other women whom she assumed he saw. Instead, she relished all
their times together—times which included the laughter and
passion she had always missed with others. They even managed a
few weekends away during which some amusing incidents, stem-
ming from their obvious age difference, always arose.

Feeling like pioneers in the new wave of older women-younger
men couples whose photos had begun appearing in movie magazines, the lovers grew closer and more confident in each other's
presence. Nevertheless, Laura kept reminding herself she was no
aging movie star with a large estate and impoverished boyfriend.
Though Matthew's attentions, in the circumstances, were even
more flattering, Laura knew they must be fleeting.

One day when Matthew began mentioning divorce, Laura
sensed there might be someone he wanted permanently, someone
he felt he could love and live with. His marriage had been awful
and Laura would be glad for his sake if it were over, but she
instinctively knew that that unhappy union was her assurance of
Matthew's continued love. Laura braced herself for the announcement of her lover's departure from her life.

The new woman's name was Sean—an auburn-haired, blue-eyed, expansive person, quick to laugh, and to become Laura's friend.

> I was heartbroken, certainly, but not because he was cruel. Never. The new girl, she's a darling. I still see both of them and Matthew is certainly my best friend to this day. All the pain was worth it. I was alive, feeling every minute during our affair.
>
> And I was never foolish enough to think it had any future. It was just . . . an enormous experience.

Laura is seventy-six now. She recently sold the bookstore and resides in Connecticut, where the younger couple visits her at least once a month. During the five years that Matthew has been living with Sean, he has seen no reason to tell her of his three-year affair with Laura.

When I was leaving Laura's home the last time we spoke, a tall, dignified lady of about sixty-five with a cane and limp came in. As Laura walked me to the door, she whispered, "Now, Isobel's got a marvelous story, and a married lover."

I got in touch with her a few days later.

During our long Chinese lunch, Isobel spoke in her deep, theatrical voice of her childhood polio, her marriage, and her divorce from a husband who left her for a former close friend of hers. *

The depression which followed that divorce and the burden of raising two children on very little money was relieved for Isobel only after finding a woman psychiatrist she remembers as "remarkable, warm, loving." In her late forties, Isobel managed to work her way from being a telephone operator to selling real estate, acquiring a better apartment than she had had, and building up her financial resources to the point where one insecurity in her life was eliminated.

She convinced herself, despite her antipathy for going out alone, that sitting home in the evenings was doing her no good. A local

---

* The story of Isobel as wife is included in Part III, "The Woman at Home."

piano bar featured classical music, which always made her feel comfortable. So five years ago, when Isobel started out one lonely Friday night, she was grateful for the three people who sat and talked with her around the piano. Through the dim lighting she could see that the more attractive of the two men was slender, with beautiful hair, high cheekbones, and a sensual mouth. She assumed his immediate attention to her had meant only boredom with his companions.

It had been years since a man had displayed anything resembling sincere interest in Isobel's past. Jack did so most convincingly and told her he had recently moved into the neighborhood and was in the process of divorcing. They listened less and less to the music as they talked until the bar closed. At 3 A.M., the other couple, whom Jack had only met that evening, were long since gone. Isobel suggested, in response to his invitation for breakfast at an all-night restaurant, that they go to her house, where she could fix them an omelet. She was self-conscious about her limp as she rose, but as Jack handed her the cane she relied on, he smiled reassuringly. She had made sure to include the polio episode in her story so there would be no unpleasant jolt for him when she got up.

Jack never did get his omelet. Something about him, his confidence, desire, gave Isobel the security to respond to his kisses. Soon she let him undress her. Jack's pleasure in her full body was genuine and obvious. The most attractive man Isobel had ever made love to in sixty-one years spent that night and many more in her welcoming bed.

After three months of much sex and very few omelets, her lover announced one day that his wife had appeared at the door the night before and had begged to be allowed to sleep there. It seemed her brother, with whom she had been staying, had sold his house. Jack said she was a decent woman, and in consideration of the years she had helped to support him before his advertising career took off, he had to allow her into his home. He depicted an extremely dependent woman with whom he swore he had not had sex in two years. "I get her tea in the morning, put her earrings on, wind her watch, and pack her lunch." Jack cried and promised Isobel he loved only her. But his wife stayed.

By the time this news arrived, Isobel wanted Jack more as a lover than a husband. She had learned during their first three months together that he had been married four times and started off each day with vodka and orange juice—not the best credentials for marriage material. Isobel preferred to forget marriage and enjoy their special times together.

Five years have elapsed since Jack's wife returned, so it is fortunate that the long afternoons in bed mean more to Isobel than weekends and holidays with her boyfriend.

> At sixty-four he's the type of lover that I didn't believe existed outside of women's erotic dreams. We are engaged in a competition to each make the other happier . . . and we both win every time.
>
> Sometimes when he comes in my door, he just holds me and the tears roll down his face while he says, "I just missed you so much." None of us can have everything, and maybe it's better to keep the romance and happiness rather than have it dwindle away in dribs and drabs. As someone once said to me, "Life is so daily."
>
> As the other woman, I suspect that if my lover found me, he could well find another if we married. I have made my peace and it feels awfully good.

As I looked at Isobel's vibrant countenance, I believed her.

Women like Laura and Isobel know they are the fortunate ones among their peers, not for having found lovers so much as understanding and acting on their needs in the most realistic way they know. Instinctively, they sense what Masters and Johnson found out: "There is no time limit drawn by advancing years to female sexuality."[*] Laura's and Isobel's abilities to make the kind of life-affirming compromises they did, even with the pain inherent

---

[*] William H. Masters, from remarks at a Lawyers' Wives Meeting, Beverly Hills, California, May 3, 1974, reported in the *Los Angeles Times*, May 4, 1974.

in them, seems admirable in a world of discontent and often passive people.

A contrast to these women is Evelyn. She accepted the tragic cliché about a woman being as old as she looks. That acceptance robbed her of dignity and satisfaction. She never found love because she thought herself unworthy of it and couldn't recognize it if it were available. The only men who ever seemed to pay attention to her turned out to be married.

A tastefully dressed widow in her fifties, Evelyn looked lost in the African Airlines section of Heathrow Airport. Set apart from others there, she neither rushed to a gate nor watched the clock, but studied the departure board confusedly. To the middle-aged man checking in for his flight home to Nairobi, she appeared to be in need of assistance. He had some time before takeoff, read his paper, bought cigarettes, but still the gentle-looking woman sat disconnected, uninvolved. "Where are you going?" he asked, gesturing to her ticket.

"I don't know, I'm trying to decide."

He judged her to be around his own age. She was trim, with an educated native London accent. Maybe she was lonely, looking for an affair, and knew none of the sophisticated conventions attached to such rituals. "Well, I live in Nairobi. Why don't you come along with me?"

"I just have an around-the-world airline ticket and not much money."

"That's all right, my cousin owns a hotel there." The invitation was exactly what she was hoping to receive.

The two left for Nairobi, where Evelyn spent several weeks making love to John on most afternoons, when he'd finished work and his wife thought he was at business meetings. He eventually took his new companion to Dar-Es-Salaam where, at the airport when they parted, she met a married Frenchman precisely as she had met John. He invited her to Madagascar, where he was drilling for oil. Two weeks later, when they said good-bye at the airport with a kiss, the Frenchman never imagined that in ten minutes Evelyn would meet an impulsive Australian who was delighted with her company for his holiday trip to Fiji. He was an earthy sort,

Evelyn discovered, and taught her things her Cambridge University education never had.

Back to the airport in Perth, Australia, and a new married fellow named Brad, who was delighted with the idea of a woman twenty years his senior as eager for sex as he.

When her around-the-world summer holiday was over, Evelyn returned to London and her high school English class. None of her students' papers on their own vacations sounded particularly fascinating anymore, but it was her last year before retirement. She needed the money for her two sons' educations.

Among the older women I met, only Evelyn acted out in such an extreme way. But a great number said they now saw married men as possibilities for affairs when earlier in life they never would have considered them. Some of these discovered the companionship and passion they thought long gone. Others made the most comfortable adjustments they were able to. One widow felt she could never be intimate with another man after forty-odd years with a husband she loved. . . . "Anyone else would just be a stranger."

Maybe one day feelings (whatever our actions) will not be tied to chronological age. The first barrier to achieving our potentials is the notion that certain emotions are only appropriate at specific ages. That notion limits the kinds of relationships people form.

A greater isolation from men is typical of women like Evelyn because our culture has trained them to believe that their age makes them unattractive. After an early, tragic widowhood, Evelyn's life became an insatiable quest to verify her desirability. After her around-the-world holiday, Evelyn realized, "The trouble is that you still want all the sex simply to make sure that you are desirable. So you pick up anybody and afterward you think maybe you should kill yourself because you're defiled and horrible."

The very opposite of Evelyn's attitude is that of one of the most popular women I have ever met—one who never lacks for men, is in her sixties and looks it. Her wrinkles and undyed gray-streaked hair do not detract from a youthfulness and strong sexuality others sense in her. There is nothing and no one she avoids because of her age. She never pays any attention to her years; hence, neither does anyone else. A perfect example of an older, independent woman, she leads a fulfilling existence which often includes a married man.

The growing similarity of the two sexes' lifestyles may eventually result in men having lifespans similar to those of women. Until that time we can educate ourselves about the assets of our older population in general and stop treating men and women differently regarding age and sex. Happily, the middle class is beginning to emulate the avant-garde in ignoring those social divisions. One sees more mature women with younger men every day.

Of all women, older ones have the strongest motives to become other women, though hopefully that will change in time. Many said they felt by their maturity that no moralistic deity was taking notes on their intimate experiences. These women aren't seeking any longer to raise families or expecting their lovers, after some forty or fifty years of marriage, to divorce. Disappointment is less likely, and thus, the mature years can be a time of a woman's emotional expansion and independence during which a married man plays an exciting part.

Sexual and spiritual fulfillment, says Dr. Ruth Weg, keep us more totally healthy at any age. "The need for intimacy and love, as with other human needs for dignity, self-concept, involvement, and intellectual growth, begins very early in the human baby and continues all through life." * The same author quotes Eve Merriam who, in the poem we began with, embraces the attitude older women will hopefully embrace:

> I'd die before I'd ever let myself
>   get old.
> I would always stay young.
> And what did I want for my life to be?
> I wanted
> the same as I want now:
> everything!

---

* "Sexual Inadequacy In The Elderly," by Ruth B. Weg, Ph.D., reprinted from *Physiology and Pathology of Human Aging* (New York: Academic Press, 1975), p. 206.

To go everywhere in the world,
to be everybody in the world,
to slide under the ocean, climb
    over the moon,
swing back and forth between them
thumbing my nose.

—Eve Merriam,
"A Conversation Against Death" *

CHAPTER 6
How Does It End?

It is the law of love that the so-called right person always comes either too soon or too late.

Lawrence Durrell,
from *Balthazar* in
The Alexandria Quartet

IT'S MAGIC . . . AND TRAGIC

ADRIENNE BELIEVED Lee was her mate. She read to me from her emotion-filled diaries during the weeks we spent together after his death. Not allowed to go to his funeral or mourn publicly, she needed to have somebody understand how she felt, what they were to each other. The sadness another might have expressed in tears or with family was unlocked to me in the pages she read.

> . . . Each time he takes me now it's like the first time, because he makes of love a ceremony. I have heard that a man kneels to enter a woman because he kneels to enter a church. I feel like a well-used and tended shrine. His hands and tongue tell me this as they caress my skin. No one ever gave love-making such deliberate importance or meticulous attention. He was of that mythical breed of men women conjure on rainy afternoons— poet and master together. How inarticulate I always felt with

one who could and did say everything. And it was the right
everything.

It was May. Los Angeles overcast mornings were somehow
conducive to Adrienne's mood and the events of her life. Every day we
went for a long walk on the foggy beach and she evoked events of the
past she suddenly felt free to talk about.

> In his eighteen-year marriage, Lee was never involved with any
> woman before me, never even a one-night fling. He buried
> most of himself in his research and practice. The little left over
> he gave to his boys—twins, eight years old when I met him.
> They always spent Saturday afternoons together.

Adrienne described Lee's cool marriage, in which work, children,
and skiing replaced the intimacy that never was. He told Adrienne he
had his one major love affair before her when he was twenty-five and
single but lost the girl's affection during his absence on a year's
fellowship in England. His marriage ten years later had been
convenient and comfortable but never a love match. He didn't fully
realize what he was missing until Adrienne came on the scene.

> "I'm the most married man you'll ever meet," Lee told me
> when we first became friends over a wonderful bottle of red
> wine. He described a life full of roots, history, and four children
> that he felt he could never leave. The last two, Lee was tricked
> into. He told his wife he definitely wanted no more children,
> but she deliberately got pregnant. He was furious, went on a ski
> trip alone for two weeks. Ironically, they turned out to be twins.
> He said it was at a time when he was really becoming restless.
> His wife obviously wanted something more to hold him because
> the other children were growing up.
>
> I thought that getting involved with a married man was the
> stupidest thing a woman could do. I considered myself smarter
> than that. Of course, it wasn't difficult to rationalize being
> together because we were working on his book. Neither of us

mentioned the fact that we met more often than was necessary. His was the most polished manuscript in the world.

Shortly after his book came out, Lee had a medical meeting in Paris. He took Adrienne with him. It was the height of her romantic life.

> We weren't committed to a long affair, but it was understood when I accepted the invitation that it was my way of saying we were going to be involved. I think we had felt before we made love that if we didn't sleep together we'd be safe. But it made no difference. By then sex was merely punctuation.
>
> Paris is a kind of lover. It was a real *ménage à trois*, the city giving herself as our partner in everything. She is one rival I would always put up with. Is there any woman so jaded that she has not, when in Paris, dreamed of living there with her man?

Adrienne read to me for hours from these highly poetic notes about their trip to Paris and the Loire Valley.

> I had to get back to New York to work, so I returned alone. Lee was attending another meeting in London. On the plane back, I realized I was in big trouble. I knew I would have to end it soon or lose myself. My phone was ringing when I walked into my apartment in New York. Lee said he couldn't wait another five days to see me. He'd fly back tomorrow.

Lee did come back and spent every spare moment he could with Adrienne. She kept promising herself she would break it off, but . . .

> He has a greater capacity for intimacy than other men. I remember one day in particular. Because we have oral sex, I don't like to have my diaphragm in when I start to make love. So until the last moment, I don't put it in. It's cold and lonely to leave him in bed and go in the bathroom to do this, but I had

no choice. I'll never forget the second or third time we had sex.
I was looking unhappy about leaving Lee. He got up—never
said one word and came with me into the bathroom. He knew I
didn't want to be apart from him at that moment and he felt the
same. It touched me deeply.

Eventually Lee became as inextricably involved with Adrienne as
she with him. When he was supposed to be staying late at the
hospital, they met in her apartment. He answered his telephone
beeper from there. Lee grew exhausted from the combination of his
bursting schedule, traveling across town to see Adrienne, and the
best sex life either had known. After six months of this Adrienne
pressed Lee to divorce, but he couldn't assuage his guilt enough to
make the break. The sex kept getting better.

> The man seems to have a perpetual erection. Sometimes he
> drapes a towel across his erect penis and walks around with it.
> We laugh a lot, but the whole situation is getting impossible.
> After months of guilt, Lee has decided that hypocrisy and
> fatigue are killing him. He will tell his wife when she gets back
> from visiting her girlfriend in Washington that he is leaving. I
> can't believe this conservative man is finally going to do it.

Three weeks later Lee had left his wife, without ever mentioning
Adrienne, and gone to visit some hospitals in Boston during the
separation. He had barely been there five days when his wife began
her suicide threats. Within another week, he was back.

> I felt there was no point in going on. He was obviously weak in
> some way, and I was frustrated beyond description. If I weren't
> so certain of his love and hadn't felt he gave himself a hundred
> percent to me, I wouldn't have gotten so involved. I'm not a
> total dummy, but I underestimated his guilt. I decided to stop
> seeing him.

Around this time, Lee was offered the department chairmanship at a Los Angeles hospital. He decided the only way to endure the separation from Adrienne was to take the position and move his family across the country. This he did, and told Adrienne he was going to try to improve his marriage.

> The last time I saw him before he left was at his Southampton summer house. We'd gone there in September when he closed it up.

Adrienne read again.

> "See how they're dying?" Lee referred to the purple and white pansies. "Summer is over."
> "It certainly is," I agreed, thinking of the summer of life, our love.
> Lee put his arms around me, attempting to ease the pain. "My child, I love you." That only made the idea of separation more senseless, a sharper cut. But Lee lived in the moment, and in his heart with which he loved me. I loved him with my mind, my whole mind that knew the destruction he had chosen.
> I will not have this thing again. Maybe one day affection, sex, which *we* never had—it was always love-making.
> Lee cleaned and organized, moved from one task to another, believing in the padding of surroundings, activities, children. And at least he would not fight the battle of indecision anymore.

Adrienne talked to me about what happened later.

> Lee reluctantly moved to Los Angeles, and I reluctantly went out with other men. Went out like crazy. I accepted any blind date and tried every opportunity I could think of to meet single men. Obviously I wasn't ready yet. Nothing worked. I spent my thirty-second birthday raking leaves at my mother's house and crying a lot.
> Lee and I spoke every two weeks or so, just to keep up on how the other one was. Despite our brave fronts, we were both

miserable. I was so depressed, I went back into therapy. I developed terrible headaches which I couldn't get rid of.

Adrienne read to me again from her diary of a year later.

The respite Lee had has been short-lived. After the distance of separation, the fading of sensory details, has come the knowledge, certainty, that it is the most refined of experiences he has let go.

I remember the day we were in Southampton. He moved quickly, unaware of the regret he tells me now fills not only his waking but sleeping hours.

As for me, the brightness of his eyes, his body's needs and strength are forever etched into my memory. I feel that I am playing some kind of game by staying away from him. But society teaches that if you can't have something in the traditional way, you must give it up.

Eleven months after their separation, Lee asked Adrienne to see him again, claiming he would try once more to leave. He was seeing a psychotherapist. Adrienne had the opportunity to move to Los Angeles with another publishing company, which was opening a West Coast office. She took the job and another chance on Lee. A few months later it looked like Lee had finally decided he wanted a real relationship. Adrienne told me what happened at the time his twins were fifteen.

He said he had decided to leave. He went to a divorce lawyer and arranged for things to proceed. The night he went to tell his wife, he came over and was very nervous; sweated, paced, but promised to call as soon as he left. The rest you know about. [He had a heart attack and died.]

Adrienne reads again.

If ever I had a mate in this world, Lee was it. I've never met a man I respected more or one so worthy of every positive thing I am or would like to become. Lee was kind. He alleviated suffering where he could, and deserved happiness. He was the best friend I ever had.

As I write this, it is several years later. Adrienne, who says she feels like a widow, is still lonely and single. Lee's wife remarried eight months after his death.

One psychiatrist said to me, "There are single women meeting married men who just happen to be the perfect guy." Adrienne feels she is one of those.

There is a moral question arising from sharing another person's legal partner. It stops some but many, like Adrienne, assume that responsibility should be to oneself and those to whom one makes commitments.

After the morality issue is resolved in favor of a married lover, the course of action of the women I interviewed became a matter of waits and measures. She determines if the measure of what she receives is worth the time she waits for it. The intervals between the lovers' assignations or the time a woman waits for a man to divorce vary. I offer the unusual story of my friend's mother.

Lillian, a warm, diminutive woman, had worked in her husband's theatrical law office with him until he died. Afterward, she became an agent for several of his clients. Julian, a lawyer who worked for Lillian's late husband, took care of the details of the estate, often dropping by in those first weeks after his death to discuss legal and business matters with Lillian.

Julian was ten years younger than my mother, who was then forty-seven. Julian and she obviously got along famously and I became used to him around the house in the evening. My sister was at college. I was a teen-ager and had a lot of after-school activities. It was always around dinner time when I finally got home. Julian was always there. I realized after about a year that he and Mom were lovers. There was a special closeness between them. They probably had sex before I came in . . . certainly I never saw any signs of it.

My mother told me and my sister after a few months that we shouldn't mention his visits to anyone because people always gossip about such things.

He was a very fine man and good to all of us, but naturally I resented him moving so quickly toward my mother right after my father died. They had known each other in the office as workmates, but I'm positive that this thing between my mother and Julian developed gradually over the course of that first year.

Much later Lillian told her daughter that Julian was never really in love with his wife but they had had a child only months before Lillian was widowed. When they became lovers, he promised, "I will get a divorce when the baby is eighteen."

"What a joke," Lillian thought. "I'm forty-seven, he's thirty-seven, and he's telling me to wait eighteen years!"

My mother certainly never expected him to keep that promise, but she seemed happy with the arrangement. Julian appeared every night for dinner. Also, Julian managed to spend some Saturdays with Mom, taking her shopping and out to lunch. There were always special presents for all of us. Frequently, he took us to the theater or movies for matinees. My mother seemed to respect and love him so much we never told her to get rid of Julian. She wasn't the kind of lady to go looking for another man, so she probably would have been alone if it weren't for him.

My friend describes a similar pattern for seventeen and a half years. Julian's wife, perfectly capable of using a phone to try to reach her husband late at the office, no doubt had the situation figured out early on.

My sister and I tried several times in those years of their affair to get Mom to come on holidays with us, but she always kept her vacations for when Julian could get away on his business trips. They went on one or two trips a year together.

My sister and I, married ourselves, never believed Julian would divorce. One day my mother called me almost hysterical. "His wife left!" she screamed. Julian's wife walked out on him with hardly a glance backward, six months before the time he had said he would leave. She had found someone herself and had gone off to live with him. Whether Julian would have kept his promise otherwise we'll never know.

My mother and Julian were married the day his divorce came through and have been together for twelve years. She's seventy-seven and he's sixty-seven. They've got the best marriage I've ever seen.

Lillian was part of the minority I met who marry their lovers. Most other women suffer with the partial love they get; so do wives. For all the suicide threats of wives who are left, I heard about more suicide attempts and successes on the part of other women.* For the majority of other women, the waiting seems to hurt more than it helps, even when the man finally divorces.

A perfect example is Vita, an athletic forty-one-year-old divorced travel agent. Attending a business conference in Vienna, she got to know Mark, a guest speaker.

I told him I'd been working up my courage to divorce. Mark said, "I wish I could say the same." There were no passes or anything—just conversation. I said, "That doesn't sound good," and he answered, "It isn't. It's absolutely horrible. We've been to marriage counselors, back and forth. I wish I had done something before this. I will eventually." He wanted to and said someday he'd try. He had four children. "As soon as my youngest graduates school, I'll do it," he said.

Mark escorted me up to my room that night, but I was making it clear that I didn't fool around because I was so straight. He was very prominent so he was careful and straight, too. I didn't think anything would happen. We said good night at the door, but all my female cells were pointing in his

---

*This is based solely on data from my own interviews.

direction. I didn't realize it was love at first sight with Mark. He
would be the greatest romance of my life.

They spent the following full day discovering each other, using
old Vienna as the excuse.

> We went to a small cafe and heard zither music. My mother
> had been to that very one on her honeymoon. We walked back
> to our hotel—it was beautiful and had stopped raining. We
> went through a long park flanked with chestnut trees and marble
> statues. Coming to a bridge with the water and the hotel lights
> across the street, we kissed a couple of times as we walked.
> When we reached our hotel it was extremely late, but the
> orchestra was still playing in the ballroom.
>
> Mark said, "Let's go in and have a couple of dances." We
> did. When we waltzed, I was overcome with the atmosphere
> and him.
>
> Then he took me up to my room and just kissed me good
> night because I'd made it very clear [she laughs heartily] that I
> wasn't interested in fooling around.

Vita and Mark resisted their passion for a couple of days. Then,
encouraged by the romantic zither music and long personal talks
on several Viennese nights, they became lovers. During the last
two days of the conference, they were inseparable.

> I was packing and it was that terrible vacuous feeling at the end
> of something, like all your insides are falling out. The last night
> we made love, and assumed we would again. He was going one
> way and I the other, but we knew we'd talk and see each other
> somewhere. Nothing specific was said. It was awful as we parted
> at the airport. This sophisticated businessman cried. We knew
> our meeting was something that should have always been.

Vita got a divorce. She and Mark corresponded and telephoned
each other all year. They met twice more while she was single. But
Mark would apparently not divorce. Then Vita convinced herself

she loved another man who was available. She married him and went to New York on her honeymoon.

> I told my husband when he went to his business meeting I wanted to see Mark for lunch. He said it was perfectly fine. Of course, he never knew the depth of my feelings for Mark.
>
> It was a bright June day. We took a picnic to the Washington Irving estate and lunched alone in the woods, holding hands. Mark said, "This is crazy. Here you are on your honeymoon." We kissed good-bye, cried, and still meant everything to each other.
>
> About a year later we both ended up in Manila alone. We tried not to get involved, so we were platonic. But Mark and I were just meant for each other, and the last day we ended up, of course, in bed. I didn't remember having that many orgasms in one day, ever. We also met in London a couple of times after that. The final occasion was terrible because my marriage was falling apart and I was an unhappy mess.

Vita's second marriage failed, and now she was alone again, still pining for Mark.

> Mark and I know we were always there for each other through everything, because it isn't just a romance but something else— a bond.

As of this meeting, ten years after the lovers met, Mark, in his sixties, has finally divorced.

> He was here six months ago and said he loves me as much as he's capable of loving anybody, but he says, "I'm not really capable of love anymore. My spirit is dead."

I asked Vita if she still wants to marry him.

> He's the only man I would consider, but the fact that he says he's not capable of love is important. Of course, we were the

greatest loves in each other's lives. It should have happened a long time ago. It's always been a very calm thing. No matter what there is in the whole world I want or need, Mark would get it if he could because he knows I would never ask for attention or telephone frivolously. We're always in touch to share good news, and we have a genuine relationship. I don't care about getting married at this stage of my life. When you have an affair like we did, it's part of you forever.

Vita's last statement is not unique. Men and women who consider each other the big romance of their lives always remain spiritually joined. Their love is not lost to time or distance. Some told me of great efforts made, even decades later, to trace one another.

Partners in such affairs stress the intimacy, the freedom of expression, they feel. Without exception, they mention honesty, superlative love-making, and a desire to please one's partner—attributes of an affair built in as surely as are its restrictions. A married man chooses his other woman romantically—practical, familial, and cultural considerations temporarily ignored. He has come to her at a later stage of development than when he was married, his tastes and needs are often those of a more evolved self. And women cherish the kind of attention married men offer.

> Since he can't express caring for his lover by offering her security or responsibility, he offers her more of his inner self instead. He can relax into behavior with his lover that's more spontaneous and expressive than he feels comfortable showing with his wife, and the result is that the affair is a good deal more intimate than the marriage.*

Repeatedly, women mentioned married men's interest in what they had to say and the men's willingness to share innermost feelings. Along with the intimacy the couple feels comes a sense of

---

* Daniel Goldstine, et al., *The Dance Away Lover* (New York: Ballantine Books, 1977), p. 203.

liberty. Anything can be told between such lovers. A husband need not lie to the other woman about where he is going and with whom. His girlfriend knows and has accepted the situation for her own reasons. There is security even in her secondary role. She senses he is faithful . . . in his way. They are partners in a confidence drawing them close. If only because her lover *elects* to visit her, the other woman feels wanted. There is no legal or moral obligation to carry on. She is a lone star in his life—not one of numerous burdens which he must carry.

But lone stars get cold in the dark. The other woman's man is not going to call or be there in the middle of the night, or when she is sick or celebrating a promotion. He is not going to be there most of the time. Maybe they will have vacations, a friendship for life, but the fact is that relationships generally progress toward commitment or regress to distance. It really is magic and tragic.

The view from a mountaintop is spectacular. We sometimes glimpse it once only. Perhaps not seeing it at all is the wiser choice. Through years of listening I have been convinced that people want to take risks. As one man pointed out, "It was the only time in my life I was incandescent."

SUCCESS AND DEFEAT

I wish my wife were more like you so I could leave her.
—A man who didn't

The only rule about when a man leaves his marriage for the other woman is—he usually doesn't. Of all the other women and married men I interviewed, only about 15 percent of the men having affairs divorced. Those divorces were not necessarily caused by the affair, though; nor did they guarantee a successful long-term relationship between husband and lady lover.

The other woman, I have found, cannot destroy a successful marriage. The psychiatrists and other experts I consulted agree that when a man turns to another woman for a relationship, the marriage is already in trouble. Good marriages survive a husband's strictly sexual encounters. And if he falls in love inadvertently with someone else, which satisfied husbands rarely let happen, a strong marriage can surmount even that crisis.

The other woman's best chance for success in marrying her lover is when he is a sincerely unfulfilled man, rather than one who is merely experimenting. A fellow who feels emotionally *choked* (a word I heard again and again) might be ripe for divorce. But judging his unhappiness can be difficult. The image of the husband whining, "She doesn't understand me," comes from a lot of real married men's complaints. Al Lerner, the private investigator, told me that in restaurants and bars men still give women that same old line. And staying in the marriage is usually blamed on children and money. But whether or not they are excuses he gives himself and his lover, the lady does well to realize he probably won't leave.

Here are a few maxims for other women which evolved from years of listening to both them and married men.

If you are the other woman in a long-term affair during which your man has assured you he loves you, has provided numerous examples of his suffering at home, hasn't got any children or money problems yet hasn't divorced, there is a solid reason. It is not simply that he doesn't know any lawyers. Probably the man is taking care of unconscious needs of his own. He may be satisfying masochistic desires. Maybe he only feels comfortable getting love—from you—when it is meted out with punishment—from his wife. The needs may be subtler and all three people in the triangle might be entangled in a complex mental game. The best help your man can get is psychotherapy or counseling to work out these conflicts. That is, if he wants to leave. He may very well not want to.

By staying where he is and apparently doing nothing, he gets exactly what he yearns for—fulfillment of different desires from both you and his wife. This type of behavior, sometimes dubbed passive-aggressive, is the most stressful to deal with. He claims to be "alive" only in your presence, yet some kind of guilt keeps him home. When he starts calling guilt "loyalty," your chances are narrowing. We are all slow to condemn loyalty. But what about loyalty to you? It is forgotten during teary speeches in his arms. He convinces you that a force greater than his will keeps him locked in an unhappy marriage while his soul is pledged to you.

When your lover paints himself a victim of circumstance, watch out! "Darling, what can we do?" may elicit your sympathy for a while until you realize *you* are the victim. For that to happen it may take a friend, pointing out that it has been two, three, five, ten years of waiting for the fulfillment of this relationship, while he still waves the loyalty flag, though the children are grown and the house is paid for.

The issue is not whether he leaves you or is lying to you. It is whether you want to buy another set of bath towels alone or have harried weeks with empty weekends. A pattern which became clear to me after many interviews was that the unhappy husband who focuses on his wife's needs rather than his mistress's almost never leaves his marriage. *His* important emotional needs are somehow being satisfied. It is the other woman who, after years of waiting, gets fed up and ends the relationship. It was rare to hear of a man ending it. Psychiatrists all over the country are treating women devastated by years of such disappointed fantasies.

In a recent article,* Dr. Helen Kaplan gave an excellent hint on how to distinguish between husbands likely to leave their marriages and those not. If a man is always nervous about calling home or being caught, he is a poor candidate for an exit visa. Conversely, the one who considers his relationship to his lover the more significant one is more worried about rejection from her. This sort of man might well divorce.

A big problem the other woman has is determining how much time a man needs to make up his mind. It is easy to rationalize long delays when she is enjoying the best or maybe the only real love she has ever known. Dr. Kaplan states, "Almost every married man is ambivalent. He's waffling. He's worried about alimony, the children. The woman who has no conflict about winning, who

---

*"Beware the Affair With a Married Man," by Dr. Helen Kaplan, *Savvy*, June 1980, pp. 73-74.

wants to really love this man, knows instantly when to force a crisis and say: 'Okay, I can't take it anymore. We have to get married or good-bye.'" *

Women have found that timing these crises is not as easy as Dr. Kaplan suggests. Many do not possess that instinct. My research indicates that most men who leave wives do so sooner rather than later—in the first year or two of the affair. But that is only the majority. Merry's lover took twelve years, and Lillian's marvelous marriage was preceded by an eighteen-year romance!

If you are in that holding pattern—while he is deciding (presuming *you* have)—forget hiring someone to shoot or seduce his wife. And dismiss the plan to act as dependent as you think she does. If he wants someone who cries and locks herself in the bathroom, he can stay home. The man will finally make up his mind based on his own goals, strengths, and needs. Do not nag him about divorcing. A husband will make a move if he is really unhappy and

—if he is in love with you.

—if he can handle the separation from his children and money, both of which may, in his mind or reality, be too little.

—if he is not neurotic—requiring a daily dose of misery.

—if his value system does not place greater weight on tradition or appearance than on love.

—if he is not using the affair to avoid real intimacy with either you or his wife.

Before all that is decided, you can help yourself by continuing to build and grow in your own world. If a woman relinquishes all her support systems before she has new ones, she will be left desolate when the affair ends. As mentioned in the last chapter, I heard

* Kaplan, p. 74.

about more suicide attempts and successes by abandoned other women than by abandoned wives. Probably these women felt sure of winning their men, then did not win them and had given up real lives of their own in the meantime.

A single woman might want to end an affair but no longer has the emotional equipment or social set-up to do so. Exactly like a wife or husband wanting to leave an empty marriage, the single woman with no lover and few friends is frightened and insecure and dares not venture out on her own. During an affair, married women with lovers fare far better than single women. They have the whole network of home and family to lean on when their lovers are absent. Married men tell me it is easier to have affairs with married women because of this. They don't feel as guilty as with single women who have no one else in their lives.

But a single woman can have more to depend on if she wants to. Here is some advice from women comfortable with their affairs, and those few who won away their men:

1. Don't give up dating other men.

2. Don't give up your career or move to his city on the presumption that it will help him decide in your favor.

3. Don't stop your income-producing work, even if you are kept in the grandest of styles. The affair may end abruptly and you will need to have a job. More significantly, it is better for your self-esteem to know you're not with your lover because of financial dependence.

4. Don't stop seeing friends or family because you are involved in a *secret* life.

5. Don't spend your time and energy competing with the unknown "enemy." His wife may be no more your enemy now than you could be someone else's three years from now, if you become wife number two.

6. Don't wait around for his phone calls.

7. Make sure your lover understands you are not stopping your independent life when he enters the scene. Your own long-range plans should be made excluding him, no matter how fervent the talk. And convey the message, in some way, that you believe only actions, not words.

8. See him on your terms.

On your terms means when it is psychologically comfortable. For some women is it easier to handle sexual encounters only when the man can stay overnight. Others prefer seeing their men out of town, when they can spend days or weeks together. On the other hand, many find any of this closeness too binding. They want to be with the men only on their own home turf, where jobs and other male friends limit the time and attachment they have together. Some women are even more comfortable when their lovers go home to sleep.

None of us wants to doubt someone she loves. A man may be completely honest with his lover and lie only to himself. It is more important that she does not lie to *herself*. If she takes the best she can from the experience, it can be a wonderful transition to another relationship or stage of development. It might be the height of her love life. If she is not ignoring her long-range goals and her man makes her happy, why, the other woman reasons, shouldn't she enjoy it? When the pain outweighs the pleasure, when she is obviously not getting what she wants, it is time to think about a change.

II
THE MAN
in
THE MIDDLE

CHAPTER 7
A Strange Perfume

It is easier to be a lover than a husband for the simple reason that it is more difficult to be witty every day than to say pretty things from time to time.

Honoré de Balzac,
Physiologie du Mariage

WHY MARRIED MEN HAVE AFFAIRS

A PSYCHOLOGIST who did an experiment with rats "found that if immediately after the male rat reached (sexual) exhaustion he replaced the original female with a new one the exhausted male suddenly had no difficulty performing. Moreover, if the male were supplied with a new partner after that—and still another partner after that—he managed to double or even triple the number of ejaculations he had before again becoming exhausted."* Plenty of wives discovering similar patterns in their husbands' reactions to new partners feel certain those men belong to the same species.

Close to 75 percent of the one hundred men I interviewed described themselves as happily or fairly happily married. Fifteen percent of the remaining 25 percent were either divorced or have since divorced.

---

*Allen Fisher, cited in F. Beach, "Copulation In Rats," *Psychology Today*, July 1967, p. 8. Also cited in Elaine and G. William Walster, *A New Look at Love* (Reading, Ma.: Addison-Wesley, 1978).

The final 10 percent I spoke to said they were unhappy with their wives, though they chose to remain married.

After hearing their stories, I concluded that many who said they were happy were trying to convince themselves of that fact. They rationalize, it seems, that what they have established is superior to what it is. People don't like to feel, after all, that they have wasted their lives. Then too, men with lovers possibly feel better tempered in marriage because of the satisfaction they are getting outside their homes.

The interviews that follow were chosen either because they express directly common attitudes or inform us as to a significant but less commonly expressed point of view. The dialogues have been edited for repetitive or irrelevant comments.

I have chosen to present the husbands' views in interview form rather than create narratives of personal experiences supplemented by verbatim dialogue, as I did in the other woman's section. This decision was based on some interesting differences which arose between the men and the women I interviewed, the most significant of which was that the women almost always stressed one or two major relationships in their interviews with me, while the men focused on their general philosophy on the subject. I found that my discussions with men tended to be, more or less, question and answer sessions whereas with other women, I was usually listening to a long and complex story.

The men speak for themselves in the following interviews. Strangely, I found in reading them over that the answers they provided sometimes suggested far less sensitivity than the men seemed, in person, to have, and certainly they appear less sensitive than the men the other women described—even when they were those very men! Most of these men are college-educated; many are professional.

The striking differences between the two sets of interviews points to there being some truth to the myth that women are still far more in touch with their feelings than are men. Nevertheless, the men were, I believe, admitting their own conflicts and feelings as honestly as they could. Their manners, vulnerability, and warmth are lost in the printed word; the interviews do, though, provide a good sense of their needs, fears, and struggles.

Greg is a fifty-year-old business manager from Dallas, now living in San Diego with his second wife.

Q: Greg, how do your affairs affect your marriage?
A: They don't. I differentiate between sex and love.
Q: Okay, let's talk about just sex. How does this outside sex affect your married life?
A: Not at all. I don't have a pound of sex and a pound of love that I have to divide equally among the people I'm having sex or love with. I have an unlimited amount of both.
Q: If you have great sex, isn't it hard to come home and make love?
A: No.
Q: So it has no effect.
A: The only way it has ever affected me negatively is that I brought home a case of crabs.
Q: How did you explain that?
A: It happens in the best of families.
Q: How about a deep love affair, how would that affect your marriage?
A: Severely.
Q: Negatively?
A: Negatively. I don't think people can have a deep love affair and stay married to another woman. It would be very difficult.
Q: Why do married men have affairs?
A: In my experience, a lot of guys don't like themselves, they just don't like themselves. They can't form close relationships because the person they're close to is going to find out how rotten they are and not like them. But their need to be close is great, so they form very short-term close relationships—one bed tonight, another bed the next night. It's a close relationship of three minutes, or four hours, or twenty-four hours, or three

weeks duration. That's what fills their need for closeness without divulging how horrible they are to the person.

Q: Do you think more men have affairs than women?

A: I don't know, I'm polygamous. That's a one-woman man who has affairs with a lot of other women.

Q: Do you think you have a double standard for men and women?

A: No.

Q: How would you feel if your wife did the same thing as you?

A: I would hope she enjoys it.

Q: As long as you didn't know about it?

A: I wouldn't care if I knew about it.

Q: If you found out about something she didn't tell you, would you be upset?

A: If I thought she was being hurt.

Q: Otherwise, it wouldn't bother you?

A: I don't know what jealousy means. I lost that somewhere when I was fourteen. I think it's an immature emotion.

Q: Do you think it makes a difference if someone wears a wedding band?

A: I think it makes a difference if a man wears a wedding band. It's very attractive to women.

Q: In what way?

A: It makes them feel safe.

Q: You think it makes any difference to the person wearing it?

A: I know some men who take off their rings when they go away. I've never taken mine off. I've found it to be an asset.

Q: Is sex better in an affair than it is in marriage?

A: Yes. More excitement.

Q: Because of the kind of women you choose?

A: Yep. Also, I'm inhibited sexually in my married life whereas I'm not inhibited in my affairs.

Q: What do you think is the psychological reason?

A: Background, childhood, old wives' tales. I've rid myself of a great deal of my negative associations with sex, and while intellectually I understand them, I'm still bound up in them to some degree. I can do a lot of things I couldn't do before with my wife, but I'm not capable of doing as much as I could with a stranger.

Q: In other words, you're not blaming it on your wife because she's inhibited or conservative.

A: Hell no.

Q: If you fell madly in love with another woman, would you leave your wife?

A: Yes, but it's unlikely.

Q: In other words, you give great importance to love.

A: It's much more important than sex and very different. But I think everybody should get as much sex as they possibly can. We would have a much better world if a woman had periods of heat like dogs. Let's say, every December for thirty days we were turned on. Everybody would fuck for thirty days and the rest of the year we'd go about our business doing things and sex wouldn't be on our minds. And you wouldn't have to write this book, because no one would have any problems.

Q: Then your motivation for affairs is purely sexual?

A: Sexual, but you can say sex is fun. The thrill of a seduction. Look, I grew up in an age when sex wasn't as easy for a man as it is today, because women are so readily available. Women didn't just give sex or want sex, you had to steal it, you had to win it. In Dallas, the fifteen- or sixteen-year-old kids I hung around with, they had a phrase they used to say when you went out with a girl—"Did you get it off her?" Do you understand what that means? That means you stole it. It wasn't something two people did together, it was something you stole from a woman. And five years of psychiatry never changed it for me. The idea of stealing it in some way is exciting in the same way it was when I was sixteen years old and I stole it from a twenty-year-old girl.

Q: Do you have a moral viewpoint about what you do?

A: When I was single, I never felt it was immoral. It was something people did. I don't think it's immoral because my father always had affairs, I was used to it. I met a lot of women my father had affairs with. On the other hand, I feel my wife would be hurt if she found out. I don't want her to find out and be made a fool of, but that doesn't stop me from making it with her best friends. And somewhere she knows. I guess I feel guilty.

Q: Do you try to insure the fact that she won't find out?

A: I try, but you can never be sure. You're always going to run across a girl who will say, "No one will know but you and I," and then lets it out in little ways, even when she's unaware of it—especially if she's married.

Q: Why especially if she's married?

A: The desire for punishment.

Q: Her desire for her own punishment from her spouse?

A: Yes.

Q: Did you ever fall in love with a woman, other than your wife, while you were married?

A: Yes. During my first marriage.

Q: How did you handle this?

A: I told the woman I loved her. She was also married. We saw each other as often as we could, and we carried on a mad, passionate love affair for almost ten years.

Q: What prevented you from leaving your wife?

A: I did leave my wife.

Q: But she didn't leave her husband?

A: No. He was a very weak man and it would have been his destruction. At least, that's how we both saw it.

Q: You knew him?

A: Oh yes.

Q: How did you feel toward him?

A: I liked him, he was a very nice guy.

Q: When you were involved with his wife, were you angry with him, did you pity him, feel jealousy?

A: None of those feelings.

Q: What has happened as a result of this affair?

A: Nothing. I see her occasionally now, but not sexually.

Q: Did you get hurt as a result of this affair?

A: No, not at all. It was one of the most beautiful things in my life. Any time I've had sex with love, it's been beautiful.

Q: Does your financial position affect your ability to have affairs?

A: Of course. The man who's able to say, "Let's get out of here and have lunch at the Regency," and already have a suite of rooms waiting upstairs with champagne, caviar, and so forth is ten steps ahead of the guy who says, "How about it, baby?" It allows you to plan elaborate affairs, it allows you to seduce easily. You bring a girl a diamond necklace or a beautiful watch, and whether she wants to or not she feels grateful. She may even feel loved, even though you haven't said anything.

Q: And her gratitude and emotions may be a little bit mixed up?

A: In most cases. Also, if you have money and you're bald, you can go and get the finest toupee in town. You can get facials, you can get suntans, you can wear good clothes that hide your potbelly. There are any number of things you can do to make yourself attractive and pick the woman of your choice. Anyway, money is power and women are attracted to power.

Q: Did you ever have a purely sexual affair?

A: Oh yes, a wild, tumultuous two-year one with a girl I couldn't stand.

Q: What do you mean?

A: We were animals—she couldn't wait for me to walk through the door and I couldn't wait to get through the door and frequently we didn't. We did it on car tops and hallways, anywhere—restaurants.

Q: You didn't actually do it in restaurants?

A: Yeah, she went down on me in restaurants.

Q: What made you end that affair?

A: She started to blackmail me. Insisted I come around when I couldn't and threatened to tell my wife. Eventually, I had to end it.

Q: In your most profound emotional relationship outside your marriage, did you treat your wife and your mistress differently financially?

A: Yes.

Q: Who did you treat better?

A: My wife. Emotionally, my mistress.

Q: Did you treat them differently any other way?

A: Sexually. I was much better sexually with my mistress than with my wife—first wife.

Q: Do you think men marry one kind of woman and are turned on by another?

A: Yes, I can say that about me. I marry ladies and have affairs with whores. I say whores because I'm trying to explain them. I'm attracted to girls who come on very strong sexually, wear black lace, wiggle their behinds, don't wear bras, and flaunt sex. I get very excited.

Q: Are these women always the best sexually?

A: Not always, but they turn me on.

Q: Do you mean to say that a man of your intelligence couldn't find a "lady"—or hasn't—who's very good sexually?

A: You said a man of my intelligence. My cock doesn't have any intelligence at all.

Q: And can the ladies you marry also be sexual?

A: Oh sure. I enjoy my married sex life too, but I'm very turned on by those girls who usually have dirty sheets and so forth. Real pigs.

Q: But you look so immaculate.

A: What does that have to do with it?

Q: How can you tolerate someone who's dirty?

A: Maybe they're turned on by immaculate guys, so it works out.

Q: Tell me about how one of your affairs began.

A: Once, my wife and I were having dinner with friends of ours. We were sitting with a man and woman on my left, with the woman closest to me and my wife on the right. Somewhere during the meal, I found this other woman's hand on my leg, which came as a big surprise to me. I thought they were happily married. I didn't know how to react because my wife was sitting next to me and this woman's husband on the other side. When I didn't react, she took that for consent and worked her way up in my crotch and unzipped my pants and played with me inside my pants.

Q: What did you do about this?

A: I didn't say anything to her that evening, but I called her a few days later and said, "Did I dream that? That something went on in the restaurant the other night?" She said no. I was very glad to hear that and asked if she would like to get together. She said, "Certainly. Where, when?" And I made arrangements to meet her at a hotel.

Q: Just that simple?

A: It's sometimes much simpler.

Greg displays conflict in his sexual relationships. "I marry ladies and have affairs with whores." With "whores" he can apparently express aspects of himself that he hides or represses in his social persona as well as in his marriage. The "whores" are the "dirty" parts of himself. Greg protects this unacceptable aspect of himself with a personal fastidiousness but plays out the feelings with women who are "piggy."

Another benefit of neatly dividing women into categories of good and bad, often called a madonna/prostitute complex, is that he can easily avoid a committed relationship. Greg admits to this: "[Men] don't like themselves. They can't form close relationships because the person they're close to is going to find out how rotten they are and not like them." How can you have one fulfilling relationship when you must go to different kinds of women to satisfy different needs? Greg's language suggests he is generally contemptuous of women and enjoys a sense of superiority with them. The one notable exception was the girlfriend he had during his first marriage.

Greg sees himself as the modern, liberal husband—no jealousy, no double standards. He hopes his wife would enjoy any affair she might have. I interviewed a fair number of men who said they felt this way. I wonder how calmly Greg would actually react if he discovered she were involved in an affair. Men's reactions, I found, are as diverse as women's—some ignore jealousy, others are passive, but many more confront their wives angrily. I have known of a few men who demand the details and receive vicarious pleasure from them. Others are turned off completely. The important fact here is that what they said they would do and how they actually react are frequently quite different.

Franklin is a professor of philosophy, in his late sixties.

Q: Have you ever had an affair?
A: I would say I've had three major affairs in my life.
Q: What was your motivation?
A: After the children were born, my wife wasn't interested in sex.
Q: Were you in love with the women you had affairs with?
A: I was in love with all three of them and also with my wife. She is an intelligent and wonderful woman and we had a tremendous relationship and family life, but sex had no meaning for her.
Q: When you got married, did you expect to have affairs?
A: I never thought about it. I was always involved with sex since I was fourteen and never really intended to get married. But I met someone who was fascinating and her social set-up required marriage.
Q: How would you feel if your wife was to have an affair?
A: I wouldn't mind at all. It wouldn't bother me if she had physical needs and couldn't fulfill them with me.
Q: Tell me about the affairs.
A: I'm not promiscuous. The first affair lasted four years, but the woman was completely neurotic.
Q: Did she expect you to leave your wife?
A: Yes. I told her I wouldn't. She was married when I met her, and when we got together she left her husband. The second affair was with a woman in my academic world. It went on for five or six years and the problem was we lived in different cities. She had an unhappy experience and didn't want to get married. The third time I fell in love has lasted over twenty-five years.
Q: Why don't you live with her?
A: We have independent lives and no desire to get married. It's a

very satisfactory relationship in the sense that we are interested in each other. The matter of marriage never came up.

Q: Do you think your love affair has affected your marriage?

A: I don't think so, though it's a very strong relationship. My wife has a suspicion—she's too smart a woman not to suspect.

Q: If you had no outlet for your sexual needs, perhaps your marriage would not have been so tolerable.

A: Well, you must remember I owe a great deal to my wife. She bolstered me in my career, we raised children, and how do you desert a woman when she's sixty, especially when she's someone you like?

Q: Do you believe men are polygamous?

A: Absolutely.

Q: If your wife died, would you remarry?

A: No. I believe a polygamous life is more suitable now.

Q: Does your financial position affect your ability to have relationships?

A: I never used it to seduce showgirls or anything. I don't think my economic situation made any difference. With the kind of women I know, money never had anything to do with it.

Q: Did anything funny or embarrassing ever happen?

A: I have never, at any time, tried to hide any relationship I have ever had. I assume that the society I move in would not misunderstand a lunch. But my wife's best friend called up once and said I was having an affair with a famous person. I told her that she shouldn't listen to gossip. I was actually having a fling, and I don't think I fooled her.

Q: How did your affairs affect you?

A: I call them relationships. The first one made me rather unhappy, the second one was long distance, and the third one has been extremely satisfactory.

Q: Why do you think women want to have an affair with a married man?

A: Because there aren't that many single men. A woman would rather have a man who was completely available to go out with, but there just aren't that many around.

Q: Why not?

A: There are two kinds of men. Married ones who play around and unmarried men who are into quickies. Then there are a lot of men looking for the ideal princess who don't love real women but their fantasies.

Q: Is sex better in an affair?

A: Christ, yes. But sex is not enough. It slows down very quickly where the trees shake and all that. I would say in a love affair, sex is twenty or twenty-five percent of it.

Q: Do you think men have more affairs than women?

A: In my youth that was true. The double standard meant that men could be forgiven.

Q: What advice would you give to a wife who discovers that her husband is having an affair?

A: Forgive him. For the reason that otherwise her life would be miserable and lonely. There's nothing worse than a middle-aged woman discovering her husband is having an affair who rushes to her lawyer and gets a divorce.

Q: Do you think most married men are faithful?

A: I think most are frightened and have inhibitions. I think they have religion and morals. I guess that doesn't hold true as much anymore, but many of them are incapable of affairs. They have quickies.

Q: You think women are more capable of having prolonged affairs?

A: Probably. I have found women more intelligent and interesting. Maybe that's because they relate more to what I'm interested in.

Q: In the past, most marriages were arranged. Today, people marry for love. Shouldn't there be a decline in the necessity of mistresses or other women?

A: You're talking about married men. Men after marriage for fifteen or twenty years rise to the fear that they are becoming impotent, they're missing something, and pretty soon they'll be old. It's part of the pattern of our society.

Q: Why don't women feel that way?

A: I think that women are going to feel that way, but the

opportunities are still not open to them. There are not as many single men around.

Q: Why is that?

A: We're discovering that the population is very homosexually inclined.

Q: Do you have any advice for married men?

A: If you have no guilt feelings, it's better to have sexual relationships. If you have guilt feelings, then don't. If you're going to suffer, if you're going to lie on a couch at sixty dollars an hour, then don't do it. But if you're a human being, you're rational, intelligent . . . you're reasonable . . . I see nothing wrong.

Franklin is a more integrated person than Greg. While Greg is inwardly chaotic, having a conflict between his sexual and emotional standards, Franklin's choice is more conscious and he comfortably accommodates his needs.

Franklin loves his wife and his other woman. His life is divided into family activities at home and sex outside. Both are real relationships. His wife and he have intellectual interests in common, and possibly there is mutual nurturing. As Franklin's wife has no interest in sex and his lover none in marriage, there seems to be no conflict here. Some men would probably view Franklin's situation as ideal.

I have spoken with the other woman in Franklin's life. She expresses a strong belief that love stays alive better in relationships where two people live apart. Actually, she gives signs that she is quietly lonely—but seems to know it is pointless to push Franklin for anything more. Undoubtedly her conscious belief in the separation that kindles love explains her long-term satisfaction with her lover. Whatever compromises she might have made provide her with an affectionate relationship.

Alex is a forty-one-year-old publisher from England.

Q: Do you have many affairs?

A: Once in a while I have an affair.

Q: Before you got married, did you think you'd have affairs?

A: No.

Q: What changed your mind?

A: Travel and opportunity.

Q: Do you feel guilty?

A: Yes.

Q: Do you consider yourself happily married?

A: Yes.

Q: How would you feel if your wife did the same thing?

A: Bad.

Q: What would you do if she found you out?

A: Explain it as best I could.

Q: What if she were adamant that you not see this woman again?

A: I'd have to think seriously about it.

Q: What if she said it's her or me?

A: I'd say don't be so bloody silly. I'd get so damned mad I'd say, "Okay, it's her." But I wouldn't mean it.

Q: Do most of the men you know have affairs?

A: Most of my friends don't have affairs. They have strictly sex and pretend to themselves that flesh is art.

Q: What do you mean?

A: They sleep with someone and think that's a relationship. Americans, I believe, have far more affairs and far fewer hang-ups than we do.

Q: Do you think it's possible to be faithful to one woman?

A: Yes, if other opportunities rarely present themselves.

Q: How would you summarize your feelings about your affairs?

A: I like the meal at home. I want an occasional different dessert.

Opportunity and contact through travel can prove irresistible. Alex keeps his affairs limited so that he can avoid entanglements which would create feelings of guilt in him. At the same time he protects his relationship with his wife, whom he cherishes. Yet if she discovered him, he would apparently jeopardize their union. If his wife pushed him, he would bluff and choose the outside woman . . . even though "I don't mean it."

I know from Alex's lover that he really is happily married. He is possessive of his wife and takes care that his escapades remain just that. But perhaps a desire for control motivates him more than he knows. When his independence is threatened in a hypothetical situation, he verbally moves to the brink of separation.

Dr. Judd Marmor, Professor of Psychiatry at U.S.C., in discussing the psychological importance of control, mentioned to me some husbands' "need to do something to enhance their sense of power." This desire for power or freedom was blatant in the conversations of men who had reasonably good marriages but carried on affairs. Even though Alex may have been content, an imagined threat to his independence sparked an aggressive response. "I'd have to think seriously about giving up the other woman," he says. In reality, he might be less cavalier.

Conrad is a thirty-eight-year-old man who is part of the current power structure of Washington.

Q: Why do married men, specifically you, have affairs?
A: I, we, are psychologically sex starved. Sex with a new partner is more psychologically satisfying. You can pursue your fantasies.
Q: With whom do you prefer affairs, single or married women?
A: Married women, because the risks are the same for her and for me.
Q: Why do you think single women have affairs with married men?
A: The single men today are arrogant and have inflated egos. I see it in men I interview for jobs. They overvalue themselves because they have their hands on so many women—single and married.
Q: Do you feel guilty about affairs?
A: Yes.
Q: How do you handle the guilt?
A: Screw the devil out of my wife for a few days.
Q: Do you think your wife has ever had an affair?
A: I know she has.
Q: How did you feel when you found out?

A: Desolate.

Q: Did you consider divorce?

A: Yes.

Q: Why didn't you?

A: I like her. But what infuriated me was that the affair was with my best friend and she's done that twice!

Q: Did you discover it yourself?

A: Oh no. Women are much more expert at deception than men. They go and choose a safe partner, like his best friend, who'll never tell. A man doesn't generally get involved with women's friends. I would never do that. But a woman's instinct for deception is so sophisticated it causes them to preselect people who are safe.

Q: How did you then react to those men she was involved with?

A: I never spoke to either of them again.

Q: How did you get your wife to tell you about these affairs?

A: After a woman has had four orgasms, she'll tell you practically anything. The difference between married women having an affair and married men is that women go for the big affair. Husbands go for one-night stands and feel very guilty about the long-term affair. I guess we're more childishly romantic.

Q: When you got married, did you expect to have affairs?

A: No.

Q: How long were you married when you began?

A: Four or five months.

Q: Did you ever fall in love?

A: I was in a deep affair for two years. She tried to kill herself. It was horrible, but I was not in love with her.

Q: Do you think most wives know when their husbands are having affairs?

A: No, they're blind. But so are husbands. I remember one married woman I had an affair with who said that her husband was joining us for dinner because he unexpectedly came to town. I knew him, so he didn't suspect anything when I "accidentally" ran into them both. After dinner the wife excused herself because she didn't feel well. He and I were alone and he asked me to fix him up because his wife was four months pregnant and "didn't do it anymore." I was caught in the irony of all times. I had just screwed his wife and her husband wanted me to take care of his needs too!

Q: Is monogamy still possible?

A: Yes, but not if you travel the way many men do.

Q: Do you know many men who are still faithful?

A: I would have said my minister, but he just got a divorce because his wife caught him in an affair.

Q: Now that you know about your wife, does she know about you?

A: Yes. We've agreed never to do anything with any friends, but since we travel so much, we know it's inevitable to have some sort of affairs. If she ever sleeps with another friend of mine, it's absolutely over with us.

"We're psychologically sex starved," Conrad says of married men. He was the first person capable of describing his need so precisely. It's not a physical deficiency to him but rather the irresistible thrill of someone new. "You can pursue your fantasies," he says.

Conrad is perfectly satisfied with his wife, physically. Sex is not what he is missing at home—just the psychological thrill of exploring someone new. Neither does he use sex, as Greg or Franklin seem to, as a substitute for affectionate experience. There are people, Dr. Judd Marmor pointed out to me, who are incapable of strong emotional attachment. In those instances, sex substitutes for other strong feelings.

Conrad claims women have a sinister side . . . "They're much more deceptive." He doesn't think they share the same guilt as men feel when they stray from their marital beds. At the same time he acknowledges that they don't go for one-night stands but always "the big affair," an involvement as emotional as it is physical. (It is well to remember, though, that psychological sex starvation is also valid for wives.)

Women today are more actively reaching out for their own happiness and sexual fulfillment in ways men classically have.

While they have less opportunity to meet new people than their husbands, they may get involved with friends or neighborhood men; but they do find partners.

Conrad's wife, however, has a job affording her ample travel. Her affairs with his best friends very likely relate more to dynamics underlying her relationship with her husband than they do to lack of opportunity with other men. Competition between the spouses, or the wish to hurt one another, lead to friends' beds, men and women tell me. Conrad and his wife have now made a pact to stay away from friends. Their marriage affords them both enough satisfaction to have survived until now.

Brian is a sixty-year-old international businessman from Portland, Oregon, now living in Hong Kong with his wife. Two of their four children live there as well.

Q: What is your motivation in having affairs?

A: The sheer pleasure and thrill. Not living the day to day drudgery. We can role-play like kids.

Q: Do you ever lie about being married?

A: I cannot operate with deceit anymore. I used to say whatever was necessary to get a woman to bed.

Q: Have you ever loved any of the women you had affairs with?

A: Anyone I have a continuous relationship with I love. I don't believe any love is exclusive.

Q: Are you happily married?

A: If I were in a normal job, I wouldn't be happily married, but the way I travel it works. I think a sea captain has the right idea. He's off six to eight weeks at a time, so when he comes home it's a honeymoon. Marriage was invented as an arrangement for economic protection of a family to assume bloodlines. It was never a romantic love thing until Hollywood. Hollywood's influence in the 1920s changed our concept of romance and marriage.

Q: Do or did you have a moral viewpoint?

A: No. The hang-up I had was Irish-Catholic, but I brought up my children with no religion. I just told them that we need more kindness and less religion. Religion was invented for men to control women, because they recognized that there are animal aspects in women and it frightened them that they might be cuckolded. So they used religion to give themselves security. They invented the concepts of decent and indecent women and the women bought it.

Q: Do most men have affairs?

A: Men don't confide in each other that much and there are damned few I'd trust. He'd tell his wife and that would be the end.

Q: Did you ever think of leaving your wife?

A: I once thought of leaving without saying I would.

Q: What prevented you?

A: My family. My mother and her reactions. I've considered it even when there was no one else. I was fed up with the whole idea, the competitiveness and the jealousy in marriage.

Q: How would you feel if your wife had affairs?

A: I'd prefer not to know. I'd be pleased if she were enjoying herself, but I don't wish to be embarrassed.

Q: Do you think if your wife found out and confronted you, you would change your lifestyle?

A: My wife would have to be a complete ignoramus not to figure out that if I travel for twenty-five years and have sexual needs and enjoy people, I have extramarital relationships. But she doesn't care to confront me on this because it would cause a situation. I'm quite convinced in my own mind that she's had a couple of affairs herself.

Q: What convinces you?

A: She was a very beautiful girl and I would be quite surprised if she hadn't. I'm certainly not going to confront her on it.

Q: You once told me about a special relationship that has gone on twenty years.

A: Yes, it started when I was single. She married my boss very soon after I met her.

Q: And has your love affair continued even until now?

A: Oh yes, all these years.

Q: How would you say your love affairs affect your marriage?

A: They're usually positive relationships, because I won't put up with them unless they are. They give me a greater joy and this means I can be much more compassionate, thoughtful, and understanding than if I had no other satisfactions. I enjoy myself a great deal. I'm known as having a good nature at home. I feel that much of the unhappiness and dissatisfaction I see in life comes from frustration. So many married people lash out at each other, and yet they're sweet to strangers.

Q: Tell me about competition.

A: Married people compete for the favor of children, the attention of friends, everything. Life is a tough situation. I think it's very easy if the wife is a mothering figure and the husband is a child; then it works out beautifully.

Q: Why do you think, in general, a woman wants to have an affair with a married man?

A: I think she can experiment with a bit of safety, with someone experienced. She might feel a little more tenderness from a married man. She might feel like a piece of meat with the younger men and their urgencies. They might not have as much time for romance, so it's flattering if someone in an accomplished position spends a little time with her. That includes a lot of married men.

Q: Do you think that mystery is the great thing that attracts men to women?

A: Yes. When there's nothing more to learn, you're on to the next book.

Q: Do you think women feel differently than men?

A: I certainly do.

Q: It's been said that men are polygamous and women are monogamous. Do you believe that?

A: In a sense, I think a woman can love ten men and a man can love ten women, but a woman can only love one man a day.

Q: You're saying one at a time. I'm talking about in marriage.

A: Women are monogamous but fickle. Monogamy can change and with a woman when it's over it's dead, absolutely dead. A woman can live or breathe this man, but when something happens, it stops and she never cares if she never sees him or talks to him.

Q: I notice you don't wear a wedding band. Do you think that makes a difference?

A: I don't like wedding bands because to me it indicates a ring through the nose.

Q: How would you feel if your wife wouldn't wear a wedding ring?

A: She doesn't have to; it would have saved me a lot of money.

Q: Is sex better in an affair, and why?

A: Marriage is just like the same meal every night.

Q: If you fell madly in love with another woman, would you leave your wife?

A: Who knows?

Q: Well, you did, and you didn't!

A: Maybe I wasn't really in love—then. Love is not absolute. There are degrees of anything.

Q: What would you say to the women of America about having affairs with married men?

A: I think it's very good training. It's important.

Q: Do you have a daughter?

A: Yes.

Q: How would you feel if she had an affair with a married man?

A: I would recommend it highly. Absolutely.

Q: What advice would you have for women between twenty and forty?

A: I'll put it this way. The best thing that could happen to my daughter would be for her to meet an older married man. If her only input were boys of her own age, because of their physiognomy, they have only a one-track interest in young girls. That's normal. There's something wrong with them if they don't. I have no objection to this and I understand the interest, but the older person would be genuinely fond of her. He wouldn't be as selfish.

Q: Wouldn't you be afraid that she would fall in love and get hurt?

A: Nonsense. Women are not the weaker sex, they're very good recoverers.

Brian, who is older than many in my sampling, has developed a personal philosophy which suits his lifestyle. He acknowledges his wife's intelligence, expects that she is subject to similar appetites and entitled to the same privileges he assumes himself. He likes his life just as it is and would probably feel stifled in a career which required him to live at home fifty-two weeks a year.

When he thought of divorcing, it was his mother's restrictions above all else that stopped him. The focus on the mother figure is further underscored by his statement that the perfect marriage is between a maternal woman and a man who relates as her son. Brian states he is missing that kind of connection to his wife, that his wife and he are competitors. That complaint crops up a lot in the men's interviews.

In Brian's case, the familiar wife/mother association is actually emphasized by the inclusion of his mother as the disapproving figure. She may be the conscience for the activities about which he feels unconsciously guilty. Brian finds a rationale to act on his sexual and emotional needs ("I don't think love is exclusive") while his family and Irish-Catholic background keep him committed to his home base. He is aware that while certain aspects of domesticity repel him, there is a certain security in them.

Charles is a forty-three-year-old accountant.

Q: Before you got married, did you expect to be monogamous?
A: No, but a man wants a nest.
Q: Have you had any long, deep affairs?
A: Yes, several.
Q: When you were in love, why didn't you leave?
A: I guess I wasn't sufficiently in love.
Q: What were your motivations for affairs?
A: Sexual, adventure. I don't believe any man can go through life sexually with one woman.
Q: Are you happily married?
A: Relatively so.
Q: How would you feel if she did the same thing?

A: I wouldn't mind.

Q: Isn't there a danger you might fall in love?

A: You risk that.

Q: Do you feel guilty?

A: No.

Q: Do most married men have affairs?

A: Most married men with any imagination or intelligence, at some point in their lives. Within a few blocks of home.

Q: Do they ever ask you to cover for them?

A: Yes.

Q: Do as many married women have affairs?

A: No, not as much opportunity. In twenty years, it will be on an equal basis. Religion and bourgeois values make us sneak around. I don't know if I could have an open marriage.

Charles believes and lives the historic notion that a penis is not monogamous—that no man can go through life sexually with one woman. Married now for the second time, Charles didn't mention marrying again for love but because "a man wants a nest."

Taking a popular stance, Charles says he wouldn't mind if his wife had an affair, yet he is not prepared to have a sexually open marriage. He is bound by tradition and cultural mores. I suspect part of the reason he prefers things status quo is that he knows his wife would refuse the open marriage idea, and he is not sure he could tolerate the jealousy he might feel in such a set-up himself. More significantly, he says religious and bourgeois values make us sneak around . . . but he probably senses the adventure would disappear if those shackles were loosed. An affair just wouldn't be as much fun if he could tell his wife about it.

Sal is a thirty-six-year-old Canadian real estate developer.

Q: How long have you been married?

A: Ten years.

Q: Do you have affairs?

A: Occasionally.

Q: What is your motivation?

A: The first time was entertainment. I was, to put it bluntly, putting on an orgy.

Q: How did this happen?

A: Well, I went to Hawaii with a group of Americans to buy a hotel. Halfway through the week, we arranged about fifteen young girls for about five of us.

Q: What did you do with them?

A: We shared them.

Q: You mean simultaneously?

A: Two of us were lying in the big king bed—across the bed—and the girls were blowing us and the other guys were fucking them from behind.

Q: Did you enjoy this?

A: It wasn't sexually enjoyable . . . it was entertainment.

Q: Had you been faithful up to this time?

A: Yes.

Q: How many years?

A: Seven.

Q: After this time, you started having affairs?

A: I relaxed.

Q: You mean it didn't affect your marriage?

A: No.

Q: What made you change after this orgy?

A: The realization that my family life is one thing and that, occasionally, my personal life is something else.

Q: Did you have a moral viewpoint about married men having affairs before you were married?

A: Yes.

Q: Did you decide you were not going to have affairs?

A: Yes.

Q: What made you change?

A: Time alters you, changes your beliefs. I still believe in what should be.

Q: So you disapprove of what you do?

A: I don't disapprove. I just don't shout about it.

Q: But you somehow decided it's not so terrible.

A: That's right.

Q: What was your motivation for your first real affair?

A: I liked her when I was single and I liked her again. It's that simple. She was a girl from my past.

Q: How would you feel if your wife did the same thing?

A: As a matter of fact, I can answer that because two nights ago I dreamed she did and I woke up furious from my sleep.

Q: What would you do if you found out your wife was actually having an affair?

A: Well, in my dream I got very annoyed and upset. I think I would go crazy, mad. Maybe I would try to swallow it. *Maybe.*

Q: Would you confront her and try to stop her?

A: Of course.

Q: Would you divorce her?

A: Oh, Christ. No.

Q: What if she said she wouldn't stop?

A: I think the kids would come into play as the number one thing.

Q: Did you ever fall in love with another woman?

A: No, and I don't think I will.

Q: Do you think your wife is the best person for you?

A: Certainly, I think highly of her. The question here is what is love? Married love? Family love? Or, love in the sense of going crazy about another woman? What I don't like happening is being fifty years old and going crazy over a twenty-year-old.

Q: Why would you hate that to happen?

A: It's ridiculous to do that. I would be the unhappy one, not her. I would be the one to suffer.

Q: Why not her?

A: Because I don't think young girls, in general, can fall for a man fifty years old . . . it's a very special situation.

Q: If your wife died, would you remarry?

A: The question again depends on the children. If they were of an age and out on their own, I would probably not although I think I would be lonely. Men are notorious for not being able to live alone.

Q. Does your financial position affect your ability to have affairs?

A: Well, in the sense of doing it away from home, yes.

Q: Did anything odd or funny ever happen?

A: Well, the same night of the orgy we went to a night club and found some very old whores, Danish. One was the ugliest thing I ever saw in my life, the other was quite nice, but very old. I proceeded to jump on her. After all our efforts of the whole night, we finally got them to bed at five in the morning. They wouldn't make love in the same room together, so I went into the bathroom with this woman and tried to make love with her there and just couldn't.

Q: Why did you pick up a girl who you thought was ugly?

A: We ran into them and we liked them.

Q: Did you ever have a platonic lover?

A: You're kidding. I have no time for that.

Q: Does a wedding band make any difference, do you think?

Q: Well, I certainly haven't worn mine on occasions. I was sure it would not work out.

Q: So you lied about it?

A: Right. I was at a famous actress's party once and lied.

Q: Did you feel guilty about it?

A: Yes, because I was trying to keep track of whether I had it on or not and when I would see these people again.

Q: Does a wedding band make a difference?

A: Yes.

Q: Is sex better in an affair?

A: It's more refreshing, naturally.

Q: Do you think most married men have affairs?

A: I don't think so.

Q: Do you have double standards?

A: Yes, but I don't think it's right.

Q: Do you intend to continue to have affairs for the rest of your married life?

A: I don't know. I have a suspicion that my wife doesn't even care. It would depend on with whom I did what. If I did it with her best friend, she'd flip. I think she would leave. If I said I did it with the wife of a tailor in Beaumont, Texas, she'd say, "You bastard," and then ignore it.

Q: Do you think extramarital affairs keep some marriages together?
A: No question.
Q: Do most of your married friends have affairs?
A: Not all of them.
Q: Do any of their wives know?
A: Yes, some of them divorced them.

Sal acted out a fantasy many men only imagine. He participated in an orgy that he helped arrange. Afterward, this previously faithful husband decided there is no harm in clandestine relationships as long as they are conducted away from where he lives. "My family is one thing and my personal life something else." In fact, several professionals observed to me that these brief interludes don't generally affect men one way or the other. They simply come under the category of things one should keep to oneself.

Sal dreamed his wife admitted an affair of hers and he became furious. His double standard, if only in a dream, typified most of the men's attitudes.

DIVORCED MEN TALK ABOUT THEIR AFFAIRS

The divorced men I spoke with are viewing their extramarital affairs from some distance now, having come to a particular stance on the subject. Rather than living with the conflict of an adulterous relationship, these men have chosen to, or circumstances have forced them to, leave unsatisfactory marriages. The men who do leave of their own volition generally do so during the first couple of years of the affair. These are the ones, like Warren (the last interview in this section), who are unable to live the double life. Regardless of how their divorces came about, the divorced men I interviewed who had known deep love affairs during marriage suffered far less than those who were still wed and maintaining secret involvements with girlfriends they really loved.

Randall is a forty-eight-year-old writer.

Q: Did you have one or numerous affairs?
A: Numerous.
Q: What was your major motivation?
A: I think emotional.
Q: Would you say you considered yourself happily married?
A: Only in the early stages.
Q: How many affairs did you have?
A: Which time?
Q: How many times were you married?
A: Twice.
Q: For each marriage.
A: The first one, two affairs. The second, sixteen.
Q: Which marriage was happier?
A: The second, I suppose.
Q: Would you say that you were happy with your wives when you started having affairs?
A: No. I think the problems that came up early in the marriages justified it for me.
Q: In both marriages you had problems?
A: Yes. I left my first wife because she would not let me penetrate her.
Q: Ever?
A: Ever.
Q: What did she expect?
A: I don't know, but she couldn't. Little tears would come down her little face. I went to Vegas on my honeymoon and went out looking for pussy.
Q: But you stayed for six years; why?
A: Maybe because my father had been married five times and I saw myself repeating his lifestyle.
Q: What about your second marriage?
A: She said, "I don't care what you do as long as you don't do it around our lives."
Q: But you had some sort of sex with her?
A: Basically oral. She liked that better.

Q: So neither wife wanted complete sex and you didn't push it.

A: Right.

Q: Did you feel guilty about affairs?

A: I don't think I ever really felt guilty.

Q: Did you have children?

A: No.

Q: How would you have felt if either wife had had an affair?

A: In those days, I would probably have killed. I had that double standard I no longer have. Today, I'd just leave casually.

Q: Did you ever fall in love with any of the women you had affairs with?

A: Yes.

Q: One or many times?

A: Not many.

Q: How long were your affairs?

A: Basically, a couple of years.

Q: What prevented you from leaving your wives?

A: I loved the first, but couldn't live with her . . . temperament. The second one—a lot of reasons—guilt, a need for roots, a fantasy I live with, a dog. I had a dog for a number of years I wouldn't have left anybody for.

Q: Do you like being married?

A: I think so.

Q: Would you ever consider remarrying?

A: Now? I don't think so.

Q: Did your financial position ever affect your ability to have affairs?

A: My financial position had nothing to do with anything.

Q: Did you ever get caught?

A: No. I'm an expert at cheating. I could write a book on it. The first thing you have to not deal with is fear. You have to stop at gas stations and wash off lipstick and perfume. Jump in and do it with both feet. I was never seen for twenty-five years. I was on the prowl. The second thing is to cover yourself. Call your buddies and friends who you are using for an excuse.

Q: We've gotten through authorization and no fear, what's next?

A: A sense of believability and honesty to the wife. Never look at another woman in public when you're with your wife. And you put down men who do. You say, "Look at that. Isn't it disgusting?" Or you say, "I saw Harry with a young broad, do you believe it?"

Q: What comes next? What about when you get caught?

A: I've never been caught.

Q: What about a man who does get caught?

A: Okay, I was on the island of Capri and involved with a young lady who was an extra in a movie I was writing. I also wanted another lady. The first one had some trouble with her teeth and we sent her to a dentist. Right away, I got the Italian lady and brought her to my room. As we were coming out of the room, the first lady returned home and saw this and went into her room and slammed the door. I said, "Well, I finally got caught." But innately I am a wonderful liar. I went into her room, forced my way in, and told her, "Would you believe this? She saw you get in the car and knocked on my door and told me that she wanted me and had wanted me the whole time."

Q: Did she believe you?

A: Yes.

Q: Were you sincere?

A: I'm an awfully sincere liar.

Q: What do you do if you get caught?

A: As an old friend said, "If you're caught with your ass in the air, deny it."

Q: Any other advice to men?

A: Yes, very early in the marriage begin to brainwash the lady as to your lifestyle. Such as moodiness . . . you drive into the desert for five hours. You must do this early in the marriage when all is well, so later on, when it begins to go bad, you have an excuse to get away for a day . . . to go to the beach. Build up that side of your life. Develop a need to paint, take photographs, anything. Buy season's tickets to the fights or ball game.

Q: Is there a male conspiracy to protect each other in these situations?

A: It's not a conspiracy . . . but there's some kind of fraternal feelings.

Q: It's understood?

A: Oh yes. We're absolutely supportive of one another.

Q: But you never actually discussed it?

A: Oh, all of my friends know what a scoundrel I was.

Q: And were they, too?

A: Some of them were. I've only known, in my wide range of friends, two men who were faithful and I'm not sure of them.

Q: So most married men do have affairs?

A: I think so.

Q: What about women?

A: More men do.

Q: Did you ever have a platonic love affair?

A: No. I always had to care passionately.

Q: How did your affairs affect you?

A: They never made me confused, guilty, or any of that. Happiness, I don't know. I think you lose your perspective the more you do these things. It makes you less able to relate to one person.

Q: How did affairs affect your marriages?

A: It certainly didn't help the marriage. Maybe it helped keep the bad marriage going . . . gave me a certain amount of freedom.

Q: Do you ever wear a wedding band?

A: Yes. I used to take it off when I was around cruising, but I rarely do that now, because I always meet people in a more natural way. Sometimes the ring was on and I didn't pay any attention. Generally, the way to work your way into the heart of a woman is to say that you're lonely or misunderstood, or your wife is sick, something like that.

Q: Did you ever lie about being married?

A: Yes, I would try to make a judgment about whether it would make an effect or not.

Q: Did you ever eventually tell them you were married?

A: If the affair ever went on long enough.

Q: What about wives who find out their husbands are having affairs?

A: It would take a great lady to maintain the relationship.

Q: What would be your advice?

A: Confront the man and discuss it. If he denied it, the man is a creep . . . I think as you get older, you change. I think I will miss not having children.

Q: Why didn't you have children?

A: I didn't want them with the ladies I married.

Q: Did they want them?

A: I don't think so.

Q: That's unusual.

A: Well, I sought them out. I wanted my virgin goddess. I wanted a virgin goddess and I married her—twice.

Q: What do you mean a virgin goddess?

A: Probably sexually frigid.

Q: Sixteen years is a long time to be married to somebody who's frigid.

A: Well, I was away for a lot of that time and I had my dog for eleven years and I would not have traded that dog for anything.

Q: Is the dog still around?

A: She's dead.

Q: Is that why you finally left?

A: Probably. What can I tell you? This dog is probably the only thing I ever loved. It was not an evil thing. If I had had kids, I would never have left the marriage either.

Q: Was sex generally better in an affair than in marriage?

A: I think with anyone, after a while, it ain't what it was. You can't have that for ten to twenty years.

Q: Do you think men are generally polygamous and women are monogamous?

A: I think there's an emotional factor with women—whether it's false or not, I don't know. I think that women are somewhat promiscuous, despite the double standard. But, instinctively, there's a difference. I'm involved with a woman now and for two years I have not been unfaithful. Two reasons—I'm getting old and I don't have the same drive and, second, I just haven't met anybody.

Q: How old are you?

A: Forty-eight.

Q: Did you expect that you would have affairs when you got married?

A: No. But I married the wrong kind of women for me. They did not fulfill or even approach satisfying my needs. I should have married hot-blooded broads.

Q: And your wives were not?

A: Not at all. Very virginal.

Q: What about the second one?

A: It was always a problem because she was Catholic.

Q: What is your advice to single women having affairs with married men?

A: I think it's very bad because they generally will wind up with nothing except a dick and they can get that anywhere. I think the pain involved in an affair for a young woman who doesn't really know where it's at yet is sad. There's a romantic fantasy that surrounds the unhappy, older married man. "I can do something for him. I have something more." It's all horse-feathers.

Meeting this articulate, rather attractive man, you would never suspect he is the awful scoundrel and "sincere liar" he paints himself. Intrigue and lying are his game. Though he instructs men to deny affairs, even if caught with their asses in the air, he claims a fellow found out by his wife who denies it is "a creep."

Randall, confused, full of contradiction, rejects the possibility of confronting his marital problems. He lived his sexual life outside of marriage and a less sexual life with "virginal goddesses" at home. To last as long as they did, the marriages obviously held strong, deep attractions for him. His wives may have been beautiful women who projected the kind of image he wanted and provided the bases from which he could pursue sexual women.

When I asked Randall why he didn't leave his first wife, who wouldn't allow him to penetrate her, he answered, "I loved her, but couldn't live with her temperament." Lack of sex was never mentioned as the focal problem either with her or the second wife.

With the second, staying married was attributed to "A lot of reasons . . . guilt, a need for roots, a fantasy I lived with, a dog."

"I should have married hot-blooded broads," he claims. But not doing so suggests he suspected that such women would have made demands on him he was not prepared to handle. His wives didn't want children and remained "pure," leaving Randall free to live his erotic life elsewhere.

Separating women the way he does, into good and bad categories, the same way Greg does, turns them into nonpersons who are easy to lie to and to manipulate. In this division he loses any feelings for the woman, and the only real sentiment Randall expressed was for his dog—a creature who could make no demands on him.

The dog, like children in some instances, is used as a rationalization to remain in a marriage which lacks real sharing. Men who do not want to break up marriages often use children as an excuse because they are incapable of confronting the fact that their own immature needs are fulfilled in the marital partnership.

Jed is a thirty-seven-year-old engineer.

Q: You were telling me about swinging in your marriage. I don't know too much about that. Was everyone who swung at this club you belonged to married?

A: Most were married, a few couples lived together. One club only allowed couples.

Q: Did you pay a fee?

A: It was ten dollars per party per couple to pay for clean-up, towels, and beds.

Q: Beds were provided?

A: All over the place.

Q: Were these big houses?

A: Three bedrooms, mostly.

Q: There were four or five couples then?

A: No, thirty.

Q: How did you do it? Take turns?

A: No. This one house had the garage made into little cabins with maybe fifteen bunks built in and weird lighting.

Q: All in one room?

A: Yeah, but we all had our own little cubbyholes. You would have five or six couples trading off. Then sometimes you got to know people and invited them over to your house. Just four or five couples. Had a party.

Q: So when you went to the club, it was for the initial contact?

A: Well, it was a place to go every Saturday night.

Q: How long did you do that?

A: About a year and a half.

Q: And both you and your wife thought this was a terrific idea?

A: Well, I always talked about it, but it was my wife who found the place and dragged me over there.

Q: Before you got involved with this, did you have affairs?

A: A few.

Q: Anything very serious?

A: No.

Q: How about your wife?

A: No, as far as I know.

Q: Did she know about yours?

A: No.

Q: How did they happen?

A: They were just sexual things that happened.

Q: You were saying that most people who go to cocktail parties wear social masks, but that at swinging parties no one has any pretensions.

A: Right. Everybody is there for one reason—to get laid.

Q: Do you think cocktail parties are the same?

A: I think that a lot of boy-girl games are played.

Q: Do you think that swinging is good for most marriages?

A: I think that at the beginning it had a positive effect on mine, but then it became negative.

Q: How does swinging positively affect a marriage?

A: There were people at the club where the wife was frigid, so they tried swinging to loosen her up. Sometimes it worked. There were a lot of new things one could learn.

Q: How did it affect your marriage?

A: It was just something new to talk about and do.

Q: How about the negatives?

A: It became like an obsession with one person more than the other. Sometimes I wanted to go more than my wife did. Never at the same time.

Q: Did you stop doing it after a while?

A: Yes.

Q: Did you continue to have affairs?

A: No.

Q: Did anyone at the club become emotionally involved?

A: Not that I know of. You become really close friends, though. When you go to bed with someone, you're never strangers again.

Q: What would happen if you went to bed with someone one week and the next week you didn't want to but they did?

A: You tell them. I'm not interested now.

Q: Were there a lot of hurt feelings?

A: No.

Q: Are you sorry that you got married now that you're divorced?

A: No.

Q: Did your financial position affect your ability to have affairs?

A: It didn't enter into it.

Q: Do you think men are polygamous and women monogamous?

A: I think both are polygamous.

Q: Did you ever wear a wedding band?

A: For a while.

Q: Why did you take it off?

A: Actually, I found a wedding band encouraged outside action. There are girls who are looking for casual affairs. It's quick, easy, and there are no strings.

Q: Why did you stop wearing it?

A: I hurt my hand when I was in the service.

Q: Is the best sex in an affair?

A: No, the best sex is with someone you love.

Q: Do you think married men are having more relationships than married women?

A: Actually, I think more women are. The way it's going today, women are a lot more liberal, and when they want to have an affair they just go out and do it.

Q: Do men talk about their affairs with each other?

A: Not gentlemen. I don't. High school kids do.

Q: But there seems to be a conspiracy to cover for each other.

A: Well, once in a while. You know, at the poker game sometimes a guy will say, "If anyone asks you if I was here the other night, tell them I was," when we know he wasn't. But wives do that too. I think it's the same for both sexes.

Q: If you remarried, would you expect to have affairs?

A: I don't think so.

Q: If you did, would you think that your wife was entitled to do the same thing?

A: Yes.

Q: Do you believe in open marriage?

A: I think as I get older, I'm more old-fashioned. I think if I got married, it would be a one-to-one thing and I would not seek affairs. I would turn them down.

Q: Do you think affairs are more prevalent now than they were?

A: No, I think we talk about it more.

Q: Do you know a lot of people who belong to swing clubs?

A: You don't have to belong, you can just go and pay the fee at a lot of them.

Q: You're an attractive man. It would seem to me that if you wanted to sleep with someone, you would have no trouble finding somebody. Why go to a club?

A: In swing parties, you don't have to play any games. I meet girls all the time, and if I'm in the mood I go out or don't. But at parties, everybody is there for the same thing. I meet all kinds of neat people. Sex is just part of getting to know somebody.

Q: How many of these clubs are there?

A: Hundreds. There's a whole book on it—a guideline. We have truckdrivers, cops, politicians. But there was an ethic at the swing clubs where you just don't recognize anybody away from the party. It was such a cross section of life. People were careful not to do anything against the law, like bring dope or grass or anything like that. If you wanted to, you could bring your own wine. After a while you'd be undressed. There were always stag films showing.

There are people who instead of having a clandestine affair want to swing with their spouses. It seems like a possible attempt to have shared experiences. It might be a desperate effort to save the marriage before the divorce, or speed it up. Jed and those like him seem to feel it is more moral or virtuous to swing with their wives than to have furtive liaisons. It is certainly more honest toward the wife but an entirely different matter than an affair. The thrill of secret romantic meetings and deep feelings certainly has nothing to do with swinging.

This modern variation of an orgy clearly expresses a desire to try someone different, and perhaps a lot else. Is it to degrade his wife or himself or other men that Jed goes? Is there a competitive element with these men? His wife? Or only sexual equality? Boredom? Jed says, "It was a place to go every Saturday night."

The few affairs Jed had during his marriage were strictly sexual. Swinging with his wife appears to be an effort to avoid secret sex which excluded her. There is some fantasy element in those Saturday night parties. "Next time it's going to be different," people think, "and better than before." In this case, the effort is not to create a new relationship. Jed says, "You don't have to play any games. Everybody is there for the same thing." He has no demands made on him in such a situation.

He recognizes that "the best sex is with someone you love," and that you need strong feelings for a real sexual high. Also, Jed feels that if he got married again it would be a one-to-one relationship and he wouldn't look for outside affairs. I think he has seen the whole spectrum of sexual choice and is forming his values from experience. His new fantasy is stability instead of variety.

Jerry is a forty-one-year-old stockbroker.

Q: Did you have one or more affairs?
A: I had one-night stands and then an affair.

Q: How long did the affair last?

A: About a year.

Q: When you had the affair, did you consider yourself happily married?

A: In some areas.

Q: Was it one of the things that broke up your marriage?

A: It was *the* thing.

Q: How did you meet this woman?

A: At the supermarket. We were parked next to each other and were driving the same kind of car.

Q: You started talking about your cars?

A: Yes.

Q: Was she very attractive?

A: She was then, possibly . . . today, no.

Q: What do you mean?

A: In my eyes, she has lost the most substantial part of her attractiveness.

Q: How did this happen?

A: I resent the fact that the relationship broke up my marriage and do not find her in the best of light anymore.

Q: Was your motivation more emotional or physical?

A: Probably physical.

Q: Did you fall in love with her?

A: No.

Q: What were the logistics of how you met?

A: She was a housewife. I called her during the day. We met at friends' apartments, hotels, sometimes in her place, but she had a full-time maid.

Q: In the logistics of meeting, did anything funny or embarrassing happen?

A: I called my wife her name several times.

Q: What was her reaction?

A: She went berserk.

Q: Was this during love-making that you called her this name?

A: God, no. My wife was pregnant at the time.

Q: How did your wife find out about the affair?

A: My secretary left a note for her saying just that.

Q: Why did your secretary do this?

A: I don't know. A vindictive little bitch.

Q: What did the note say?

A: Exactly that I was having an affair with Stephanie. I told my wife it was a lie, but then I called her Stephanie shortly after that.

Q: You say that Stephanie's husband was your lawyer. How did that happen?

A: I just needed a lawyer and she recommended him.

Q: Did he ask how you got to him?

A: Yes, I said through his wife. I had helped her one day when her car had broken down.

Q: How did you feel toward him?

A: I liked him. I still like him.

Q: Did you feel sorry for him?

A: To a degree, because of his wife. They say once someone has affairs, they always do.

Q: But you didn't feel guilty toward him?

A: At first I did.

Q: Did you feel guilty toward your wife?

A: Horribly.

Q: Why did you keep on with the affair?

A: It was pretty good and my wife was pregnant and I didn't find her at all attractive.

Q: Do you think that if your wife hadn't been pregnant you wouldn't have gotten involved?

A: Probably not.

Q: Then what happened that the marriage broke up?

A: One night I decided to sleep in the den when I was really pissed off, and the next morning she came in and said, "I think you'd better move out." I said, "Fine," and I moved out.

Q: If she hadn't told you to move out, would you have gone?

A: Probably not.

Q: Do you think you would have continued to have affairs?

A: I don't know, I think it would have stopped.

Q: Why did you stop seeing Stephanie?

A: I was divorced and single. Dating a married woman got a little raspy at times. I didn't need the aggravation of having an affair with a married woman.

Q: Do you think most married men have affairs?

A: Yes.

Q: Do you think most married women do?

A: I'd say a decent number.

Q: Did most of the men you know marry one kind of woman and get turned on by another?

A: Yes.

Q: Explain.

A: Well, people wanted to marry women who represented what they wanted for the rest of their lives—a young, upper-class, Jewish, Catholic, WASP attractive girl who has money, maybe. Now it's more someone you can relate to physically, intellectually, and emotionally.

Q: Do you think men are basically polygamous and women monogamous?

A: I think the nicest thing in the world is to have an affair with one woman. But I think that occasionally both wives and husbands stray.

Q: Do you think a man's financial position affects his ability to have an affair?

A: Oh God, yes. When I drive my four-fifty, the girls all smile. The best car to pick up girls in is a Jaguar; they *follow* me. The next is a four-fifty.

Q: Have you ever thought of going back to your wife?

A: I have, but we've never discussed it.

Q: Did she develop a career since your split?

A: She's an insurance broker, plus she's quite wealthy in her own right.

Q: Any advice to married men?

A: It's okay to have a little fun on the side, but I wouldn't get emotionally involved.

Q: What if they're not happily married?

A: I think they're better off getting a divorce.

Q: What is your advice to women who discover their husbands are having an affair?

A: Buy a copy of *Forbidden Gardens* and read it. Turn your husband on, that's usually the problem. That and the emotional support that a woman can give a man.

Q: Any advice to the woman? Should she confront her husband?
A: I think the first thing she should do is to find out what attracts him to the other woman.
Q: Have you anything to say in retrospect?
A: My personal opinion is that the affair ultimately wasn't worth it, but I have a very lovely girlfriend now and so it's okay.

Jerry was not unhappy with his wife and still thinks of going back to her. Never, though, has he mentioned it to her. Maybe his passivity where she is concerned is only an excuse for not trying to work things out between them or has to do with male pride. Remember Alex, who also cared for his wife but would not accede to her demand to make a choice between herself or the other woman? These examples reveal an apparent need some men have to protect their self-images; again, a need for control. Apparently Jerry had no need for other women until his wife's pregnancy. Was the forthcoming baby a threat to Jerry? Was he punishing his wife for changing the composition of their relationship?

Jerry also totally blames his other woman for breaking up his marriage, though it was his secretary who spilled the beans. His own carelessness probably made that possible. Other men keep affairs secret from secretaries for years.

There is a possibility that Jerry may have manipulated his wife into acting out his own wishes—to end the marriage. This may explain why although he "thinks" about reconciliation with his wife, he never does anything about it.

Dr. Katherina Marmor pointed out to me "the inadequate personality structure Jerry's behavior suggests." Not only didn't he keep his affair hidden, but he insured that his wife was further irritated by calling her Stephanie after she knew his girlfriend's name. In this way, and probably others, Jerry forced the issue.

His wife probably reached a point where she felt she had to ask him to leave. It looks like he maneuvered her into the position so that she, the secretary, the other woman, anybody but he, was responsible for the failure of his marriage. In a later chapter on the wife's discovery of the affair, this behavior pattern is almost the garden variety.

Peter is a thirty-eight-year-old clergyman.

Q: Have you ever had an affair?
A: I've had many.
Q: What is your chief motivation?
A: I need excitement outside of my house, and I like sex very much.
Q: Do you have sex in your marriage?
A: Yes, but it's not sufficient.
Q: Not sufficient in quality, quantity, or both?
A: Quality. When I started having affairs, I think I used to delude myself and my lovers by indicating that there were areas of unfulfillment in my house other than sexuality. I looked outside for the special quality and gifts they had. I think I am coming more and more to the realization that it is a sex drive and a need for excitement and variety. By and large, the relationship at home is a good one.
Q: So your motivation at this point is mainly sexual?
A: Mainly sexual, but also excitement. I think I have to live on the edge of danger, also. To do it outside the house makes the sex more stimulating. As a married man who happens to be in the public eye, the elements of danger add to the total stimulation. But I always seek out women who enjoy sex thoroughly.
Q: Do you personally have a moral viewpoint?
A: I think the ideal is to have a marriage that would satisfy all the aspects of life. To pursue an ideal can sometimes be destructive. I think part of civilization and morality is an adjustment and recognition of the fact that the world and the people we relate to are not ideal or perfect. Therefore, while in one sense I am certainly depriving my wife of the depths of the feelings I have and the fact that I am capable of deep sensuality she will never know, at least I stay with her.
Q: Do you feel that sexually your wife is for one thing and your lover is for another?
A: No, I don't have an image of that, but it's the pattern that has emerged.

Q: Have you ever attempted to change it?

A: No, not really. I suppose I seek out this existence. When I was younger, I sought all the stimulation in the house. But another moral aspect is that if I insisted on restricting my sexual relations to the woman I was married to, I would probably divorce her and that would be even more immoral. What I'm doing now is not much more moral, but my affairs have something to do with the competitive aspect of my relationship with my wife.

Q: Did you expect to have affairs before you were married?

A: I didn't think about it until very shortly after marriage.

Q: What about guilt?

A: Sure I have guilt.

Q: Did your moral viewpoint change after your got married?

A: I think my morality was determined in very large measure by my existence. The clash of my values is an intellectual position that I arrived at afterward. My wife is probably a more interesting human being and better company than most of the women in the affairs I've had.

Q: How would you feel if your wife had an affair?

A: On the one hand, I would be honest with her for the first time and try to establish an open marriage. But my wife lives by a very traditional morality and that would be devastating for her. On the other hand, I would be jealous because I'm a very jealous man.

Q: How would you handle it? Would you confront her?

A: Sure I would confront her.

Q: Did you ever fall in love with anyone you had an affair with?

A: Yes, I let myself because I'm a romantic. Sex is better when I can tell a woman I love her.

Q: How did you handle it?

A: Each time I have an important affair, I feel that that is the best sexually. In my second big affair, the sex was better only in the sense that she was capable of an indeterminate number of orgasms. This feeds a man's ego.

Q: What do you get sexually from women you don't fall in love with?

A: Oral sex. Also, I like the variety of anal entry, and that most women do not do. That's an example of what I can't get at home. My wife is capable of orgasms, but maybe I didn't bring her along. I have gone further sexually than she.

Q: Did you ever contemplate marrying these women you have had great sex with?

A: Two of them. But I have a traditional view of the way I have to live my life, and because of the way I live in the community, I have to be a model. Leaving didn't fit into my life script. The only way I was capable of extricating myself from those other two affairs was that I changed jobs and moved.

Q: Are you sorry you got married?

A: No.

Q: Are most of the women you get involved with married or single?

A: They're married.

Q: Are they ever single?

A: Yes. One got divorced in the middle of the affair. But now in addition to and during these affairs, I have had outside little things.

Q: Why?

A: Validation of my masculinity? I don't know. The outside ones are very young and single. I did have an affair with an eighteen-year-old.

Q: Does your financial position affect your affairs?

A: I am upper-middle-class, but not upper enough to take off for Switzerland. There are courtship elements to affairs and they cost money in addition to running a household.

Q: Do you treat your wife and the other woman the same?

A: I'm more free with the other woman.

Q: Did you ever have another woman call you at your house?

A: Yes.

Q: Have you ever worried about women becoming vengeful?

A: No.

Q: How do affairs affect you in general?

A: They always make me more efficient at work, because you have to get done in three hours what it takes others ten hours to do.

Q: Do you think your affairs have improved your marriage?

A: No, they weaken it. Affairs focus you away from the primary relationship. I suppose they decrease the frequency of sex at home and the marriage stops growing. There are times when I become angry and hostile, almost enough to provoke a divorce. I was once in love and in love with love. Then I contemplated having a child with my lover, but I recognized that was to remain a fantasy.

Q: Why do you think women prefer to have affairs with married men?

A: I don't think they prefer to, I think they have an affair with whoever's available.

Q: If you fell madly in love with another woman, would you marry her?

A: Maybe after the kids grew up.

Q: Would you say that most married men have affairs?

A: More than fifty percent.

Q: Do you think men have a double standard about what they should do and what their wives should do?

A: I think they probably do.

I interviewed Peter on his knowledge about married men's affairs based on his role as a professional clergyman.

Q: Do married people ever come to you to say that their spouses are having affairs, and ask what they do about it?

A: Sometimes. More women do. Men almost never come, because they don't want to show you their horns. Men are macho.

Q: What do women come to you for when they know that their husbands are having affairs?

A: They say, "Should I tell him that I know? What should I do?"

Q: What do you tell them?

A: I ask them if they want to stay married. I try and find out how well they know their husbands and help them decide what to do vis à vis that. Men don't come because they are not open; don't want to admit failure.

Q: What is your advice to men?

A: Enjoy women.

Q: Why do people value these relationships so much when they are happily married?

A: They are not happily married. I am not happily married.

Q: Why do you think this intense love always seems to take place outside of marriage?

A: The generation I am from got married and were inexperienced.

Unlike Franklin, whose relationships indicate long-term nurturing, Peter's affairs focus on physical love. Like many men I interviewed, Peter feels it is more moral to have his physical fulfillment outside the marriage than to end that union. He pursues affairs though he admits they distract him from his primary relationship. He claims not to be able to get what he wants at home but grants that he never tried to bring his wife along sexually.

Peter, like most married men I spoke with, made minimal efforts to change his sexual relationship with his wife. Men seemed to establish a role in a marriage—authoritarian, filial, whatever—and hesitate to experiment with it. They relate to their wives in a pattern, however unsatisfactory, which they believe will not upset the whole house of cards.

Men such as Peter reason, "Why work on keeping sex in marriage fresh when it's easier to find someone whose sexual tastes are the same as my own?" Maybe part of the motive for leaving inferior sex alone is that it provides a rationale for getting it elsewhere.

Many people do not want an integrated emotional existence. It requires responsibility. One psychiatrist who asked not to be identified observed, "Very few men seem capable of long-term intimacy." The division they make in their lives can easily be observed in the different treatment they accord their wives and girlfriends. As Dr. Olsen succinctly put it, "Men don't like their own wives to be screwed by anyone, including themselves."

To today's young men and women that may sound like an overstatement. It is perhaps truer for people over forty, but it still applies to many in their twenties and thirties. In 95 percent of the marriages described to me in which an affair was going on, emotional integration and intimacy were missing.

Peter, reflecting this awareness, is honest enough with himself to admit that affairs prevent a couple from growing together. "Sex is always better when I can tell a woman I love her," he states. Love is obviously more a fleeting sensation in his experiences than in Franklin's affairs. Nonetheless, no matter how much shouting there is about sex, everyone says it is better with love. Evidently, what is happening outside the bedroom or inside the mind is more significant than skin on skin, even when that is superb. It follows that new partners are exciting because we mentally project on them all the wonderful qualities we hope or imagine will make us love them.

Warren is a forty-three-year-old film editor who lives with the woman he met during his marriage.

Q: When you were married, did you ever have affairs?
A: None, except the woman I met at the end of my marriage.
Q: Did you have a moral viewpoint about this?
A: No.
Q: How would you have felt if your wife were involved in an extramarital affair?
A: Early in the marriage, shocked and very upset—all the usual things.
Q: What was the result of your affair?
A: I live with the woman I'm in love with.
Q: Are you sorry you got married the first time?
A: Two answers. Number one, I'm not sorry I did anything philosophically because it brought me to a place that I'm glad to be in right now. Emotionally, at times, sure. That's mainly when I'm depressed.
Q: Did you treat your girlfriend and wife differently financially?
A: Sure. The woman I live with now is entirely self-sufficient financially. My wife, since the advent of the children, was not.
Q: Did you treat them differently otherwise?

A: Yes. There's less anger and more openness with the second. Later in my marriage, the sense of play and the sense of my freedom left—they became sort of vanished concepts and I was depressed a great deal of the time for a number of years. Although I can still get depressed, there's a sense of play, a sense of purpose, and a great sense of sharing. There is also a remarkable absence of competition.

Q: Did you ever meet your lover clandestinely?

A: Only for a short time. I told my wife I met someone else. There wasn't time to set up anything clandestine, nor was I of a mind to. Two weeks after I'd started seeing her, I broke the news. I had known her for some time through work, but I only spent that kind of close time with her for two weeks before.

Q: What was your wife's reaction?

A: Negative, of course, but within bounds. I really don't think she was surprised. Our marriage hadn't been good for some time.

Q: What was the result of your love affair and the divorce for her?

A: There was a lot of emotion at first—shock. She reacted later with some depression, but I wasn't around to see the entire sweep of emotion.

Q: Has she remarried?

A: No, but she went back and got her doctorate, and she is dating.

Q: Would she have gotten her doctorate anyway?

A: I think so but in a much slower way.

Warren is the most integrated and direct man of those I interviewed. Admitting and allowing himself to experience anger, depression, and sadness, he deals with both himself and the women in his life honestly.

Though Warren might easily have set up a clandestine relationship with his current lady, the conflicts of that lifestyle, with its inherent deceptions, did not suit him or fit in with his self-image. Also, Warren seems to have as much respect for the brains and integrity of both women as he does for himself. No one was treated lightly.

Rather than safeguarding himself against negative emotions with excuses, rationalizations, and self-deceptions, Warren faced his conflict, acted on, and resolved it. He built a mature, satisfactory relationship with someone he could live with and be faithful to. Simultaneously, his wife was able to evaluate realistically her own life instead of depending on an illusory love relationship.

Married men pursue extramarital activities for reasons both obvious and subtle. Those having no sex at home (and there is a legitimate number of them) are one group that have a considerable amount of internal pressure. Both Franklin and Randall (the one who married "virgin brides") worked that problem out quite neatly. They were not the only ones.

Almost 10 percent of the men I interviewed said they have had no sexual relations with their wives for years. Such marriages, one might conclude, have little holding them together. On the contrary, many of those sexless unions go on for decades. Strong psychological and emotional needs of both parties are fulfilled in the marriages—needs greater than any inconvenience caused by having to go elsewhere for sex. Almost all these husbands wanted to stay with their wives.

Usually abstinence is due, they say, to a wife's physical or psychological problem. None of the no-sex-at-home husbands mentioned the possibility that the wives were having sex outside the marriage. Three men, though, told me it was their own choice to withhold sex. One of these stated that his reason for remaining wed was financial. At the point at which I interviewed him, he claimed to have his entire savings tied up in their house. The market was poor for selling it then.

An unhappily married man may leave his wife or establish a long-term, profound love relationship which becomes his entire inner life or keep moving around the world and among its women. Once he finds a woman to love, he might stay with her faithfully until he feels he can leave his marriage, or until the other woman leaves him. I heard of a few instances in which the other woman was married and wouldn't leave her husband. The closeness the lovers build will ultimately lead to the man's loneliness in marriage unless they get together. Of the men I interviewed who had such love affairs, about 15 percent have thus far left their original marriages (though only 10 percent of these are still with their former lovers). The guilt involved in the clandestine romance, they felt, was far worse than that of divorce. If the man waited beyond the endurance of his girlfriend, he regretted having let the grand amour go.

The largest group of men having brief encounters are, according to them, fairly happy in wedlock. They say they pursue women for more or different kinds of sex. A good example is Alex—"I like the meal at home, but occasionally I want a new dessert." He is a candidate, one would imagine, only for one-night or short stands. But looking for different tastes often leads to a whole new diet.

More self-searching was Conrad. He said, "Married men are psychologically sex starved." Recognizing the emotional element dominating sex, Conrad knows it is the excitement, mystery, discovery, and idea of another person rather than sheer physicality drawing him to other beds.

If the first encounter seems uncomplicated, the process is easier to repeat. Unable to find sufficient prohibitions in their own values against adultery, Conrad, Sal, Alex, and men like them take a good portion of their sensual and sexual pleasures away from home. Travel provides them with easy access to women who, they reason, will never interfere with their family lives. Sometimes they are wrong. A good half of the men I interviewed wanted only to fool around, but got fooled themselves by their own emotions!

Other conclusions I was led to were that pressures having nothing to do with the marriage partners push men to seek out other women. Financial difficulties, the desire to experiment, to be one of the boys (especially at conventions and business meetings), or to test their own potency are a few of these. Dr. George Dubin, a Los Angeles psychiatrist who treats Latin Americans, pointed out that a part of that community's tendency is for married men to prove their virility with affairs.

Even husbands who are content in marriage and have, by their own descriptions, sexually satisfying wives occasionally go to other women. If a man meets someone special with whom a rapport is instant, he need not be looking for someone else to begin an affair. Often he is terrified of any involvement. But the excitement, he senses, is too much to resist. If the marriage is solid, these detours either remain superficial or eventually sink of their own weight.

For a large percentage of these men, adultery is a matter of sheer action. They seek plain old adventure to break up business, domestic, and sexual routines. I give you the example of a fellow who when visiting the other woman never called home to say he would be late. "It would take away the spontaneity," he told me. Rather than offer a cogent excuse, this man wanted danger, excitement, and jeopardy at the cost of his wife's worry and his own probable punishment—an argument. To him it was worth the discomfort his wife might have, and the verbal hassle with her later for an hour of passion without reporting in. He felt in control and free.

Husbands, I found, prize independence. Their anger in traditional marriage seems to stem from their dependent position: their everyday needs taken care of by a woman, the housewife, as they were in childhood. Is it any wonder that wives become merged in their minds with mother figures? And when the female spouse becomes a biological mother, the image is reinforced twofold. A wife's attention is then divided between child and husband, just as man's own mother's was in childhood. Altogether, his wife is then busier than she used to be before marriage.

Other women may have the same chores wives do, but the married man doesn't observe them. Their meetings are briefer, usually include sex, and take place when both look well and focus on the present and each other. Even though other commitments limit his time with her, a man goes to another woman when she pays attention to him mentally and physically. Additionally, he chooses when to see her rather than finding her in bed every night expecting or hoping to be made love to. The wife may have no such wish, but her presence alone belies that.

A man may also use affairs as a remedy for his frustrations. Dr. Katherina Marmor suggested to me that when a man feels defeated by life in general, a lover may reinforce the self-image he wants. These relationships can also be an expression of hostility toward his wife, especially when the man is having difficulty with sex at home. The psychiatrist who asked not to be identified noted, "It proves he has a penis and knows how to use it." Randall is a perfect example. Men like him do their sexual or "dirty" deeds away from the wife/ mother figure. And Greg even says he went to a woman with "dirty sheets."

A few of the men I interviewed wanted the woman to act out fantasies they would never dare suggest to their wives. One such businessman went to a high-priced call girl every week only to be powdered and diapered. (Who says you can't go home again?) Overwhelmingly, though, the majority have simpler needs. They want jeopardy, the thrill of secret lust, more oral sex, escape from routine, the intimacy that is missing elsewhere, and, emphatically, the irresistible sensation of falling in love again.

Pursuing others is more understandable in men who never married for love. Unaware that they were delineating their social, cultural, and emotional needs, they picked wives who would give them what they wanted—career, status, money, family background, beauty, strength, and so forth. These marriages may even satisfy unresolved childhood needs. Dr. Olsen suggested to me that omnipotence—the desire to feel all powerful—is one of them. The replication of the marriage a man's parents had is another. As several professionals have expressed to me, the resulting partnerships generally exclude requisites like sexual satisfaction; but these can be met elsewhere. With structural security at home and love, sex, or both on the outside, husbands, and an increasing number of wives, manage quite well.

Marriage is unlikely to be the large part of a man's life that it is of a woman's. His major identity and status come from work, though this is slowly changing as women grow more career-oriented and men develop their tenderer inner selves. The relative unimportance of marriage as compared to work is especially common among high-achieving men. When they love an outside woman, this may still be peripheral to the core of their lives and doesn't, therefore, herald divorce.

Loving may be, for these husbands with girlfriends, a thing apart from marriage, not the criterion for choosing whom they live with. The biggest mistake other women seem to make is assuming that if their men love them, they will eventually leave their wives for them. What they forget is that many men have stronger demands than those of love—neurotic, practical, or cultural. These needs are potent.

Additionally, middle-, upper-middle-, and upper-class men have large social, financial, and familial investments they are loath to disturb. If they travel, much of their unhappiness in poor marriages is reduced. About 85 percent of the men with whom I spoke opted for the structural status quo over divorce, unless they could not stand living at home or with the hypocrisy of a double life. Those comfortable but uninspired husbands who had no new genuine love partners were least ready to consider divorce. "Why should we divorce," the husband reasons, "when we're used to each other and there's no one else I want to live with?" Even the women they love are sometimes let go in favor of property, family tradition, habit, and the need to avoid commitment to one person. As long as their marriages are satisfactory on some level, many stay put.

In the preceding interviews men stressed the physical when talking about other women, but loneliness and boredom underlie what they said. They seek closeness and appreciation as well as new bed partners. As Jed, the "swinger," ultimately put it, "Sex is best with someone you love." I am convinced that in affairs, as opposed to incidents, emotional factors far outweigh physical ones. If they did not, why would anyone develop an affair? He would find a new sex partner every time he wanted one. Men have told me, "I have affairs to talk—my wife and I have nothing left to say." Another insisted, "I go to other women to kiss—my wife loves screwing but not kissing." Even when sex is the strongest feeling in a man's life and a substitute for an affectionate experience, his need for various kinds of touching seems to be what motivates him. And inability to handle long-term intimacy does not indicate a lack of desire for it.

Dr. Judd Marmor, among the many who have written about conflicts during a so-called mid-life crisis when adulterous affairs peak, most clearly explains the reasons why at that time we reach toward closeness with another.

1. the somatic or physical changes

2. our American cultural emphasis on youth and physical vigor and individual success

3. economic stresses

4. psychological stresses

He gives greatest weight to the last one, specifically to "separation loss."

> . . . the loss of one's youthful self-image, the increased frequency of illness and death among relatives, the loss of children who leave home, and the loss of love in the "tired" marriage where intimacy has been replaced by mutual toleration and sex is without passion or tenderness.*

Two additional factors are cited as more important than the preceding:

> . . . the *loss of the fantasy hopes of youth:* the hopes of fame, of wealth, of romance . . . The second factor, and perhaps even a more challenging one, is the fact that the somatic changes of middle age carry with them the inescapable *confrontation of mortality.***

As we move into the middle stage of life, we yearn for the sense of, if not the reality of, symbiosis. If his marriage is not fulfilling, a man may seek this missing interdependence with another. Moreover, many men still do not enjoy the same close friendships with each other that women do, so a lover often becomes more important. He may even go to her strictly for friendship.

There are those, however, who only mouth a desire for oneness.

Psychiatry in Transition. Selected papers of Judd Marmor, M.D. (New York: Brunner-Mazel, Inc., 1974), p. 73. Reprinted by permission.
**Marmor, p. 73.

They are actually uncomfortable when someone gets too near. Men repeatedly used the image of strangulation or choking when discussing their marriages.

"It chokes me to death."*

"I'm being smothered."

"I have dozens of people hanging on my neck."

Each marriage partner finds his modus vivendi. A husband can tell his other woman, "I can't really be with you because of my first commitment." At the same time, he offers only part of himself at home so that he isn't sharing his whole self with anyone. If a man requires no open, intimate relationship with his wife, several women can be managed. When he becomes more integrated, that solution is disturbing. It doesn't work well. Like Warren, the man who cannot manage this, such a man divorces and tries to establish one fulfilling relationship. Sometimes he does. In other instances, the pattern of his first marriage repeats itself. It probably depends upon whether or not the man resolves the conflicts that created the original need for his other woman.

RING AROUND THE ROMANCE

Oh, how many torments lie in the small circle of a wedding ring.
—Colley Cibber,
The Double Gallant

I wondered if the presence of a ring made any difference to the wearer. "I consider it an early warning sign," a receptionist said. Nonetheless, she got involved with her boss, a married man wearing a ring. Naturally, he had the advantages of being an authority figure and being able to see her every day.

There is a warranty that comes with a married man. Someone else found him attractive enough to marry him. If there are women scared or put off by a wedding band, a growing number do not care.

---

* A reference to this gentleman's wedding band.

A few find it provocative. Wives insisting on or wishing their husbands wear rings might rethink this whole issue. Although at the first flash of gold certain women eliminate the wearer as a possibility, others say they never even notice such things.

Dr. Sandra Allenburg told me, "Some men wear it to say, 'I'm untouchable in one way. I am interested in having a different kind of relationship with you.'"

Somewhere along the line women know they will probably have a lot of pain with someone else's husband. Estelle, the woman who fell for the Episcopal priest, assured me wedding bands turned her off instantly: "To me the ring means hands off." The man she had met had taken off his ring. Before she knew of his marriage, they had a few memorable days together. Women like her feel it is unfair for a man not to wear a wedding band.

According to my interviews, as many men wearing wedding bands as not had outside affairs. Some slipped them off until the other woman was sufficiently "snared." Some took them off during the affair and never put them back on. Frequently the request to remove their rings, at least in their presence, came from other women finding such symbolism embarrassing or upsetting.

A wife need not despair because a husband has recently removed his ring or does not wear one. Let it quickly be added he is not necessarily having an affair, or looking for romance. As a second wife and former other woman explained of her husband, "When we got married, he said he didn't want to wear a ring. Who knew better than I that it makes no difference? He had been wearing one when we met."

Refusing to wear a ring may, in fact, have more to do with a man's relations with other men than other women.

Dr. Olsen remarked:

> Men don't particularly like them because it's a symbol of bondage to them. I never actually met a man who said, "Oh yeah, I've always wanted to wear one. It was our mutual idea."
> A wedding ring comes with a goal of the woman's mid-twenties. It's a showpiece: "I'm married." That's a good thing for a woman. I know for men it's a badge of heterosexuality to be

married, but they also consider a ring a badge of bondage. They kid each other about this in locker rooms and at lunch. It's the modern variation of being henpecked. Men are very sensitive to this issue.

Considering the number of excuses I have heard men concoct about why they don't wear their rings, I find Dr. Olsen's statement deadly accurate.

"I'm allergic to gold."

"My finger expanded."

"I can't play [fill in any sport]."

"It chokes me to death."

"I'm afraid it'll slip down the drain."

"My boss is gay and prefers not to see symbols of heterosexuality."

"Since I broke my finger, it's impossible to get on."

"I don't wear jewelry."

Such folderol can well be avoidance of heckling from the boys rather than any need to play with the girls. On the other hand (precisely where it may turn up), rings for some men are the same protection they are for women. "I'm married; don't try me," is the message. The protection can be from temptation rather than attack. It helps bolster a potentially shaky fidelity.

The "small circle" means different things to different people—it seems there are no rules for rings.

CHAPTER 8
Maintenance Engineering

Life is trouble. Only death is not. To be alive is to undo your belt and look for trouble.

—Zorba the Greek*

HOW MEN MANAGE TWO WOMEN

IT MAY take only the briefest half moment for a husband to find his other woman. Once he does, their lives often become convoluted, sometimes hilariously.

Lots of outside affairs should require Ph.D.'s in administration. The logistics of coordinating time and geography can boggle the best intellect and wear down the stamina of Olympic athletes. I am astonished, with today's communication devices and our easy access to each other, how so many can keep secret so much for so long.

Some men I interviewed thrive on risk. They live on the emotional edge of destruction, especially if they lead double lives. The film classic *Captain's Paradise* depicted the double life of a married man, not unlike clandestine set-ups all around us.

One such intrigue involved the theatrical agent, Lillian, who had the unusual domestic arrangement with a man, ten years her junior, living on the same block with his family. The gentleman in question ate dinner at her place every weekday night. I asked how he excused himself at home.

---

*From the original screenplay of *Zorba the Greek* © 1964 by 20th Century-Fox Corporation. Reprinted with permission.

The other woman reported, "He told his wife he had large business luncheons and couldn't eat in the evening. That's when he finished up paper work."

Living on the same block, this wife most likely knew about the affair at some point. She evidently stayed with her husband until she found someone else she wanted. On some level, wives usually do seem to know.* Often, they condone affairs by their silence. In this case, the husband married his other woman and they have been happily together for twelve years.

Having two homes makes an affair easier. One of the women I interviewed, a weekend scuba diver in Florida, had an instructor with this convenience. Unlike most men, he played bachelor on weekends and cared for the kids during the week. All of his students wanted lessons on weekends. He could "accommodate" them without seeming married.

Likewise, men whose work takes them constantly on the road or between two specific places manage double lives. (Some lovers may even reside in two different countries.) And they do not have to be rich to maintain such a double identity. Dr. George Dubin assured me many migrant farm workers have weekend jobs and families in one town and weekday ones in another.

Women sharing men in such schemes often know each other. Renee, a manicurist and the mother of two illegitimate children, began her romance with her children's father out of revenge toward his wife, Lisa. Lisa and her husband, Jean, were business friends of Renee and her husband, Jerry.

Jerry owned a restaurant where Jean was the chef. When Jerry and Lisa began their affair, Renee believed her husband was seduced by Lisa. She also thought Jean, the chef, was weak because he did nothing to stop the lovers.

Renee and Jerry soon divorced, and a few months later he split up with Lisa. Now, before all this gets too complicated . . . Renee realized that Jean, the chef, was not weak, just sensitive. "I fell in love with his cooking. When he finished at the restaurant, he'd

---

*More of this in Part III, "The Woman at Home."

come and fix me a midnight snack. One night he moved the mini banquet into the bedroom."

As the affair began, Renee didn't use birth control because her husband had always said it was obvious that she couldn't conceive. She had never had sex with anyone else. Shortly after she started the affair with Jean, Renee did get pregnant and, because of her Catholic upbringing, would not consider abortion. Her boyfriend had no children at the time. "Jean didn't divorce—only changed restaurants. He was happy, hoping our baby would be a girl."

Jean's wife knew about Renee and the child. As soon as she found out Renee was pregnant, she got pregnant too. She had a girl. Renee had a boy. The first year, Renee, still working, received one $17.50 bond per week from Jean. After that, even this pittance was withdrawn. Renee started using a diaphragm, continued seeing Jean, and almost immediately became pregnant again. This time she tried giving herself an abortion but failed. She went to a doctor. He gave her shots. They failed. She had the baby. Jean's wife again got pregnant, so the man now had four children, two girls by his wife and two boys by Renee.

Repeatedly, Renee tried to break off with Jean and couldn't. She began drinking heavily. Jean still visited four or five times a week, including weekends. Their affair has continued for nineteen years. I asked Renee about her children's relationship to their father.

> I read an article by Dr. Spock, saying if you have illegitimate children, you must tell them they were born out of love. I did, and the children love Jean. They see him all the time. The two sets of children have never met—they're all between seventeen and twenty, but Jean just recently told his legitimate two that he's got all of us. He was afraid they'd turn away from him, but they didn't.

I asked Renee how she coped with the secondary role. Like so many women in long-term affairs with whom I spoke, she believes Jean does not sleep with his wife. The last time, she tells me, was "several years ago."

"For Jean and me, it's more beautiful now than it ever was, physically and emotionally." All in all, Renee thinks she has had about an equal amount of joy and pain. "Most of Jean's men friends think he's got it made. But I don't worry about that. I just love him and accept it."

After we had spoken for some time, Renee admitted that lately she has been sorry she didn't marry. The financial burdens are wearing her down. When she thinks about why Jean doesn't give her any money, she blames his wife and what she labels "his weakness." Last week she told him that after all the children are in college, he belongs to her.

Jean laughed and said, "All right."

"What if he doesn't?" I asked.

"I'll give you another interview."

Renee seems content with her sons, has changed her last name to Jean's to protect them from any social stigma, and feels she is the rare woman who can tolerate being one end of a man's double life. She doesn't recommend it to anyone else.

KEEP MOVING

"Once I'm past the Rockies," a New York man told me, "I consider myself single."

George Segal echoed the same sentiment to Glenda Jackson in the movie A Touch of Class: "I never get involved with anyone in the same city."

Any mode of transportation is a major vehicle for outside lovers. Other women flying to see their men are a growing boon to the tourist industry. They visit the cities their lovers live in or those in which the men have business to conduct. Generally, my male interviewees prefer rendezvousing out of town. Men with a lover and wife in the same city, returning home after an afternoon's illicit love-making, find the jolt of duplicity a strain. They need a bit of distance. Additionally, they prefer avoiding possible detection. Women living at some point in a man's normal business route know how to juggle their schedules around his regular trips.

Even if he consciously seeks only dinner company on a lonely business trip, a normally faithful husband often finds a lot more. Being "available" in a new place, the hero in his own fantasy movie, he encourages encounters, brief or otherwise. People really do come together accidentally, anywhere—in the dog pound, a snowstorm, the supermarket.

Others I met purposely arrange their business plans around their lovers or instigate work projects in particular locations precisely to be near their other women. Unhappily married men, or those with long-standing liaisons, say they travel much more than business requires in order to get away from home. The airlines pick up a lot of trade from them. So do hotels.

Hotel telephone operators are accustomed to rooms where couples register as Mr. and Mrs. but receive phone messages from "Mrs. So-and-So" with the same last name. In the United States, many hotels historically did not allow unmarried couples to register in the same room. Business competition has eliminated that practice. Cautious men still book suites, though, in order to avoid the discussion of who or how many people will be staying the night. In Europe, where passports must often be handed over to the concierge, it is difficult to maintain the ruse of marriage. Of course, no one knows that the man is married . . . unless he wears a wedding ring or gets a phone message from his wife.

One other woman told me how friendly the staff of a hotel in Rome had been to her until one afternoon. She and her lover returned from sightseeing to the icy reception of the concierge: "Signora Jenkins called, Signor."

Concierges receive generous tips to keep confidences. One who obviously had not been tipped told a telephoning wife that the gentleman in question and Mrs. Gentleman just left for the airport.

Hotels are dangerous. An accountant was registered as Mrs. Lover, her lover's name. Receiving her own business calls, she told the operator she was using her professional name and to put all phone calls for Loret Paine through to their room. In the middle of the conversation with a client, Loret was disconnected. Thinking the next ring was for her, she picked up the phone to find the real Mrs. Lover asking for her husband. She pretended it was the wrong room.

While men attend business meetings, other women shop, sleep, do their own work, or accompany the men, posing as associates or assistants. Bringing one's girlfriend along as a secretary may seem an obvious ploy, but many seem to do it. A few cheeky fellows take their other women along, don't explain them, and the consequences be damned.

Lest this all sound too glamorous, not every woman gets to go on trips, exotic or otherwise. Much of the travel described to me was strictly local. Carla had a boyfriend who stayed in the city for dinner at his wife's suggestion because she was pregnant and felt too sick to eat. On those few evenings her lover did go home for dinner, Carla used to run from her office, ten blocks away, to New York's Lincoln Tunnel, in four minutes.

I drove with him from Manhattan to New Jersey, and then took a cab back to the City, just so we could have an extra hour together after work. Everyone who worked at the tunnel waved and said hello to me as I entered each day.

ALL BUSINESS

If lunchtime is taken up with real business, there is always a business drink—where a man says he is between office and home. Al Lerner, the New York investigator, at one time managed a restaurant. He saw men at the bar slip off their rings, put them in their pockets, and lie about their marital status. He heard a lot of different men tell the same old story night after night—"I'm stuck because of the kids." "Women are definitely more gullible than men," Mr. Lerner says.

Many husbands reported to me that they come straight home after work, no drinks or stops on the way. But they are not necessarily "all business." Some imaginative types work their other women into the busiest day at the office.

Wives who think their husbands couldn't possibly fit anything more into an already bursting work schedule might do well to take note of one particularly cooperative other woman, who is also a wife and mother. Her daily hair washing, manicuring, and so on take place in the back of her lover's office suite. Each day she remains there until he is free to make love, go to lunch, whatever. Her girlfriends report to her on the plots of movies and art exhibits they see so she can give a cogent account of her time to her own husband in the evenings.

Between business peers, the temptation to have affairs may be even greater than a superior's for a subordinate, or vice versa. Most people want to avoid entangling their office and personal lives. Nevertheless, a man taking up with a woman his equal maintains a sense of fair play. His secretary or assistant possibly feels obligated or fears losing her job if she rejects him. Highly placed men and subordinate women can both use the office affair to great advantage. But peers more than likely have the same or similar concerns at stake.

And for those with opulent work space, business easily slides into pleasure. A foreign student about to lose her visa thought the brilliant lawyer she hired was joking when he proposed she take a job as his bookkeeper.

"He's a good talker and listens just like a psychiatrist. After I got to know him, we began meeting at his office. He had the whole penthouse to himself, with wonderful soft couches and a fireplace."

Other daily meeting spots include turnpikes, trains, and so on. And summer-house weekend rituals notoriously lend themselves to Monday morning assignations. The trains back to the city are full of them. All along the tracks from New York's Hamptons and Fire Island communities, for example, lovers wait until their partners' trains come along before boarding for a trip to Manhattan. After a week's arduous coupling while the wife and kiddies are at the beach, the lovers return to their weekend houses. (I also spoke to wives who got "chummy" with lifeguards and tennis pros at the beach all week!)

Some cannot afford a summer house, nor do they have the convenience of travel or even private offices. For these people, public places during the week are their only sanctuary.

UNDER THE TABLE

President Carter's challenge to the martini lunch did not put all the expensive restaurants out of business. The lovers' lunch is just as reliable a trade in posh urban eateries. Restaurants with names like The Hideaway and A Quiet Little Table in the Corner know exactly how large the crowd is to whom they are appealing. Even restaurants whose names do not suggest shadows and dim lights do a booming lunchtime lovers' business. I wondered how so many men went cavalierly charging into places, occasionally in their own neighbor-hoods, with their lovers. They tell me that openly lunching with another woman appears innocent. A dark, remote restaurant implies guilt. Another fact helps—few wives go to fancy lunches unless they are in business.

More convincing still is the argument for safety made by Joanne's married dentist, who is never without at least one other woman. I was able to contact and interview him after hearing Joanne's story.

"You don't understand. There's been a universal male conspiracy for years. No one ever asks or tells."

I asked about the friends of his wife who might see him. While we were chatting, Ken spotted his wife's best friend directly across the room, having lunch with a man. I thought my presence there might cause suspicion. She and Ken nodded to each other politely before I asked, "Is she a trusted member of the male conspiracy?"

"Easy. That's not her husband. It's most certainly her lover, and there's something that helps more. For two years, she's tried to talk me into becoming her lover."

Not everyone is as lucky as Ken. Some get caught by neighbors or people in the office. One company vice-president entered a restaurant with her lover-boss. The entire company secretarial staff was lunching there. His personal secretary, correctly assessing the situation, protec-tively rushed over and greeted them, telling him who was there. After lunch, the boss and his other woman crossed the room and said hello. That is what is known as savoir faire. Frequently, I heard about an outside couple who, upon seeing people they know on the other side of the restaurant, look away. Eventually, both couples realize they are probably stuck in the same mess. As soon as the message is clear, everyone nods and relaxes.

Before having a girlfriend to take to a restaurant, a married man must find one. One Atlanta discotheque decided to assist its male patrons in looking (of course, wives could also take advantage of this opportunity). If a married man meets another woman here, time may be bought. The bar's custom-designed phone booths are equipped with recording devices and buttons to allow the caller to select one of several background sound tracks. Background noises of offices, hospitals, and highways are among the selections available to the fellow trying to substantiate his excuse for delay to his wife on the phone. How, after all, can you get mad at your husband for bringing some poor chap to the hospital?

CHAPTER 9
Slip-ups

A lover without indiscretion is no lover at all.

—Thomas Hardy,
The Hand of Ethelberta

GETTING CAUGHT

Now AND again, the best laid plans and lovers get upset. Which is what happens when neighbors or friends of the married man see him with his other woman. I understand it is a common peril, especially in his home town.

An experienced woman handles this with élan. If the man is notably older than she, a woman may call him "Mr. So-and-So." One young lady did that, referring to a friendship between her father and the man in question. Another woman, without the significant age difference to aid her, merely thanked her boyfriend for the street directions he had just supposedly given her, trotted off, and met him later at their mutual hotel. Some prefer making believe they are not themselves. Either they break into a foreign tongue (if they have got one) or deny their identity—"I'm sorry, I'm not Mrs. So-and-So's daughter."

Recognition from a man's family is more disconcerting. A steward-ess drove into a gas station with her boyfriend when his daughter arrived on bicycle. The stewardess had just gotten out of the car at that moment. She grabbed a squeegee, pretending she worked there. Her married lover tipped her generously for a topnotch job on the windshield before driving off without her. He made sure his daughter had left the area before circling back.

One day, this man had to own up. When he and the other woman later married, he was forced to explain that the girl's new stepmother did not really work in the corner gas station.

The one relative most difficult to fool is the wife. More than once, I heard of a man's spouse unexpectedly arriving at his hotel. In Neil Simon's *California Suite*, there is a marvelous scene in which a man invents agonizingly abstruse strategems to keep his wife from the bedroom. There, a woman from the previous night's antics is sound asleep.

One market researcher I know came back to her London hotel room to find a note on her door. It begged her not to knock or come in but check, instead, at the front desk for a message. There she received a note indicating that her lover's wife had arrived. She was handed her own luggage. Her boyfriend had booked her into a nearby hotel, where he promised to meet her the next morning. How did he manage his business and these two women?

"She got nights and I got days," the girlfriend told me. "His business simply went down the drain."

Romantic journeys in faraway climes have their own pitfalls. There was the husband who went to Nome, Alaska, where he figured no one he knew could possibly be. He walked into a store and there was his neighbor from Chicago.

Not all discoveries are made on the spot. Adrienne, the editor, was once in Houston with Lee. The couple was especially careful and reserved adjoining rooms. After a few days, Adrienne wanted to send her clothes to the laundry. Thoughtfully, she placed Lee's clothes in the same pile and sent one package. It was only after she returned to New York that Adrienne discovered the hotel laundry had stamped her last name into all the clothes. A pair of Lee's underpants, accidentally mixed in with hers, bore the same damning mark. By the time she discovered this, Lee was unsafely at home, with his accursed underwear. Adrienne put in a quick call to a male friend in Los Angeles asking him to call Lee's house and deliver the bad news in some sort of code. Fortunately, her mastermind scheme worked. Lee threw a lot of underpants down the trash chute, but he was never found out.

A lover's loyalty hath no bounds . . . not even in the heavens.

Everyone knows the potential dangers of flying; few have considered all of them. Suppose a man is at home one evening with his family, watching TV. Suddenly an airline commercial comes on, featuring Daddy holding hands with another lady on an airplane. That is what nearly happened to Hal when he and his girlfriend boarded a plane for their monthly trip to Montreal. Cameras and lights began flashing as a commercial was in the process of being shot. Hal quickly left for the men's room, where he stayed for a half hour. He escaped potential stardom and a possible divorce.

A prominent gentleman who ultimately did divorce told me he made the gossip columns one night with his other woman. "You really want everyone to know about it but your wife. I sort of liked that notoriety." The ambivalence he expresses was mentioned by several men, especially those who wanted to divorce but couldn't bring themselves to do it.

In the innocence of sleep, a demon may ruin a man. Stan, pining for his lover, cried "Caroline" in his sleep. His wife woke him, saying, "You're dreaming about Aunt Caroline. You were crying. You grunted and groaned." Fortunately for Stan, he had an old aunt with the same name as his girlfriend. From that day forward, Stan demonstrated his great appreciation for Aunt Caroline in many small ways.

This same husband has his other problems with names. The first time he and Caroline went on a trip, he became upset with the way she was packing his suitcase. He asked her to do it the right way, using his wife's name by mistake. "Try Caroline, and she'll do it right," his girlfriend said. Poor Stan got a migraine headache.

Life is just as full of risks under water as above. The weekend scuba diver and her instructor felt exhilarated after their run on the beach.

> We jumped into the pool naked and grabbed the tanks. I wanted to try sex underwater. All of a sudden the pool lights came on.

The janitor, hearing noise, came in and caught us in the act underwater with our tanks on. My instructor surfaced and waved him off. The old man left, turned off the lights, and we continued.

Next, the breathing apparatus went. They had to surface. Six students stood there applauding.

There are men who do not have swimming pools or go on business trips. They sometimes have to spend their limited free time babysitting. Take Justin, a good-natured fellow, who always managed his infant son on Saturdays, giving his wife a leisurely day off. The fact that the child spent his time sleeping on a motel bed across the room from his father's amorous activities went undiscovered.

Acts of God or man alter the most elaborate schemes. When a fire broke out at a famous London hotel a few years ago, a number of well-known and important men found themselves in a real hot spot at 3 A.M. They gave the fire department a terrible time. Having informed offices and families they were at points distant, they stood resolutely anonymous. They would not provide their names. It was a difficult task for the police, trying to compose a list of fatalities. A few of those men, whose names did come out, were soon divorced.

Despite the occasional bungle, it is remarkable how long outside affairs persist without anyone discovering them. Even decades go by while a wife believes, at least consciously, that her adulterous husband is exclusively hers. The men's interviews revealed some marriages of that duration where the subject was never discussed.

CHAPTER 10

A Home Away From Home

ONCE

Once
I was young
And mixed up
And unhappy
Now
I am old
And mixed up
And unhappy
In between
I was happy
Once
Once
I think.

—By a married man
who had one affair

HIS UPS AND DOWNS

HERE IS a story amalgamating all the "ups" of their affairs men told me about.

They meet at a bus stop, a party, the gym. Or he is her piano teacher, lawyer, or accountant, or she is his piano teacher, lawyer, or accountant. Instant rapport. They find some poor excuse to meet again—both know it is a poor excuse—or they have their professional relationship. His marriage is stuck in neutral or going stale. Maybe both of their marriages are. If the woman is single, she is probably lonely. The non-gay, unmarried men are treating her poorly.

Intellectually, both are against beginning anything serious. "I know it's dangerous, but we'll just have a sexual thing," he reasons. "I know it's hazardous," she thinks, "but we'll only enjoy one flirtatious lunch."

He is complimentary, sensitive, warm, mature. "Why aren't single men so open?" she wonders.

"She's so attentive, complimentary, warm, and attractive. Why isn't my wife like that?" he asks himself.

They have no social reason to be together, so the talk goes quickly from the superficial to their inner selves. "I like to take long walks between two and four A.M. because I'm a restless sleeper. My wife gets insulted, goes crazy when I do."

If the woman across the table doesn't say, "I understand," he knows it is meant anyway. How can it not be? She is vulnerable, real. They like the same food, music. The silences are intoxicating. He is cautious not to suggest anything more, but knows he wants to go to bed with her. He is certain it would be the best sex he has known. The rationale builds as he walks back to work. He reflects, "I put up with a lot this year. I've earned a lot of money, given her tennis lessons, sent her mother to Florida," or "fixed up the den, spent every weekend with the family," whatever. "I'm a good boy. I deserve it."

In his imagination our hero endows the woman with all the subtlety, understanding, warmth, or eroticism he finds missing in his marriage. The lady may or may not live up to any of this. It doesn't matter. He thinks about it more and more.

"Married men are psychologically sex starved," Conrad told us. If that is true, many married women, no doubt, are equally frustrated or hungry for variety. But men have traditionally done more about it. Society gave them unofficial sanction, especially the high achievers, whose position and money provide security for those around them. They feel entitled to special privileges because they are financially supporting the family.

Adultery is the modern middle-class adventure. Life used to be primitive, dangerous, uncertain for everyone. Today, extramarital relationships offer the challenge and adventure many find lacking in their lives. Adultery—the soothing sound of sin. Everyone we have ever known has condemned it (and billions of people we have not known). For men, the affair seems frequently to be an end in itself rather than a means to another state. It needn't go beyond the present.

An affair not only offers risks but it has got built-in success. The woman a husband chooses has accepted him and his married status by her very presence in his life. Pitting his skills against inconvenience, potential detection, and emotional vulnerability, the hero has a new sense of importance.

The man and his lady have a couple of drinks or lunches. They talk of friendship, their values, pasts, dreams. But sex is in the air. The urbane part of himself says, "Don't push." He knows she is debating. But he can't wait anymore. Nothing below his belt ever heard of sophistication. He wants her *now*—even if it is only once.

She won't invite him to her apartment because she is still consciously saying no. A hotel is premature to suggest. Something impulsive, spontaneous, daring. Maybe they duck into a building entrance for the first kiss. The kiss is more than a promise. It is another secret. They already know *it* will be sensational. They arrange to meet one afternoon after work. Each fantasizes the first sexual encounter. When they do meet, it is sensational because the beginning is all of the joy with none of the hurt. Whatever his real or imagined impotence at home, with his new woman it is vanished—she becomes an oasis of liberty.

The lovers start meeting after work. At first, he can't get enough sex. It is wild, exalted. The man asks his lover for everything he has ever fantasized but couldn't accomplish with his wife. Together they reach a sexual apex he never knew before. "Sex in the afternoon is better," he observes. "I'm not tired. I can see you in the light." She agrees that watching themselves make love heightens the eroticism.

In order to leave early, our hero becomes more efficient at work. Conspiratorial phone calls punctuate their separations. The adulterer rushes to meet his girlfriend, the sensation of falling in love now his again after five, ten, twenty years. It is even better than the first time. He is more confident, more experienced. There are no social expectations to consider. "The euphoria is worth the price," he tells himself. His fantasy life occupies more and more time at work, at home. Soon, small gifts are exchanged in restaurants where danger still lurks, but at least they can hold hands under the table.

The husband becomes nicer at home. "I'm not so frustrated now," he tells himself. One fellow who had been impotent with his wife for a while said he was cured during his affair. "In my marriage I became an observer of my own penis." After a number of unsuccessful attempts at sex, he avoided it altogether until his girlfriend broke that cycle.

Other men, like Conrad, say, "I screw the hell out of my wife for a few days to alleviate the guilt." Men with nerve may try techniques or ideas with their wives which they have learned in affairs. When questioned, answers provided include, "I read it in a magazine," or, "Don't you remember the *Kama Sutra?*"

The whole marriage apparently improves for a while when the husband is intoxicated with his new love. I talked to Dr. Judd Marmor about this phase. "When the married man has a sense of triumph over the wife/mother figure, his anger is reduced toward his wife," Dr. Marmor explained. "He has a secret which she cannot penetrate. It gives him a feeling of power." Enhancing this potency are the circumstances of seeing his lover. He determines them. She must, to an extent, cater to his schedule. Even if she is married, he knows she goes to the trouble of arranging her life to fit his timetable. He is back in control at last!

Some happily married men find the pleasure fading as the guilt arrives. They pull out of the affair because they are frightened or cannot handle the conflict. The guilt may run both ways—toward wife and lover. He is deceiving one and, at some point, involving the other too deeply. He might even become too enmeshed for his own comfort. Men themselves want to avoid intimacy. The affair is only good while it stays light and fun, according to women involved with such men. When the feelings deepen, the adulterer takes off, questing after a new beginning. As Dr. Deborah Rinzler confirmed, "A man who does not like himself may seek affirmation from a woman to provide him with good feelings. However, such a man may also feel deeply unlovable and convinced of his own inner badness and unworthiness.

"The dilemma is that he needs a woman's love and approbation, but is also certain that he does not deserve it. The possibility of closeness in a relationship calls forth all of his ambivalence of wanting love and feeling unlovable. Also, in many men, the negative self-image is habitual and comfortable; closeness would require an openness and trustworthiness many men find very difficult. In these situations the easiest solution seems to be to end the relationship."

The same reasons that drove this type of husband to one outside woman now push him to yet another. An affair is a good means of avoiding intimacy in marriage. Similarly, a new lover protects a man from getting too near his old one. Taking off before the woman does allows such a man feelings of complete control.

A perfect example is Ken, whose lover killed herself when he left her. He told Joanne (whose story is in Part I), "It took eight years of analysis before I could have another affair, but now I handle them with no guilt whatsoever." It would seem, from Joanne's experience, that he also handles them with no consideration for the other woman. Ken is the familiar Don Juan character who has given women so much pain through the ages. He seeks continued conquests to boost his ego but stays only through the first stage of the affairs. The Kens of this world, who play at life, will always be around. They are protected from defeat but cheat themselves of any meaningful success.

But men capable of tenderness choose the luxury of love in an affair and live with ambivalence. What starts out sexual often ends up profoundly emotional . . . so say half my male subjects. Letting inhibitions go physically often fosters a man's vulnerability. The softness he guards elsewhere now expresses itself. Theodore Reik found in forty years of analyzing people, that most men are often terrified of tenderness.* That fear dissolves in the affair when men feel powerful, secure.

Time passes. Our hero is exhilarated. "I have joined with an historical past, the male tradition, and privilege which are mine," he tells himself. When guilt grows, his defenses gather to assist him. "I'm still a good husband. Don't I see the kids' teachers on Open School Week? Help with the dishes? Give her orgasms?"

He begins to relax into a fuller relationship with his other woman. Sex no longer occupies the majority of their time together. One afternoon they see a movie. "At least there are no lines," he quips, because he cannot take her out at night. They go shopping or to an art exhibition. She may accompany him on a business trip.

For the man who apparently and gallantly struggles in the city all week while his family suns and recreates at the ocean or lake, summer can bring weekday honeymoons with his other woman. No longer in a rush to get home, he takes her out in a less crowded city or spends leisurely evenings in her apartment. If he has brass, he might even bring her to his own home. The guilt of the fall through spring routine, when children and wife confront him sometimes minutes after leaving his girlfriend's bed, is lessened in the hot days of heroism.

He feels he is a good father and provider, having bestowed on the family a cool, clean summer. On Fridays, the lovers may even share a car or train ride to the same resort area, where she rents a place or part of one for herself. Monday morning perhaps finds them back together in the car or train, traveling to their city of business and romance.

Sometimes the lovers fix up her apartment together or, if they are both married and there is money, they get one of their own. Domesticity sets in with all the highs and none of the lows. Now our hero has lost weight, changed his hairstyle, gone for medical checkups. Life is an exalted flight he hopes will last forever.

That is one scenario. Here is another.

The illicit lover projects so many fantasies onto the first sexual

* Referred to in Anatole Broyard, *Women, Men and Other Anticlimaxes* (New York: Methuen, 1977), p. 88.

liaison, he is immediately disappointed. She is not what he expected or he is not what she expected. It may become a one- or three-night stand. Or, let's assume he surmounts his impotence or her inhibitions and establishes a great sex life—most of his original intention.

In order to accommodate his new "account," he leaves work early, and gets chastised by the boss. Assuming he is his own boss, he cuts short meetings, is not quite as thorough as before. Business suffers. Frequently answering two women's needs, he is exhausted, torn. If he avoids sex at home, his wife wants to know why and eventually grows angry. "You go home and someone is lying in bed, but it's not the person you want," one man said sadly. "You've just finished hours of love-making, and she wants it too. I'm expected to be a Superman." The double life has begun. Commuting between his other woman's residence and his has undreamed-of demands. Time and money are only two of them.

If the other woman is single and attractive, she no doubt has other men he must put up with. "I can hardly ask her to be faithful," he knows, "when I'm married." If she is seeing him as a sexual or emotional filler rather than a fulfiller, she will have other men now or later. Even if the woman wants to be faithful and thinks he is the finest of the species, in time she becomes practical and must have others for the lonely weekends or holidays when he isn't there. It is logical. This knowledge temporarily alleviates the guilt he has developed toward her; but with growing attachment, jealousy is inevitable.

In addition to these stresses, the daytime hours and infrequent nights are too short. Languorous dinners, sunlit or moonlit sex, are not followed by rest in his beloved's arms. "As soon as I come, I'm leaving; as soon as I leave, I'm coming back," a businessman told his out-of-town girlfriend. It is back across town or on the train, highway, or plane and home to an angry, silent, or weepy wife. "Where were you? Your service had no number." Excuses, lies. He snaps out answers or hates himself for being such a skilled liar. "Why must I always account for my time?" he asks himself. A feeling of strangulation overcomes him. He had no intention of falling in love again.

Then he feels guilty toward his wife. "After all, it's been a month since we've had sex," he realizes, vowing to do it on the weekend. Obligatory sex isn't his idea of fun, but okay. Now, during most of his time at home, he is absorbed with his children as never before. Homework, chauffeuring, meaningful talks. He wants to be a good father and compensate for his offense. It is also a way to avoid confrontation with his wife. Just as his feeling of guilt increases, so does his hostility toward her.

Fantasies sustain the romantic during separations from his new love. He yearns to introduce her to friends, hold hands in public, have a month together, maybe one day a baby. She has begun to hint or tease, plead, discuss, or cry about getting married. He may consciously want to. But the family, the holy family! It is against every precept he has known and especially the image he has of himself. "That kind of guilt I can't handle," he tells himself. Besides, after years of building a career, he has no intention of substantially lowering his standard of living. Money is a factor.

By now his wife's charge bills have gotten much larger. Spending money is one way she has of avenging herself for his neglect. She is probably not even aware of it. Only a monster would criticize a neglected wife's bills, he knows. She has become demanding in other ways too. Without realizing it, she wants him to pay for her pain. Neither of them says anything relevant.

All this time he is not telling his other woman he won't marry her, and not saying he will. He isn't lying either. He wants to marry her or live with her, but feels he cannot. She is optimistic anyway. It is natural to believe in her man. He sees hope in her eyes. If she is married, maybe she has already made plans to divorce. Now he feels worse, more responsible toward everyone. Two women are waiting, one for a decision, the other, an improvement.

Our once expansive, exuberant friend becomes anxious, tense. Maybe he has developed ulcers, migraines. The doctor says, "Take a vacation." He doesn't want to take a vacation with the family. "Screw it, I'm taking her (the other woman) to Washington next week," he decides. His lover manages a few days off and they go to a conference where he knows he will run into colleagues. He is worried but depends on inveterate male loyalty. Moreover, he has become impulsive. "Life is short. How often does love happen? ("Not enough," I am told.) How long will I keep her?" Consciously, he often wants to be caught and punished. That way, his wife will get angry and leave him. That is his major fantasy. He wants her to take responsibility for their actions. Inevitably, the distance between the spouses feels unbridgeable. Then his wife challenges her husband.

As reliable as the real estate precept that only three things matter—location, location, location—likewise, with a married man the wife can usually count on three reactions—denial, denial, denial. No matter how ludicrous the explanation, men, I am told, will usually deny the accusation unless their wives have irrefutable evidence. I remember a story Greg told me about a weekend in the country with friends.

> It was New Year's Eve. A lot of drinking had gone on that day. I went up to the guest room and stripped down to my shorts and went to sleep. About three A.M. my wife woke me and said our host had gone to drive some guests to the train station and the hostess was passed out on the living room floor. Would I go down and pick her up and place her on the couch? I did. She was wearing nothing but a loose nightgown. The baby had begun to cry, and my wife attended to it. I picked up the woman and staggered over to the couch with her.
>
> As I put her down, she had her arms around my neck, spread her legs and I just accommodated myself. At the moment of climax, my bare ass sticking up in the air, the door behind me opened and her husband walked in and said, "My God." At that moment, my wife ran onto the balcony overlooking this living room and began screaming. I stood up, ejaculating, and said, "If everybody is going to scream this way, I'm going to sleep." And I did.
>
> They were all screaming downstairs. The next morning when I came down for breakfast nobody was talking to anybody. I said, "There's no point in spending the rest of the weekend if nobody's talking to anybody." I told my wife, "Let's leave." We went upstairs, packed, and left.

On the way home, she said, "How could you?"

"How could I what?"

She told me what she'd seen. I said that nothing of the sort had occurred. I was caught in the act but denied it because I instinctively knew that no one involved wanted to believe their eyes.

I said, "I may have been bending over her as I placed her down, but nothing more." Nobody wants to believe those things, so they are perfectly willing to doubt their own senses. I learned a great lesson. Always deny, no matter what.

If Greg's story sounds fantastic, I spoke with another long-term denier who was also caught in the middle of intercourse. "Don't believe every rumor you see," he told his wife. I'm not trying to suggest the woman believed him, but that men don't easily admit these things. Almost all men, I have deduced from years of interviewing, are poor at confrontation. They will go to any lengths to avoid it. That goes for marriage problems too. If a man is impotent, bored, generally discontent, he will find another woman much sooner than work through the problems with the one he has got. A few strong characters deal with conflicts squarely. Very few.

Back to our hero. If confrontation is unavoidable, he hopes one thing will come out of it. His wife will get furious and divorce him. That is his coup. If she leaves, he is off, guilt-free. Instead of taking charge of his own wishes, needs, life, he fervently wants his wife—the figure from whom he needs permission—to take matters into her own hands. But she usually doesn't, as he does, have a better alternative. There is no storming out, only around, accompanied by screaming, tears, or martyrdom. The latter may include suicide threats or attempts, claims of disease, impending death, and crises by the score. Very likely she has or will take a lover of her own.

Back at his *pied-à-terre*, the other woman is loving, sexy, good. Or assertive, withdrawing, fed up. He is in a vise from which there is no satisfactory escape. Most of the time the adulterer hangs onto everything as long as possible. In rare instances, that could be a lifetime.

Usually, the adulterer sustains both relationships a much shorter time. His lover leaves him when she is convinced he will never divorce. That was the ending to most stories I heard from other women and men in the middle.

Post affair, the man is stuck with the marriage he had, but now it is worse. In my research, no long, deep, outside love affair improved the marital relationship, shocking the partners into awareness and causing a renaissance. It is not surprising that people who dislike confrontation don't say, "Honey, why don't we go into therapy together and see how we can improve our marriage?" They have a working distance between them, and leave it alone.

Chances are he stays married. The odds always seem to be with the house. The future brings greater absorption with work and children. But children one day leave. Ultimately, there is another outside woman or a divorce. "I won't let myself get attached again. It'll be strictly sex." So he thinks until the next irresistible, willing partner comes along. If he has gone through a lot of torture, a man may initially look for women not really his type. Less ecstasy, but fewer problems.

Many a man, frustrated without his lover and further apart from his wife, divorces years after the affair ends. By then he has let the big love go. She is either married or too hurt to want him. He remarries quickly or remains alone. The wife is probably in a weaker position by having put off the divorce, and the children have understood both parents' feelings all along.

An adulterous love affair may be the most hypnotic experience a man goes through. If he knows the price ahead of time, he will be able to decide if he can emotionally afford it. I only met one man out of one hundred who said the affair wasn't worth the guilt. The psychotherapists I interviewed concur that men who stay in long affairs suffer more guilt than those who divorce. Those who win biggest in adultery, it seems, are the unhappily married men who cannot handle the guilt well. They are not slick; are unwilling to lie indefinitely or be separated from the women they love. They are the small percentage of married men having affairs who confess they have lovers and leave unsatisfactory marriages for relationships in which there is room for growth and in which they can be faithful.

The foregoing scripts are typical, not binding. There are husbands both courageous and dignified. If the wife turns out to be the woman he truly loves more than the other woman, he will attend to that relationship. In those rare instances in which he believes he can achieve and is willing to work on a really close, honest coming together with his lover, he might discuss his affair with her and/or a professional. The new relationship they form will doubtless require change on both sides. The result, according to Warren, the only man in my sample who did this, was "sensational."

CHAPTER 11
Leaving the Nest

Love is what every man seeks and so many fear when they find it.
—Anonymous

MEN WHO MARRY THEIR LOVERS

"PROMINENT PROFESSOR dismissed in adultery scandal."

There are few headlines like this in the 1980s. However, in the 1920s, when a psychology professor's wife sued him for divorce after she found love letters from him to a student, a Midwestern paper carried it.

The professor moved to New York, where he found no position in his field available to him. After marrying his former student and taking a job at a department store, he rose in a short time to an executive position. His story has an upbeat ending, but many men in similar circumstances suffered the ruination of their lives and livelihoods. Even today, no politician considers it wise to divorce while in office.

The climate, though, is wholly different. With the U.S. divorce rate at over 50 percent,* it looks like men and women are leaving spouses they are not happy with if they feel they can improve the quality of their lives. Second marriages frequently repeat the patterns of the first, particularly if there has been no long-term

---

*These are the 1978 figures from the 1979 *Statistical Abstract of the United States.*

relationship or therapy; but the men I interviewed who married their other women seem to have established quite satisfactory unions. They may be trying harder, but there is a lot of soul-searching and often professional counseling that go into making these marriage decisions; they may be made more carefully than they were the first time around. One man told me his European psychiatrist was always amazed at the elaborate investigations Americans did before buying property—assessments, title searches, appraisals—in comparison to the superficial inquiries so many made of partners before marriage.

Consider Burt. His hope all through adolescence was to develop confidence and sex appeal enough to attract the kind of glamorous women he saw in the movies and in what they used to call girlie magazines. His major concerns were good grades and doing nothing to provoke his parents. At all costs, he avoided the kind of fights he witnessed between his father and older brother, Richard. When Richard left home at seventeen to become a sailor and ultimately a fireman, a model, a manager of a porno movie house, and an actor, it was to Burt that his parents looked for their "hopes' fulfillment."

The shy Burt liked neither his accounting career nor his wife, Lois. He had no burning passion about anything except to get out of his house as soon as possible. His parents didn't say, "Be an accountant," but when his father discussed the future firm with them as partners, Mr. Kornfeld's face had a glow Burt had never seen.

The few sexual encounters Burt had before marriage were no thrill for his partners or himself. He was not, he gathered, a great lay. When Lois, a "nice girl" who had never kissed anyone but Burt and came from a good family his parents liked, professed love for him, that was all he felt he could ask out of life . . . until six months later, when he asked Lois for a divorce. The histrionics on both families' parts was enough to drive Burt back to his marriage. He would make up for the misery he caused everyone by having the children they all talked about.

Two years later, Burt decided that his extreme boredom must be due to his routine accounting work, so when he met Sandy, a manufacturer of tractors who was looking for someone to be his European and African distributor, Burt begged for the job. Sandy wanted languages, experience, sophistication, salesmanship. Burt promised persistence, quick learning ability, and a willingness to forego any salary. He asked for nothing but commissions until Sandy was confident that he deserved more. Six months was his trial period.

The happiest Mr. Kornfeld senior had ever seen his son was the day Burt took him to lunch to say he would have to find a new accounting partner. "I'm not taking the name off the door so fast. You'll probably starve." Six months later, the name came off.

Burt began to move purposefully. He learned how to dress, studied languages whenever he wasn't selling tractors, and became an asset Sandy couldn't afford to lose. He would be well compensated. His life seemed to improve. Burt sensed that his absence from home 50 percent of the time accounted for that. Lois, who took care of Burt's son and daughter and was wrapped up in decorating their new house, complained about her husband's traveling. He tried to compensate by buying her luxurious gifts, but he would never give up the job.

Burt found out how much better sex was with the right kind of partner during his first affair, in London. He was still not bold enough to approach a woman without an introduction, but he was introduced to women all the time. Surprisingly, he felt no guilt about his new hobby. One rule he made for himself: no affairs in the United States.

Life went along more or less evenly for twelve years. Sandy, after two years, made Burt a partner. Burt had many interludes. Lois gained thirty pounds and shopped a lot.

Burt called Lois from the airport as soon as he landed to say he would be home late for dinner because Sandy was waiting for him to meet a new client from Denmark. The second part was a lie, but he couldn't face Lois minutes after leaving Nina, the Italian stewardess, his acquaintance of six months with whom he had just begun an affair.

Sandy, a divorced bachelor, sat with his latest girlfriend in the

Algonquin Hotel lobby on New York's 44th Street. Burt joined them on one of the old, comfortable couches and ordered a Campari and soda. When, after ten minutes of business talk, the men began exchanging jokes, Burt heard feminine laughter coming from behind them. He turned to see a tanned, dignified young woman with an opened book having tea and toast by herself. "If you enjoy my stories so much, why don't you join us?" he asked.

"I'd much rather eavesdrop," she assured him in what sounded like a French accent. Burt continued telling jokes, now more for the approval of the woman behind him, until he delivered one punch line right to her. While she laughed, he moved to her couch.

Elizabeth was a Belgian au pair girl for a family in Tenafly, New Jersey, who had been hired primarily to teach their children French and to care for them in the summer. For her, the trip to the United States meant improving her English and recovering from a disappointing romance.

As Burt lived in Englewood Cliffs, a town not far from Tenafly, he offered to drive her home. She had an opportunity on the way to learn of his as yet unbroken policy of dating women only out of town, and of his tedious marriage which included two children to whom he was devoted.

"Why didn't you leave?" she asked as they drove over the George Washington Bridge.

"I did, six months after I was married and again five years later, but both times my family coerced me into going back."

Astonished that anyone could be so jelly-spined *and* admit to it, Elizabeth found herself at once sympathetic and repelled.

"Do you still listen to them?"

"I don't ask them if I can have lovers, if that's what you mean."

When Burt pulled up to the modern glass and wood house where Elizabeth lived, he took out his pen and pad. "May I have your phone number?" Whatever else, he seemed an honest, gentle, sensual man who attracted her despite his overweight. "What about your rule?" she asked.

"I guess it's time to break it."

Elizabeth hesitated. She studied Burt. He looked in his mid-forties, was twenty-five pounds too heavy, and smoked a lot. Well, she'd chance it.

On their first date in Manhattan one week later, Burt took Elizabeth to the best French restaurant she had been to in the United States. He prided himself on knowing the finest restaurants wherever he was, though no one in his family had ever appreciated or shared his enthusiasm.

The rain as they drove back to New Jersey seemed appropriate for the cassette of Gershwin that Burt played. Elizabeth closed her eyes, wishing the evening would last a little longer. Suddenly, they turned off the Palisades Parkway and drove up to the park. Burt leaned over, touching her cheek. "Anyone who can listen to Gershwin for an hour without talking, has my respect," he said, and kissed her. After ten minutes, both wanted to be closer but knew there was nowhere else to go.

The following Monday, Burt met Elizabeth in the City. They went to Sandy's East 86th Street apartment, which Burt had arranged to use. He poured them drinks and settled in a large chair in front of the window. Elizabeth sat on Burt's lap and he pointed out the sights in the panoramic view. As they talked, she was impressed by his ability to communicate verbally; most men she had met dived straight toward sex before any personal conversation took place.

"My problem was the simple fact that I was born fifteen or twenty years too soon. I was reared with a philosophy and set of standards which were not what I wanted, but I didn't know how to get rid of them. The next generation was living what I wanted. They have guts, respect, self-confidence, are freer sexually." Elizabeth pitied Burt his self-imposed limits.

The love-making was pleasant, emotional, but not anywhere near what Elizabeth had known. There was a holding back in him altogether. Burt needed "unlocking." He was a challenge she felt she could meet. On the way home, Elizabeth decided to become Burt's mistress, whatever that meant.

Their weekly dates continued for two months, until Burt had to go to Seattle on business and invited Elizabeth to join him. He found her not only the poised companion he had never had but a business asset he never imagined. Though she conducted herself merely as his lady friend with clients, her critical evaluation of the points of discussion, when they were there with Sandy, were searingly acute.

"We ought to hire her," Sandy suggested. Burt thought it a terrific idea but was afraid to rush the self-possessed Elizabeth. She was, even at twenty-seven, more worldly than he and might interpret that offer as a nudge toward commitment.

On the second evening, Burt and Elizabeth were in the elevator when he glanced, unnoticed he thought, at a buxom brunette who got in. "She's gorgeous," Elizabeth said, smiling, as they walked down the hall seconds later. Defensively, Burt explained that he was "only looking." It was then that Elizabeth explained that she was in favor of his completely enjoying other women in every way, in or out of her presence. "It's the healthiest thing you can do." Surprised, Burt was not sure if this were a test or a policy.

During the next few months he found Elizabeth's philosophy extraordinary. Though he had heard of open marriage, he had never actually met a woman who wanted to share her man with anyone . . . nor was he sure he could ever share Elizabeth or any other woman. The idea of his wife, Lois, having an affair was nothing less than preposterous. He had never given it a thought.

Burt was falling in love for the first time in his life with, not a photo or screen actress, but an admirable, attractive woman who seemed to love him back . . . and he didn't know why. The extramarital affairs he had before were, he assumed, something to do with the excitement of travel and the suggestion of money. Elizabeth seemed to love his most vulnerable self, but could he trust that to last? After a while he stopped questioning her motives.

Burt and Sandy did hire Elizabeth to assist them. She moved into her own apartment, where Burt spent increasingly more time. Soon he was dissatisfied with the status quo. His ego wanted Elizabeth to press him for marriage; her utter self-confidence and disregard for the future unsettled him. Nevertheless, any pressure from her would, he realized, have made things worse. He still found it difficult to leave Lois. She had never worked, made few friends, and disliked herself so much that leaving her would, he thought, only confirm all the negative feelings she had ever had about herself. When the conflict seemed insoluble, his daughter resolved it.

"You don't love Mommy. All you ever do is argue. There's somebody else, isn't there?" fifteen-year-old Ginger asked him.

Burt was stunned. "Yes, there is." He began to cry.

"What are you going to do?"

"Leave Mommy, probably."

"That would be the best thing, but don't leave us."

Her intuitive announcement, his admission, and the honest discussion which followed made Burt's course clear. He managed to torture himself for two weeks more at home before moving into Elizabeth's apartment in Manhattan. His children were understanding; his parents, difficult; Lois threatened to kill herself.

Elizabeth said nothing of future plans. She was in no hurry to marry because of a messy divorce she had seen in her family. Living together suited her temperament perfectly, and the work with Burt made them closer than either thought a man and woman could be on a daily basis.

After Burt began legal proceedings, Lois got a job and lost fifteen pounds. Burt, making sure to see the children as much as possible, moved with Elizabeth to a less fashionable neighborhood to be able to afford a larger apartment so the children could stay over on weekends.

Because Burt had not shared Elizabeth's confidence in an open relationship, it did not mean he wasn't thinking about it and looking at other women less furtively than he had always done. But Burt's insecurity, possessiveness, or healthy sense of traditionalism wouldn't immediately sanction such threats to their still-flowering love. Elizabeth did not insist on it. After all, she was content with Burt, who had become a skilled, uninhibited lover. Yet she yearned to see him utterly free for once in his life.

At a party where Burt was enjoying the company of a tall, seductive Atlanta woman, Elizabeth handed the hostess a sealed note to give him after her departure. It read, "I'll be waiting at home whenever you come. *Please* don't feel there's any hurry.

Have a great evening. Love, Elizabeth." Burt was annoyed, titillated, off balance, hesitant, and, finally, daring.

At 2 A.M., when he came in, Elizabeth woke up and they talked about Burt's evening of sex and guilt. For the first time the two explored the practicality of an open relationship. The first and foremost rule was that there would be no cheating or secrets. If one of them wanted to spend time with someone else either dining, talking, or making love, that was fine as long as the other person agreed. He or she had the right of veto power, and no explanation had to be given for its use.

Burt was ambivalent about this set-up, but he offered to try. "Will you leave me if I can't live with this?" he asked her.

"Not as long as you want me."

One and a half years of living with Elizabeth and Burt was practically unrecognizable to himself. Though he had occasional headaches, which continued until shortly after his divorce was finalized, he had lost twenty-four pounds, quit smoking, and had closer ties to both his children than when living at home.

Burt asked Sandy if he would switch places with him and travel so that Burt could spend more time in the United States with Elizabeth, who now ran the office. Sandy wasn't sure he could handle Europe and Africa, but he was delighted after years at a desk for the chance to try.

Domesticity set in and Burt discovered he could live comfortably with an open relationship. In fact, he felt, during the first year, their agreement was more important to him than to Elizabeth. In that time period, Elizabeth only wanted to see three men once or twice each. Burt on the other hand, who had grown into a much more secure man and now wanted to sample the kinds of women he had never known in his single days and even lacked the guts to date when he had secret affairs, went out with eight different women during the year. Neither Burt nor Elizabeth had invoked the veto.

The two were packing to go to Belgium to meet her parents when she asked calmly, "Why don't we get married while we're in Le Zoote" (her home town). Burt's eyes filled with tears. He was moved that Elizabeth would make the commitment to him he assumed she would never want and he, out of fear of rejection, had stopped discussing. Burt wondered if, after their wedding, the sense of liberty they had had during the first year would change. It never did.

Four months later, Elizabeth's best friend visited with them from Belgium. Claudia stayed one month before Burt proposed to Elizabeth that he spend a cozy few hours with Claudia while his wife went out with a male visitor from London for dinner. He received a definite veto. "Not as long as I'm alive," she quipped. That was that. Burt never gave it another thought. Actually, he was flattered that Elizabeth finally displayed some jealousy about him.

At the end of their second Christmas together, when Claudia returned to the United States to get a job and apartment in New York, Burt and Elizabeth received some ridiculous news. Elizabeth, beautiful, young, carefree Elizabeth, had cancer. The doctors thought it was relatively easy to contain and promptly removed the single lump from her neck. Burt's dream house was shaken, but the earthquake seemed spent.

They continued on as before, skiing through the winter together and enjoying their unique relationship. Burt soon learned not to mention their open marriage to anyone other than a woman he wanted to sleep with. People thought it wrong or maybe they envied them, but all became hostile unless they had the same arrangement. Only a few couples they knew did.

Burt thought he was the luckiest man in the world . . . his fantasy bachelor life had come true and he had a wife who loved and supported him. Nothing could ruin his happiness. Except cancer.

Again Elizabeth found a lump and again the doctors were confident of controlling it. She went into the hospital to have chemotherapy, and got better. For a year she was stable, but the following nine months were alternately hell and absence from hell. The open relationship had definitely closed. Elizabeth was too sick to have intercourse, but she and Burt continued to make love with a tenderness which was equally satisfying to both of them.

Burt prayed a lot. He knew that no matter how bad things

seemed, God would never give him everything he wanted in this world and then take it away so soon. His children and Claudia were just as disbelieving as he as they watched the energy and strength ebb out of Elizabeth's body. She was in the hospital five more times until it became clear—she would die.

Burt practically stopped working. He stayed with Elizabeth twenty hours a day until he felt his own life going. Then his wife's strength, which was greater than that of anyone he had ever before met, started to fill him. He sensed, during those last weeks together, her understanding and presence move into him. He refused to let her go to the hospital again. If she died, it would be in her own bed. Elizabeth looked smaller and frailer each time Burt returned from a few hours away from her. The doctors had done all they could. When she died, Burt and she had long since said all the words they meant to.

No matter how much of Elizabeth's gift Burt had absorbed, it wasn't enough. He moved deliberately and with relative sense, but he was not built for being alone . . . not after her. The usual grieving period passed and the standard ill-fitting dates were made until Burt, one year later, moved in with Claudia. Elizabeth had said, "Not as long as I'm alive."

As I write this, Burt and Claudia are preparing to leave for Belgium, where they will be married next month.

Though Elizabeth was Burt's liberator in numerous ways, his inner resources were abundant. He always sensed his potential and somewhere found the courage to change careers in the midst of raising a family. The mid-life crisis we hear so much about was not a sudden awakening for Burt when he met Elizabeth. He had actually been frustrated in his emotional growth before he was married and then fell into a marriage which provided a secure structure but would never call upon him to grow spiritually. It was a "safety net" kind of marriage,* with Lois the legitimate excuse for him to leave his parents' home. Burt's and Lois's life became an extension of the stifling background he had come from.

*Gail Sheehy talks at length about this security-oriented type of marriage in *Passages* (New York: Dutton, 1976), chapter 10, "Why Do Men Marry?"

Burt could have easily used his first marriage, as many do, to emotionally limit his relationship with Elizabeth. It is only logical that no honest, full commitment is made to anyone as long as there is another connection taking up time and thought. One alliance may be merely legal and the other more emotional, but the function of each—to limit the depth of the other—is the same when a man claims to love his other woman and yet stays married.

The loyalty an unhappily married man says keeps him with his wife places more value on the woman he insists makes him unhappy than it does either on himself or the one he says brings him happiness. Both women are being treated dishonestly. The wife has no idea there is a particular "other," and the girlfriend usually lives on false hopes.

If loyalty to the wife fails to stir a girlfriend's sympathy, husbands talk of obligation to children. Many delaying or avoiding divorce honestly believe this. More use it as an excuse, as evidenced by those same devoted fathers so many other women describe to me who fall back on guilt toward a wife as the excuse after the children are grown.

Yet divorced men frequently told me their children said, "I never could understand why you and Mom didn't divorce sooner," after the fact. "We thought my son and daughter would be shattered," one man said, "but they weren't at all."

Dr. Olsen's clinical experience bore out these ideas.

> Children serve as a good excuse, because it's got clout. It looks good. People underestimate children. They have no idea what complete information they pick up from vibrations in the house. They know everything that's going on. That's not to say they're geniuses. They just have senses and know exactly what's happening in a marriage; know when it's bad. To say, "It's good for my kids," is a cop-out, conscious or not. A great many broken marriages have absolutely terrific kids, who know what's going on. And very important, the kids no longer have a corrosive model of a marriage and that's crucial for what's going to happen for them later in life. The kids in a bad marriage where the two people stay together have a model of marriage

that's insincere, corrosive, corruptive, unclose and filled with strife.

One obvious advantage for children of divorce is that the non-live-in parent gives him or her focused attention during their visits as opposed to the distracted time they used to spend together. Divorced men told me their relationships with their children after leaving home were closer than before, when the children were part of the marriage-obligation complex.

Among the real reasons men stay in unhappy marriages is that affairs do not disturb a comfortable structure they have set up with their wives. These men can maintain a superficial relationship at home while looking elsewhere for their major source of emotional gratification. Additionally, they protect themselves from failure at making another relationship succeed as long as they have the marriage as an excuse to avoid trying. You can't lose a contest you don't enter.

A number of men feel downright uncomfortable with happiness. Dr. Olsen and I discussed the martyrdom implicit in the statement "I can't leave because my wife will go bananas." This implies that the woman he is married to has no resources . . . it is a subtle way of controlling her. The man may give this message to his wife, "You won't make it without me," so she doesn't, whether he physically leaves or only ignores her. Burt's wife did make it. She lost weight, got a job, and is now dating.

Burt's marriage to Elizabeth had a liberating quality missing from his first marriage. It was too short-lived to be thoroughly tested for endurance, but in the few years together neither Burt nor Elizabeth became involved with their outside lovers and, in fact, theirs was the *only* open marriage I heard about which did work. Perhaps Elizabeth recognized Burt's need to experiment because his early insecurity had robbed him of that opportunity when he was single. The open marriage may have, over time, reduced his need for any additional women in his life—which could have been Elizabeth's original plan.

Men like Burt and Warren cannot live with the hypocrisy of a split life. They become secure in the new love involvement, evaluate the integrity of each relationship, choose one life in which two people can grow, and have integrated rather than split lives. Husbands who leave may suffer some immediate guilt, but they have an easier time in the long run than those who have affairs to compensate for what is missing in their marriages. Rather than cope with the stress of not satisfying their wives, lying, and not being with the women they want, they confront their own realities and live within them.

Of the men who do leave, few are tough guys who put on their holsters, lay their wallets on the table, and walk down the road without a glance backward. They are simply people who envision better lives for themselves and the women they are involved with. They may no longer need to satisfy the immature needs taken care of in a painful marriage. When a lover is present, it makes leaving a spouse a whole lot easier. Some men do it with no one else waiting. They realize that everyone is alone with his own truth, that dependency does not mean union and independence does not mean loneliness.

III
THE WOMAN
AT HOME

CHAPTER 12
The Involuntary Partner

For men must work and women must weep . . .
—Charles Kingsley
"The Three Fishers"

THREE IS A MAGIC NUMBER

NICOLE, A conservative-looking middle-aged antique dealer, has stayed with Manny in the hopes that "one day the children will grow up and he'll leave home. At last he'll be mine." A philanthropic man, married for twenty-two years, and Nicole having been in his life for fifteen of them, Manny gave her solid, ethical reasons for not divorcing. Prominent in business and social communities, he had children, family life meant so much, and so on. But he had maintained Nicole in the same style as he did his wife.

One day Manny divorced . . . and simultaneously dissolved his affair with Nicole. She was stunned. As long as they had been together, she put up with "living on the outskirts of his life" because she thought it was his empathy and sense of duty that kept him home. Actually it was she!

I have heard of dozens of variations on the simultaneous breakup. (Remember Don who left Samantha and his wife on their mutual birthday?) Sometimes the man himself has no intention of leaving both women. He may even see his lover as a final leap to freedom and in fact marry her. Much to his own surprise, the couple divorces shortly afterward.

In these cases, the other woman is only part of what the man wants, and with exclusive togetherness the relationship falls apart. (Almost every professional I spoke with said that such husbands marry again with the same problems unresolved and they marry the same type of person. Hence, the high divorce rate for second marriages.) Apparently, the lover is a transitional woman—a bridge between marriage and divorce, no longer needed after the crossing is completed.

Again and again, women expressed amazement that one relationship ended when or shortly after the other did. Corinne found her apparently secure marriage halt abruptly—no provocative arguments, no evidence of another woman. Actually, the other woman had just departed from the scene. She had fulfilled some need for Corinne's husband that wasn't satisfied at home. It was sad hearing this wife's shock when, in her own mind, she had "maturely accepted" the inevitability of her husband's "occasional fling."

The rupture at home that follows the end of an extramarital love affair may be permanent. Suddenly, wives told me, the easygoing husband becomes restless, bored, angry. His wife's little habits they once joked about seem intolerable. These men with double lives often appear the best husbands when their specific needs are taken care of in the affair. Their emotional generosity and physical stamina are gratifying. That is how they keep both women, even when the two know of one another. The second relationship fuels the first. A number of husbands told me they are sexually active at home only when they make love to another woman, especially when the outside relationship is short-term and superficial. And even if the entanglement is profound and the marriage sexless, a husband may still satisfy his wife's other needs. Their marriage will survive as long as they both want or are willing to tolerate that kind of involvement.

Renee, the timid, sensitive mother of two illegitimate children, is animated only when discussing their father, Jean. "I just put him on a new ten-year plan," she tells me, indicating the maximum time period she will wait for him. Renee has been vigorously maintaining her half of the involuntary partnership of twenty-two years. Claiming hatred for her boyfriend's wife, she has had two children by this same man, received no financial support, worked very hard as a manicurist, and witnessed the fact that he has had two children with his wife, each one born immediately after her own. She believes Jean's conceiving those legitimate children were isolated sexual acts. "He hasn't slept with his wife since," she assures me.

Jean's double life can go on as long as his women cooperate. Renee still believes that he will leave his wife in a year or two, when both of his legal children are out of the house. (The eight years left in the ten-year plan will be the limit of her waiting, she tells me.) Renee has spent two decades despising that "partner" she claims keeps Jean from her. She cannot direct any negative emotion toward her lover; it must hurt too much, and contradicts the dynamics of the relationship with him. If she or those like her see the reality of their alliances, it might destroy them. Renee, for one, might have to admit to twenty-two years of futile sacrifice.

CHAPTER 13

Rumor Has It

WHAT THE OTHER WOMAN HEARS
ABOUT THE WIFE

RECENTLY, MY friend Julie's consciousness-raising group broke up when one of the women found out her husband was having an affair with another member of the group. Two years of devoted support among eight women was over. Within three weeks after the information came out, relationships carefully built and safeguarded were dissolved.

It seemed like the women all took several giant steps backward. The ancient bromide "Never trust another woman" was in the air. Everyone took sides. Pain and anger obscured insights that could have been gained.

Like the two women in this group, wives and lovers sharing men find themselves involuntarily partnered with each other. The faceless enemy, "she," is an awful person with terrible habits and values, or no morals or class . . . all the negative qualities one does not have oneself. Not that anyone wishes the "second woman in his life" (what everyone else is) to be run over or shot—that is a guilt-producing fantasy. Only that some starry night, as one woman put it, "she might fade away quietly, after a very good meal, with a smile on her face."

Usually perceived by her counterpart as the only obstacle keeping her man from being wholly hers, each woman in a husband's life claims she wants no association with the other. "She, the one who trapped this saint with guilt and children," or "she, the one who seduced him during a mid-life crisis," is the one I heard getting all the blame when a man couldn't make up his mind.

The potent "she" supposedly precipitates events leading to one's own divorce or—given the right personality factors—illness, life-long loneliness, or suicide. That goes for both sides, connected by a third—the man. They comprise a fluid triangle in which movement by one side affects or changes the other two.

Women assessing their feminine partners generally seemed to move toward the concept of blame—with good reason. They want to hear something that allows them to pin their suffering on the other woman rather than on the man they need or feel they need. For the other woman, hearing about the wife's shortcomings makes it easy to justify her lover's disloyalty to his marriage vows and her own involvement with him; he is not merely acting emotionally and physically delinquent.

A medical student told me of her lover's wife: "Finding out she swings made it simple to justify my boyfriend's actions." Likewise, reports of insensitive or cruel behavior on the wife's part seem to alleviate any guilt the other woman may have felt toward her. Such details carry the additional consolation of assuring her that the man is having a rotten time at home; it makes her own suffering bearable. She tolerates loneliness better when she believes he shares the same deprivation.

The other woman, I have found, feels no loyalty to a wife she cannot identify with. If she hears about awful things done to a man she finds considerate, there is no feeling of kinship with his wife.

If there *is* any familiarity about this person, it may well be as a mother figure. Dr. Rinzler confirmed that "the wife may become an authority figure to be hated and feared. She is the projection of the bad mother—depriving, cold, punitive. So while the woman enjoys her lover, she also has fantasies of tricking and rebelling against this bad mother, by whom she expects ultimately to be punished. The man's wife is on some level not recognized as a real person but is endowed with magical powers to judge and punish."

The emotional competition we've heard so much about between mother and daughter is played out again in the triangle with the other woman and the wife. They compete for the husband/father's attention. This expression of a classical Oedipal triangle may be more blatant if the other woman is single, and the wife, a mother. All these feelings are reinforced when the husband's attitude toward his wife seems like that of a child dominated by a mother figure.

Let's take the opposite case. The man tells his other woman that his wife is a marvelous person and his marriage is satisfying. It is just that he finds the other woman irresistible. If the outside woman is not fulfilling immature needs and denying the obvious reality of her lover's good marriage, she will try, in her own interests, to keep the relationship superficial. If she is already in love with the man, chagrin is bound to follow this glowing portrait. One girlfriend lamented, "If she weren't so terrific, there would be a better chance of his leaving." When a wife sounds too saintly, the girlfriend could transfer negative emotions from the wife to the man, on account of his not being faithful to the deserving lady.

The kind, loving, or admirable wife is a figure the other woman identifies with. In these cases I heard about, an affair with the woman's husband did not make her feel guilty so much as hesitant about getting hurt herself. She cannot, she instinctively knows, divide a union that is solid. Similarly, the daughter is less likely to continue her battle to replace Mother if she feels it is a hopeless aspiration, that Mother has and deserves Daddy's loyalty.

Unless the other woman maintains a very light relationship with her lover, an unflattering description of the wife is what she wants and generally hears, according to my sample. If there is any negative information to provide, a man who is unhappy will supply it. This is evidence to the girlfriend that she has a chance to win her man away from the competition.

When either woman discovers inadequacies in the other, she feels more secure that her own is the most important relationship to the husband. Until ready to face the reality of shared responsibility for the triangle as it exists, both women appear to direct the greatest part of their rage at a fantasized version of the other.

There are times, however, when a girlfriend pities a wife,

resolving never to occupy her position. One woman said that her boyfriend used his only car to take her away for weekends, leaving his wife at home, stranded, with the children. "He'd say it was a business trip, but I thought doing a thing like that was terrible." The girlfriend soon ended the affair.

Many women in these love triangles compete for an impossible prize. Both wife and girlfriend support the husband's double life by their continued participation in it. Taking no positive step to alter the status quo, or defending the man's "weakness," they acquiesce by their passivity. Each woman is unknowingly the other's ally in supporting the man's other relationship. The irony is that each woman spends her anger on the very person unwillingly sharing her own dissatisfied state.

Actually, the man in the middle may be too guilt-ridden or weak to take action, or simply unaware that he is manipulating the women to satisfy immature needs of his own. One wife who had reluctantly accepted the outside affair and decided to live with it found herself at a Broadway show in which her husband's lover was appearing—the husband having bought the tickets for himself and his wife with this awareness. She finally realized her husband was the puppeteer in this triangle, but she nonetheless aimed all her hatred and revenge toward the other woman.

The wife, who was friendly with the wardrobe mistress for this show, convinced her to put some itching powder into the lady's costume a few days later and settled down in the audience to enjoy the show for the second time. When the unfortunate actress came on stage, the wife delighted to see her jump and twitch throughout the performance.

In a truly involuntary partnership where the wife or other woman neither consciously nor subconsciously wants the connection to continue, she may try to change things so that the partnership becomes a twosome between herself and the man, or end the relationship altogether. But as long as the women are unable to do one and afraid to do the other, and many of those I spoke with are, the man in the middle is unlikely to cut the three-way ties.

CHAPTER 14
The Willing Victim

A WIFE WHO HELPS HIM HAVE AFFAIRS

THE SCENE is a wedding reception on Long Island. A wife feels sorry for her divorced neighbor. "Honey, she's all alone," she tells her husband. "Why don't you ask her to dance?" He does, and they dance right out of his wife's life forever.

In many instances, say other women and husbands, a wife acts as the unsuspecting matchmaker for her husband. "I knew both of them," a designer remembers. "She went to Europe and asked me to take care of her husband, go out with him, have fun. We were just friends. I didn't expect anything to happen, and neither did he. That eventually became a six-year affair between us." Although the dressmaker saw to it that her friendship with her lover's wife tapered off, she still feels badly about the whole business. She had promised to meet her friend's boat when it returned from Europe. But when the boat docked, "I just turned around and left. The only thing I could have done was to ask what I was there for at the beginning."

Sometimes the push from a wife is so blatant one wonders what she could have been thinking. Leslie was twenty when her girlfriend's husband, who was thirty-eight, made it clear that he would like them to be intimate. Leslie was somewhat in love with Irwin but staunchly refused involvement with him because of her friendship with his wife, Judy.

Instead of keeping his feelings a secret, Irwin told me he'd told Judy and "it's all right with her." I said, "I'm not a free cow and nobody else can give me permission to do it." But even after I definitely refused, Judy would tell me, "If I don't let him have you, he won't want me and he'll never forgive me." No matter how I reiterated that I couldn't sleep with her husband, she kept pushing me to do so, and I knew she loved him desperately. Finally, she picked up the maid, grandparents, and children and went to their farm in Vermont, leaving us together.

Leslie lived nearby and knew Judy had left her with Irwin to break the deadlock.

She actually asked me to sleep with him, to get it over with. "He'll never be happy until he does, and I want him to be happy," she said. So I did go to bed with Irwin and he was completely impotent in that situation. Probably he was nervous and guilty because of the emotional trauma.

Not surprisingly, Irwin had difficulties when Judy gave him permission to have sex with Leslie. He probably felt that Judy was a kind of witness to the act. Like a boy told he may do something naughty, Irwin found the fun and his ability had disappeared.

Leslie moved to Washington shortly thereafter and didn't see the couple for five years. She was still in love with Irwin despite their failed physical encounter, and when she returned to New Hampshire, they all had a good visit until the same situation arose.

Irwin and I went off together as Judy waved bravely good-bye. The identical scenario took place. He couldn't do anything and admitted he had become the cocksman of the whole area, laying every girl he could in order to prove he was okay. Of course, none of this affected the tremendous feelings I had for him.

Years later, during a visit to Washington, D.C., Judy and Irwin saw Leslie and the man she had married in the interim. When Leslie divorced, the other couple stayed in touch with both of them. Prior to a visit to Washington, when he was in his fifties, Irwin told Judy he was going to see Leslie. At dinner with her, Irwin admitted that he had always felt a failure as far as she was concerned. The irony to Leslie was that he had been the central man in her life and an ideal against which she had always measured others. The two old friends did not try a third physical consummation. Irwin died shortly afterward.

> Judy and I have remained close friends, and she told me once that she'd always feared losing him to me and everyone else. I explained that I never even wanted to marry Irwin because he and Judy were really good together and I never thought he and I were suited for marriage. It may not sound it, but despite her problems, Judy did have a glorious marriage with Irwin for twenty-seven years.

Women may not condone lovers for their husbands outright, I've found, so much as agree to or ignore specific friendships that include clandestine sex. Friends are likely candidates because they are easily accessible and have time to develop an attraction toward and fantasies about the husband. Wives say hostility, insecurity, competition, or simple jealousy of a couple's socio-economic level or relationship may be the friend's motive. And when the friend is herself married, the affair could be motivated by anger toward her own husband. She may be trying to punish him by means of an affair that he is likely to sense.

The wife also has certain psychological advantages in permitting this friend to share her husband. It is logical that there exists some feeling of control in knowing whom he is with (the same might be said about the motivation for an open marriage), and perhaps she counts on some degree of loyalty from her friend in not finally, permanently taking her man away. She might also expect a measure of gratitude from her husband for being so apparently broad-minded.

Michelle no doubt consciously or subconsciously knew that her husband, Richard, was having an affair with her friend Sandy while both married couples continued to be close friends.

Sandy said:

> Richard and I saw each other socially without spouses several times weekly. Additionally, he usually came to visit me on his way home from work; my husband often worked later. Everything went smoothly for us. Sometimes it even seemed as if Michelle wanted Richard for me as well as herself. There were many instances she'd offer Richard's services to help me if I needed someone and Ed was off working. Or if Richard had to go somewhere and Michelle couldn't join him, she'd say, "Sandy, please go with him so he won't be alone." She knew he loved me as a friend, but of course never knew we were lovers.
>
> All four of us frequently went to Michelle and Richard's Cape Cod house. Once, I remember lying down on a great big day bed where Richard joined me. We were lying spoon fashion. Michelle said to my husband, "They're so adorable together." Then she covered us.

It is possible that Michelle never perceived the affair on any level. Much more likely is that she wanted to evade the truth because that was too painful The consenting wife's self-devaluation rests on the theory that she alone cannot hold her husband. Even if she feels confident about her own attractiveness, she may realize her husband is not capable of fidelity to anyone. Much has been written about identity conflict, such as the latent homosexual element, between the women in these situations. It is only one of a number of complex possibilities, which are difficult to evaluate. The woman's motivation can only be determined by knowing her individual internal problems

One wife who actually interviewed and picked someone for her husband to sleep with did so, admittedly, precisely for control . . . and "medicinal" purposes. After her first trip away alone, Pat found out her husband, in her absence, had had an affair with their neighbor. She said nothing. The next time she left town, her husband was ill and confined to bed. Pat hired a gorgeous nurse to take care of him. She explained, "It had two advantages. She was such a dummy that after three days with her, I knew he would be bored and dying for me. Also, he was an impossible patient who wouldn't get better. I figured he'd be too embarrassed to stay sick long with the knockout I hired." She was right and returned to a smiling recovered man.

The majority of women, of course, are terribly hurt and angry to discover it is a friend or neighbor who has betrayed them. When the other woman is the one to whom they have been confiding their innermost thoughts, the pain is greatly increased.

CHAPTER 15
Blindfolds

IGNORING THE EVIDENCE

A POPULAR way to avoid all pain and disappointment of betrayal by one or two close companions is to ignore the evidence of the affair. Denying or refusing to admit to herself that both husband and friend are conspiratorially partnered was a commonly voiced theme among wives who were eventually forced to face the facts. One wife never noticed the other woman's phone number which her husband had placed in her personal address book.

Unhappy wives told me they had denied the evidence of their husbands' outside interests because they knew their marriages were a tenuous business and had decided nonetheless to maintain them. Satisfied wives have different but equally strong reasons to wear blindfolds. Their men, refreshed or stimulated by new sexual partners, frequently become lustier at home. They turn on to their wives anew when they are more passionate in general. Sometimes their guilt alone motivates them.

Conrad again: "I screw the devil out of my wife for a few days."

Even if sex is rare between the spouses, the unfaithful husband can be an attractive marriage partner, becoming more loving or a better family man because he is fulfilled somewhere else. This is the likeliest instance in which a wife denies the other woman. Living with a solicitous, attentive mate is easy. Daily pleasantries help her miss the messages he sends. Why should she look at them when she senses no betrayal?

Women can drift contentedly through married life for years never knowing what a loving husband's full romantic existence is like unless he asks for a divorce. We rarely stop to analyze our lives when they are flying along successfully, our joys abundant. We only pause to see what has gone wrong, what we missed, after we are deep in conflict. Cruel or unusual behavior gets the message across more quickly.

Isobel, who in her sixties became the other woman, was once on the other side of the triangle. Her marriage to Jeff, after her 90 percent recovery from polio at nineteen, was chiefly an escape from her dominating mother. In theory, the young couple had everything in common, but Isobel soon found that Jeff's inability to communicate in and out of bed left her terribly lonely.

> Sex was only that. Never did he connect it to feelings. In thirteen years he never put his arm around me. If I hadn't had my son and daughter to hold and kiss and hug, I would have felt starved, because I came from a very affectionate family.

Isobel was also concerned with her inability to change Jeff's three-minute sex routine. They were both virgins when they married, so she assumed Jeff just lacked knowledge. Isobel bought books on sexual technique and left them around with markers at the salient pages, but Jeff never looked at them.

> It was very hard for me to tell him what I wanted because he felt that foreplay was a lot of baloney and time wasted. He never paid any attention to my requests. I would make suggestions, but he did not listen. Instead, he told me I was a frigid woman. I didn't really believe him, but my ego was smashed. Though I'd never had an orgasm except in my dreams, I decided after ten years to find out if I really was frigid. I set about deliberately learning to masturbate. I did and found out I was all right. I just never had had any proper attentive loving. Strangely, Jeff was an excellent father and there was never any conflict about the children, so I thought we should stay together.

When he changed jobs, Jeff met an old high school buddy and his wife, Paula. They became the couple's new friends. Paula was an attractive woman who, she confessed to Isobel, had had an extramarital affair during her former marriage. Isobel never supposed, when she attended her father's funeral out of town, that Paula, who had professed affection for her and had taken Isobel to visit her own parents, would sleep with Jeff. It was shortly after that time that Jeff began working evenings.

Though Jeff often didn't come home until three or four in the morning, Isobel accepted his explanation of playing poker with the boys. "I believed him. I'd been afraid it was a woman and guess I was grateful it wasn't."

Despite Isobel's conscious efforts to ignore Jeff's affair, some part of her registered the change in their marriage.

> Suddenly I developed symptoms like heart trouble. I couldn't get my breath. I realized my subconscious was trying to tell me something I couldn't accept: that Jeff was having an affair. Although I wasn't happy, we had two small children who needed us. Also, I couldn't face the facts squarely.

The evidence mounted of Jeff's need to show Isobel what he was doing, but still she ignored it. In a nightclub with Paula and her husband, Ralph, Jeff and Isobel were dancing when he suddenly said, "I never thought I would mind being married to a cripple, but I do mind." It was the cruelest remark Isobel had ever suffered. In a daze, she walked onto the street alone, with no money or way to get home. Soon, the others came out and drove to Ralph and Paula's house. Ralph drove the babysitter home while Jeff, leaving Isobel in their car for twenty minutes, remained in the house with Paula. Still Isobel said nothing.

A few weeks later, Jeff, a pack leader, announced he was taking his cub scout troop to a lake for the weekend. On Saturday, Isobel called headquarters to get a phone number where she could reach Jeff to ask him about some legal papers she needed. As soon as she learned there was no camp at that particular lake, she phoned Paula's house and was told that both she and Ralph had gone away for the weekend. Whether they were together or not the babysitter didn't know.

> Jeff had obviously lied to me. I was furious to think that one of our children could have been run over and I wouldn't have been able to get in touch with him. When he came back, I said, "How was the weekend on the lake?" He said, "It's gone down a couple of inches." I called him a liar. Jeff knew he had to leave. He moved out and after a week begged me to take him back for the sake of the children. I did.
>
> I know I made a mistake, but hindsight is always twenty-twenty. He kept seeing Paula. Her husband had a night job, so she and Jeff had it made. He'd get out of bed with her and come home and make love to me. I felt like a whore; I just hated it. But I reasoned that if I got up and out of that bed, I would completely forfeit my husband. I had to try and win the game.
>
> Paula continued to seek my friendship after she was sleeping with Jeff. Once I found out about them, I wouldn't see her, but she still wanted to. Jeff said to me, "What's the matter? Paula still likes *you*." He couldn't understand why we couldn't be one big, happy family.
>
> We spent another year and a half together before Jeff left for the last time. The children were crying when he left and I said to them, "Okay. Tomorrow I'm going to find a job and we're going to start a whole new life as the three musketeers."

Isobel was a telephone operator, secretary, and real estate broker, all within six months. Paula left Ralph in that period and moved with Jeff into a house which Isobel sold them. "I decided, dammit, if he's going to buy a house two blocks away, I'm going to get the commission."

When Isobel saw their baby, she thought it looked more like Jeff than had either of their own children. Paula had conceived the baby when she was still married to Ralph and convinced both men it was Ralph's. Jeff went to court to adopt the child.

When Isobel wasn't ready to face her husband's infidelity, she wore blindfolds about her marriage. More noteworthy is the fact that she never tried to resolve the problem or avenge her anger and pain once she acknowledged the affair. She didn't tell Paula's husband, or do anything after her first confrontation with Jeff but accept him back on his own terms. She thought she would win him with passivity and accommodation. The total self-abnegation she underwent is the price many women seem to pay to preserve the marriage they believe they cannot live without. Such a weak marriage has no substance against which the frame can lean. External pressure can easily destroy it.

Jeff and Paula, in socializing together with their spouses, were involved in dangerous games. There is a great deal of upsmanship in these situations where the lovers act out complicated, competitive feelings toward one another. Jeff was no doubt competing with Ralph, his old boyhood friend, and Paula with Isobel, by consenting to continue their social contact. Though the bringing together of a wife and lover is not necessarily sinister, Jeff's desire to hurt Isobel can be clearly seen. The set-up may easily work in reverse. According to several psychotherapists I consulted, when a husband is affectionate or solicitous toward his wife in front of his lover, some sadism or hostility toward the other woman is at the base of this behavior.

Cooperating in these dangerous games may also indicate a degree of self-devaluation on the part of the woman lover. Perhaps punishment for duping her friend is what she is after. Complicated internal needs, Dr. Katherina Marmor theorizes, underlie even apparently benign social situations where lovers and wives mix.

Isobel finally confronted Jeff verbally, but she never really dealt with the problems in their marriage that led to his affair. Without attempting or insisting that the two of them work on their marriage together, she took Jeff back and suffered the continued humiliation and agony of consciously sharing her husband with a former friend. This deceit by her presumably closest allies is one of the worst kinds of betrayal a wife endures. The pain and anger I heard in their voices, as I played back those wives' tapes, were heart-wrenching.

Wives like Isobel whom I interviewed, who feel emotionally and financially dependent, practice denial in large part because they fear striking out on their own. They believe on some level that ignorance is bliss. The problem is that real ignorance is impossible—a woman knows her husband. Part of her is aware that the ignorance or innocence is only a willingness to keep one step behind the truth.

According to most men I interviewed, those whose wives do not challenge their right to have affairs will rarely give up having them once they begin. Some are more active than others but they all feel their wives have accepted or are totally unaware of their outside lives. Husbands who find the double life intolerable make sure their wives discover it. But when sex is not too important to a wife anymore, or both partners are comfortable avoiding the physical side of the marriage, the triangle, it seems, will generally stay intact.

The added advantage of a wife's denial system is the elimination of any sense of participation in the triangle. While feeling blameless, she escapes the chaos others could be injecting into her life. She avoids pulling loose the thread she thinks may unravel the whole fabric of her security. Even after she takes the blindfolds off for a quick, unpleasant look at reality, she may put them back on.

Christine is an obvious example. An attractive, amicable woman in her mid-thirties, she found out that her husband behaved like a bachelor whenever he traveled for business. None of the episodes was emotionally entangling. Christine, nonetheless, felt devastated. She was under the impression that her marriage had been mutually satisfying and faithful. Christine confronted her husband and found that he was vulnerable when traveling and wished that she would accompany him. He promised to be faithful in the future and very much wanted their marriage intact.

Though her children were in school and they had a full-time housekeeper, Christine did not feel comfortable about leaving them even for a few days at a time. After the first couple of trips with her husband, she announced that it was more important to remain at home. "Anyway, he didn't fool around anymore. Jack really made an effort. He always called and told me where he was and exactly whom he was with. Things were great between us."

Christine sensed their marriage was back on solid ground and wanted to have a third child. Jack refused. He claimed to need more of his wife's attention and, as the children grew, more freedom to be by themselves. Christine insisted that they have another child, crying for weeks until Jack reluctantly consented. Now, with a six-month-old to care for, as well as the other two, Christine tells me, between sobs, that, "Jack is screwing around again. The whole thing has fallen apart." The couple has just separated. Unfortunately, Christine chose to ignore the thin ice in her marriage and skated right over it. Jack evidently wanted more of Christine's attention than he was getting.

As much as a wife may desire to reestablish an emotional rapport with her husband, it may be impossible. No marriage is unaffected by an important outside relationship. But she who is hopeful about a marriage that is in jeopardy removes the blindfolds and works on the conflicts. If after examination with her husband and/or a professional her marriage cannot be improved, she may make a decision to accept her husband's affair rather than divorce. Knowing that the decision is consciously hers provides at least some feeling of control over her life and its direction.

CHAPTER 16
Friends Later

Heaven has no rage like love to hatred turned,
Nor hell a fury like a woman scorned.
> —William Congreve,
> *The Mourning Bride*

When the Wife and Mistress Get Together

IT WAS midnight. Beth had another hour of reading to do. Between taking care of the kids and finishing up her last semester of course work for her master's in psychology, she sometimes felt she wasn't going to make it. This night was one of those times. The phone rang.

"Beth? I'm the other woman, I'm Linda."

Beth was in no mood for this call. She had always sensed Pete had someone else because he was away a lot on unnecessary business trips, but she didn't want any more pain from him and had ignored his comings and goings. In the last few years, she had realized he was a selfish, immature man and had decided to concentrate on her own self-realization. She had heard through friends that Pete had moved in with another woman, but she didn't know whether this was an extension of his former extramarital affair or not.

"You take a size eight dress, seven shoe, thirty-four sweater, ten pants, and have a gorgeous mauve silk raincoat which you have never worn," the voice said.

"He provides a lot of information!"

"I bought it for you."

"What?!"

"By the way, the last book you read for pleasure was *Report to Greco*. I liked it too."

Beth discovered in their four-and-a-half-hour conversation that her estranged husband had not only told this woman every detail about her and their life but had set up a cruel one-way competition in which Linda emulated the brainy Beth, whom Pete claimed he admired. Linda, while denigrated by him, served him for three years as a manageable version of his wife. Linda read the books Beth read, tried to participate in conversations the way she did, saw all the films she had seen, and mouthed the same opinions. Linda tried to become his wife because Pete convinced her he wanted her to be Beth. But a controllable Beth.

Without his willful, unpredictable spouse, however, the malleable version of the same woman was a flat, warmed-over, dressed-up edition who soon bored him. After two months exclusively with Linda, during which time Beth had initiated divorce proceedings, Pete decided he had had enough. Without discussion, he ended his three-year relationship with his girlfriend.

Beth was hypnotized by the idea of her twin self, created from Pete's descriptions, and Linda's own observation of their home. "During your weeks in Washington, I stayed at your apartment with Pete."

Beth, rather than being angry, felt sympathy for Linda, who was much more hurt by Pete's absence than she herself was. Beth was preparing for self-sufficiency while Linda, the injured party, found herself stranded. She had given, she felt, the best years of her life to Pete.

Beth insisted on hanging up the phone in the hopes of getting some sleep. Beth, who learned that Pete had taken much better financial care of Linda than he had of her, resented that. Linda expressed concern for Beth toward whom, she felt, Pete would be vindictive; he was already trying to get custody of the children. Not only would Linda help in Beth's divorce, she would be her star witness.

Although she did sound concerned about Beth's welfare, Beth also detected in Linda's voice a frustration that she could do nothing more to Pete for leaving her. Linda had no recourse like a divorce to use against him. In fact, the generous "settlement" he had given her was meant, no doubt, to buy her loyalty.

Beth empathized with what this woman had gone through with the hostile and narcissistic Pete. She also understood that Linda was handing her tens of thousands of dollars worth of private investigation fees.

The *pièce de résistance* of the phone conversation came just before they hung up. It was Linda's announcement that, "Oh, tomorrow or the next day, you'll be getting your period."

"Now how could you know that?"

"Because we've been on the same cycle for the last three years." Beth grew angrier at Pete for having allowed her privacy to be so invaded, and she was dizzy at the thought of an alien self moving around every day in the same city. As soon as her lawyer's office opened, Beth called him. "You've got to get her down here today. She's hurt now but may change her mind in a few days," he said.

Beth telephoned Linda, who was anxious to meet her. When they walked into the lawyer's office on Manhattan's East Side, Linda in a fur coat and carrying two Gucci bags full of evidence, Beth in her turtleneck and jeans, he said, "You look like the wife," pointing to Linda, "and you like the other woman," indicating Beth.

After their appointment, Linda invited Beth to lunch.

"And Pete's paying for it. He owes us a lunch. Doesn't he?" Beth agreed. They put her ten-speed bike in the back of the black Cadillac Pete had given Linda and they went for an expensive lunch.

Sex lives, feelings, lifestyles were thoroughly compared. "Did you know we were sleeping with each other almost to the end?" Beth asked.

"Yes, he told me." The psychology-oriented Beth wondered how strong the homosexual element was in this woman's participation in the *ménage à trois*. Beth had unknowingly been part of the triangle for three years.

Linda said, "Every day after the chauffeur dropped you off in the Village with your bike, he picked me up and I went to the department stores to buy our clothes, when I wasn't seeing films, reading, or going to museums Pete mentioned."

"And while I was at school, you were buying me a wardrobe appropriate for the life with Pete that I had abandoned. He kept bringing home these things I wouldn't wear." Beth liked Linda. She was not a stimulating, original mind, but a supportive person bent on obtaining revenge for the suffering they had both undergone. The lunch cemented a close interdependence.

Beth was as anxious to see Linda as the other way around. "I felt lousy, vulnerable. Here was a person who had no other purpose in life but to hold my hand and be a star witness in my divorce." They became quick friends, hungry for the company of the only other person on earth who understood and sympathized with the misery each felt. While Linda wanted to ease her pain in losing Pete, Beth wanted to forget the years of hurt and to insure herself custody of the children. For months, both were absorbed with discussing their mutual experiences and with the upcoming divorce trial.

Linda still echoed all Beth's opinions and imitated her actions, but now she had the living, warm original for a model and no longer had to copy an imaginary figure. Being attached to someone who was in a position to revenge Pete's insensitivity, someone who was smarter than she yet kind, and who never put her down the way Pete had gave Linda a sense of security.

After the first few weeks as friends, Beth discovered Linda's phone number and address in the first page of her address book.* Pete had obviously put it there long ago, hoping Beth would find it. All the other blatant hints concerning the affair which he had dropped over the years now dawned on her. Evidently, Pete had wanted to win Beth's love back by convincing her someone else wanted his. She understood that her ignoring such evidence indicated how much she wanted to avoid the fact that he had another woman. Thinking that their real relationship had died long ago, she was surprised that her feelings for Pete still ran so deep.

*Mentioned in chapter 15, "Blindfolds."

Maintaining the marriage was a good way to sidestep the confrontation for which she was not ready until she could emotionally take care of herself and the children.

The day of the divorce trial finally came. Linda decided to wear a simple man-tailored shirt and skirt similar to the one Beth picked out. Pete looked miserable as he watched the two women fortifying each other and the case against him. Even though his lawyer had warned him of Linda's appearance, he was never prepared for the solidity of his two female adversaries. And on top of everything else the judge was a woman! Pete ended up giving Beth a large settlement and custody of their children.

After enjoying a celebratory dinner with Linda and the attorney, Beth began cramming for exams. Now on her own and at ease with that, she was doubly eager to succeed, leave behind the old life with Pete, and take a vacation with the children. When exams came and went, Beth cheered up. She rented a modest cottage on a lake in Connecticut where she would meet new people and have no chance of mixing in the social circle associated with her marriage.

For Linda, the trial was an emotional climax that led to nothing. Her settlement didn't change, she had no idea what she wanted to do with her life, and Beth was still the most important friend she had. After the trial, however, Beth had begun to cool off a little toward her. She disregarded the hint that Linda wanted to share the cottage that she rented. For Beth, Linda had not only become a part of the old life she wanted to shed but a boring, albeit sweet, carbon copy of herself.

Beth was packing to leave for Connecticut when Linda, very depressed, visited her. She couldn't understand Beth's not wanting her along. "I explained to Linda during a long walk that the divorce closed an unpleasant chapter in my life. I was ready to conquer new things and implied to Linda that our friendship would certainly not remain as it had been."

Beth went to Connecticut, and Linda, even more hurt by Beth's absence than Pete's, drifted sadly around the city for a week, going to movies and wandering around the Village, where she was sorely out of place with the musicians and painters who were part of Beth's world.

Beth spent the first week of vacation getting acquainted with the community, enjoying her children, and looking over the single men. She had shed a skin—it went with the conventions of wife and mother which were associated in her old life with the possibility of a part-time or unimportant job. She realized now she had the chance to reach as high as she liked. After a week in Connecticut, she decided to apply to a doctoral program in psychology. The challenge was exhilarating. Once it would have only scared her.

Linda also made a decision . . . to try once again to keep Beth's friendship. She drove to the lake in Connecticut and found Beth and the children, with a man, digging in the sand. Beth had met the man playing volleyball.

"Hello."

"Hello, Linda."

"I just decided to take a drive and see how you were doing."

"Fine . . . really fine."

"I probably won't be staying very long. I'm just going to take a walk in town and drive back."

"Have a good summer if I don't see you. And take good care of yourself; you deserve it."

Linda walked away. "Why didn't you introduce me to your friend?" Beth's male companion asked after Linda walked away.

"I'm very possessive," she answered smilingly.

Over the next few years, the women spoke a few times. Linda got married. She was divorced four months later. Beth is practically finished with her doctorate.

Linda's detailed knowledge of Beth and her participation in personal and even biological routines indicate a powerful desire to fuse with this woman. Her fantasy was to be like Beth, and she got as close to that ideal as she could. Linda was trying to compensate for feelings of inadequacy by emulating Beth. Sadly, she had little identity of her own and sensed that by adopting the personality of someone strong like Beth she could be accepted by a person like Pete. When Linda absorbed Beth's personality, she began to believe in it and wanted to get as near to the source of her new self as possible. It worked until their common anger and need for revenge were discharged by the divorce finalization. Then, it pleased Beth to be free and independent, but Linda was left floating, undirected.

Unlike these two women, a few involuntary partners I interviewed stayed friends after the marriage breakup. This seemed more likely if the wife's and husband's relationship did not contain passion anymore but those two retained some affection for one another.

When Steve's wife began getting friendly with her over the telephone, Ellen couldn't really understand it. Ellen had been having an affair with Steve, her boss, for six months and she intended to keep her distance from his wife, Margot.

But out of curiosity and a desire to be polite, Ellen accepted Margot's invitation to lunch one day when Steve was out of town on business. She discovered that not only was Margot lovely and bright, but that she was having an affair of her own! At first she wondered why Margot had told her this. Although she had been Steve's personal secretary for two years, the women had really just met. Ellen supposed that Margot suspected her and thought this confidence would encourage a confession. It did, three lunches later.

Ellen at this point felt closer to Margot than to Steve and confessed the affair, trusting her new comrade's discretion. Both women felt they had been treated badly by Steve and wanted more from a relationship. Margot said she had indeed suspected it and wanted Ellen's help (in the form of adultery evidence) in her efforts to divorce Steve. Because she had planned to leave her job anyway and was fed up with Steve's insensitivity, Ellen consented to help Margot. The married couple's divorce trial was the end of Steve's affair as well as the beginning of a solid, long friendship between the women.

Another woman, Adele, was furious with a woman colleague who had had an affair with her former husband until Adele once again felt warmly toward the man himself. In time she understood the motivations on both the lovers' sides and found out her husband had had other lovers before her friend. After a few years in therapy, he proposed to Adele but she refused to remarry him. In these circumstances the two women and the man all resumed their friendship. That can happen when the husband of contention is removed from a sexual involvement with either.

Bonds are destroyed by sharing men far more frequently than they are created. In rare instances, as with Margot and Ellen, when the women are naturally compatible and each feels the other is more deserving than the man involved, a friendship of empathy and shared suffering can be forged. At that point, in all the cases I have heard about, both affair and marriage are over.

CHAPTER 17
Discovery

People change and forget to tell each other.

—Lillian Hellman,
*Toys in the Attic**

FINDING OUT ABOUT HIS AFFAIR

THE HUSBAND who told me, "My wife never before opened a bill in thirty-two years of marriage," took an unnecessary chance by charging his girlfriend's lingerie to an account sent to his house. It precipitated events ultimately leading to his divorce. If his wife never before opened a bill, chances are she had gleaned other hints of his affair before doing so. Possibly there were changes in his behavior. Men who leave overt clues such as bills, photographs, and phone numbers, lipstick-stained and perfume-laden shirts, are unaware, at least at that moment, of "asking" their wives to confront them or give them a kind of permission for an ongoing affair.

A confrontation which results from such evidence can end either the liaison or the marriage, something the man is incapable or unwilling to do himself, or it punishes his wife, toward whom he feels hostility, or it provides punishment for his own guilt-producing deed. Whatever the motive, it is apparent he wants his

---

* Lillian Hellman, *Toys in the Attic* (New York: Random House, 1960), Act III. Reprinted with permission.

spouse to share responsibility for the outcome. The wife who reacts to these clues with silence is tacitly agreeing to the situation he has set up. Though she may feel very strongly that she does not want it to continue and in fact tries in roundabout ways to wrest his attention back toward her, saying nothing to her husband generally indicates to him acquiescence.

"My wife is no dope—obviously she knows if I'm gone so much, I must have other relationships. She just accepts it," a long-time traveler said. Wives like his have their own reasons to go along with their husbands' affairs. But if a man is leaving blatant hints around the house, on some level he must want his wife to know.

Phil wasn't telling Denise he had a girlfriend, but the advertisement for a heart necklace gave her a good idea. She saw it lying in his open briefcase when he went into the shower. As Phil had been particularly distant of late, Denise intuitively knew the necklace was not for her. She waited a few days and went to the jewelry store mentioned in the ad. She told them her brother had sent the heart necklace to his fiancé. Denise wanted, she explained, to send the woman another piece of jewelry for a gift. She picked something out, paid for it, pretended to have misplaced the address, and asked if they would look it up. She discovered the address was in Chicago, a place Phil frequented on business. (Later Denise cancelled the order.) When she confronted Phil with the name and address, he turned red and said little. Six months later the couple split up "because the whole marriage was so rotten," Denise said.

Some wives are told of the second woman by their own husbands. But unless the man considers the affair over or he wants to end his marriage, he has no reason to share this information directly. The wife may suspect her husband; still, when no one tells her and she ignores the hints, she is, as the cliché goes, the last to know.

Cindy was visiting relatives out of town when she received a call from one of her neighbors. "We're sorry to interfere in your life, but since we're friends we thought you should come back right away—your husband's got another lady in your apartment." Cindy returned to find Hal in bed with a blonde stewardess. The lovers were asleep. She woke the woman, gave her cab fare, and sent her quietly on her way while her lawyer husband snored on. Cindy crawled into bed with him. As he turned, half asleep, and began fondling her amorously, she said, "Don't touch me." He woke up, confused, assessed the situation, took a pillow and blanket, and went on his way to the living room couch. He announced, "I'm not discussing this because I have to be in court in five hours." Cindy was dumbfounded. Later that day she found photos of the blonde in his dresser drawer. Eventually, this couple was divorced.

Relatives and friends (frequently women friends, who are jealous of the married couple's relationship or who have tried unsuccessfully to seduce the husband) often carried the bad news to the wives with whom I spoke. The other woman can also let a wife know by means of conscious or subconscious gestures—keeping her lover with her past the hour he is expected; or insisting that they shower together, knowing the wet hair he goes home with will be suspect. Girlfriends may even be deliberately vengeful like Patricia, who left her nightgown in her lover's wife's drawer to "give her a little hint. It was exciting. I wanted to punish her for being stupid," she said, "for not realizing that her husband really didn't love her."

Patricia's blatant hostility and acting out are very rare. Actually, it was surprising to this interviewer how long so much was kept secret by so many. Unless the husband has specifically hurt or left the other woman, as Pete did in Beth's and Linda's story, most girlfriends feel that the decision about his affair is up to him; they don't want to purposely hurt another woman or incur their lover's wrath with underhanded offenses.

The twist of fate, an ironic moment, whatever, can expose many a meticulous planner. Out for a day of shopping in a Boston department store, a wife, feeling particularly affectionate toward her husband, decided to buy him a new briefcase. At the leather goods counter, she admired the briefcase the woman next to her had picked out. She commented to her about how handsome it was while the first woman ordered a man's initials inscribed onto the lock plate. They were the same as the second woman's husband's initials. Then the first woman asked that the briefcase be sent to the second woman's husband's office. The latter blanched, then said to the salesgirl, "Make that two, same initials, same name and address." The women had lunch; the man's affair soon ended. His marriage continued, and his wife began an affair of her own.

Traps lie everywhere, even for the most discreet lovers. A fellow who hadn't been discovered in fifteen years of adultery never knew that his girlfriend owed her new sultry look to false eyelashes. He rushed home from her apartment one night, got undressed, and turned to hang up his clothes. A strip of eyelashes was stuck where no one should have been looking. "Someone has been batting her eyelashes at you in the strangest places," his wife began. That was the beginning of a long, long line of questioning and sarcastic remarks—eight years worth . . . and still counting.

Wives who view their husbands' adulterous behavior as the men's exclusive responsibility may end up sympathizing with the girlfriend and taking her side in the ensuing conflict. That was how Karen reacted. There was a knock on her door one day. Her husband, Leo, had to play pro football that evening and was sleeping late. A very pregnant girl introduced herself as Irene, the secretary for another football team in another state.

She said, "I have a problem. I'm pregnant and it's Leo's baby." Karen at first refused to believe it.

"Is Leo here?" she asked.

"Yes, he's sleeping."

"Well, I have nowhere to go. I was fired and have no friends to turn to. I came here by bus."

Karen woke her husband, who claimed this woman had had no contact with him in many months and had never told him she was pregnant. He could hardly deny knowing her but asked what she wanted.

"She looks like she's eight months pregnant."

"I'm not going out there."

"Yes you are going out there."

After an argument between them, Leo came into the foyer. Karen left for a nearby coffee shop.

> I thought I was going to come back and it would be all over. But I came back and she was still there. He said, "I have to go to the stadium," which is where ballplayers always go for protection.

He left me with this girl. He claimed not to know what to do. The poor girl was crying hysterically.

After giving the expectant mother some money and getting her settled in a hotel, Karen learned that her husband told his coach what had happened. The older man got the whole team mobilized to help this girl and took her into his home himself. In the meantime, Karen was more angry at Leo for not visiting the pregnant girl and for abdicating all his responsibility than she was for his illicit behavior.

Karen was too attached to Leo to leave him but wanted to hurt him in some way. "After that, I fucked every player on the team I could." Leo never found out about her revenge, but six months later another chain of events was set into motion.

Karen found it flattering when a new neighbor and friend began dressing and wearing her hair like she did. One day she noticed the woman had Leo's picture in her wallet and was told that her friend had sent to the football stadium for it. Coming in from dinner one night, Karen and Leo saw dark stains on the hall carpeting and then blood all over their apartment door. Leo, who obviously knew what it meant, raced down the stairs, with Karen after him, and busted in the door of the neighbor's apartment. She had slit her wrists and had come to stage a death scene at the married couple's home. When they weren't in, she had stumbled back to her own apartment. Leo and Karen got her to the hospital, where her life was saved.

Karen understood Leo had been having an affair with her, moved out, and called Leo's former roommate. "He was three hundred twenty-five pounds, but I fucked his brains out. I just wanted to fuck everybody who was around him." Karen finally realized she was doing herself no good, and she wanted to escape the sickness of the atmosphere in which she felt she had involved herself. After moving cross country, she read in the newspaper two weeks later that her neighbor had once again slit her wrists, killing herself and leaving Leo her sizeable inheritance.

Like Karen, wives, I've heard, react emotionally to news of their husbands' infidelities and often seek revenge. But their acts of vengeance are frequently more self-destructive than painful to the man in question. It is noteworthy that both women in Karen's husband's life became involved with her. One came to her in need and the other, like Linda in the Beth and Linda story, tried to take on her identity. Realizing that Leo was a man who would continue to need other women, and weak women at that, Karen finally extricated herself from his life and began a new one of her own.

The dramatic or obvious indications of a man's other life are unavoidable. Subtler signs, wised-up wives say, are much easier to miss. A husband's guilt and dissatisfaction can lead to increased travel, emotional distance, irritability, silence, later working hours, and/or more involvement with the children. Add to the list insomnia, tension, new physical ailments, and any other worrisome changes in his behavior. They can be construed as merely mid-life crisis symptoms.

Conversely, men motivated to improve themselves during an affair may become better tempered, sexier, more interested in clothes, new hairstyles, losing weight, exercise, and health. Wives told me they had seen these signs as signs of enlightenment—"My lectures on diet and exercise have finally gotten through." It is tempting to think of these alterations as another phase in a marriage or her husband's development. Unless a wife feels she needs, or already has, someone else to love, she likely wants her marriage to continue. Avoiding those hints of another woman—wearing blindfolds—is comfortable for her.

Alicia felt that way. She was delighted that Danny had lost the extra fifteen pounds he had been carrying for years, had started jogging, and had finally bought some new clothes. One morning while making sandwiches for the kids she discovered that her large jar of peanut butter was practically empty. The kids never ate that much and the jar was new three days ago. Obviously, Danny, who deprived himself all day, was ravenous at night and was sneaking into the kitchen for peanut butter. Alicia called him at work.

"I found you out."

"What do you mean?"

"I know what you've been doing—you bad boy."

"What do you mean, Alicia?"

"Come on, you know exactly what I mean."

"I'll talk to you when I get home."

Danny came home from work early, extremely agitated. He said to Alicia, "Now calm down and let's discuss this thing."

"What's there to discuss?"

"Well, what we're going to do."

"About what?"

"Well, what did you call me about?"

By this time Alicia gathered that Danny was guilty of more than closet peanut butter eating. Any explanations he could manufacture were useless.

The couple separated shortly after that discussion, and Alicia learned that Danny had been seeing many other women over the course of several years. The couple remained separated for three years before divorcing.

Alicia says she is not sorry she began the "peanut butter charade," as she refers to it, because "the marriage already had problems." Divorce led her back to school, to her master's degree and, ultimately, to an unusually good job with a museum. She said, "Our problems would have come out eventually. I'm glad it wasn't ten years later."

An outside love affair of deep emotion and sufficient length is bound to affect a marriage. Even relationships never consummated by the sex act, like the one depicted in the classic movie *Brief Encounter*, affect a man's behavior and moods. A mate sensitive to him detects the change. I believe now that if a wife consciously wants to know, she will. How she reacts to the knowledge depends on her awareness of her immediate and long-term needs.

CHAPTER 18
Attack or Retreat?

The life which is unexamined is not worth living.

—Plato,
Dialogues, Apology

REACTION TO A MAN'S AFFAIR

WOMEN FIRST discovering their husbands' infidelities are shocked, angered, hurt, humiliated, and even guilty. A wife's anger is largely directed toward the other woman and, at times, at both lovers. Only rarely, it seems, does she blame solely her husband or share the responsibility herself. If she did, the implication would be that there is something wrong with their relationship, her love object, or her own conduct; it is easier to displace any self-anger for what happened onto the other woman and/or the husband.

Except for the wife who wants out of her marriage and tries to improve her financial leverage by waiting for her husband to make some "mistake" like infidelity, or the one enjoying an affair herself and wanting to alleviate her own guilt, wives can hardly wish to share their husbands. Some, though, handle their pain or jealousy with more grace than others.

There was a celebrated Monte Carlo couple who opened a dancing school in New York. The wife, on meeting her husband's current mistress, a prominent New York socialite, said, "We were married when we were both young. The best of Phillip I've already had. If you want what's left of him, you're welcome to it." Less cavalier wives can't do that. The initial reactions of most wives I spoke to included hysteria, suicide attempts and threats, angry outbursts, affairs of their own (maybe with one of their husbands' friends), or trips to their lawyers' offices.

If they are insecure, like Judy, who sent her husband, Irwin, off with her friend, they may actually encourage a man's extramarital activities. Because they sense there is nothing they can do to stop his wandering, women like Judy figure they might as well get credit for a liberal stance. All of these reactions are comprehensible but do nothing to resolve the problem. My conclusions about the three kinds of reactions wives have to discovery of their husbands' affairs follow.

Silence

If the wife finds wedlock otherwise satisfactory, the transgression of the marriage vow does not always interfere with the central aspects of the spouses' relationship. Even if jealousy and mistrust inhibit her full enjoyment of that, a wife may stay silent on the subject forever. Possibly recognizing that her man is narcissistic, that he had been made the center of the universe by his mother and wants to perpetuate that feeling with other women, she will say nothing about what he does outside their home.

Another passive group believe their mates are in love with them and the affair is a meaningless fling. Still a third silent variety suffer from low self-esteem and think they have no viable options to their present marriages. These women will accept unfaithful behavior because they are afraid of confronting and destroying whatever connections, however tenuous, they maintain to their men. They usually claim it is love that keeps them hanging on, but as marriage counselor Sandra Allenburg observed, "The major reason they stay that I have seen is usually financial. When we get down to the nitty gritty, they really don't care about the men and they're not interested in an intimate relationship. They want security." Certainly there is nothing wrong with wanting security, but being aware of what she wants and why lets a woman acknowledge her choice, at least to herself.

A lot of men, like Brian, the urbane traveler, take their wives' silence for acquiesence.

> My wife would have to be a complete ignoramus not to figure out that if I travel for twenty-five years and have sexual needs and enjoy people, I have extramarital relationships. But she doesn't confront me on this because it would cause a situation. I'm quite convinced that she's had a couple of affairs herself.

Brian assumes his wife accepts his way of life and he obviously accepts hers. Other men also claimed their wives knew and, without protest, tolerated their affairs. They can be right. Women, particularly those sexually disinterested or with lovers of their own, sometimes find the marriage a comfortable accommodation and see no gain in leaving. If a wife has a lover who is also married, she has reasons to stay married. Divorcing her husband for her lover will give her all the disadvantages of being the other woman and none of the advantages of being the wife. This way she has both. Others are passive only because they see nothing beyond their present circumstances as a possible choice. In either case, on some level, the husband very likely interprets his wife's silence as permission for his affair.

Before deciding on the appropriate response to discovering the man's liaison, a wife does well to understand on what basis her marital contract has been operating and if that is satisfactory. If she has accepted her husband's affairs and simply chosen not to confront him or change their relationship, she may decide that whatever they had between them was good enough. If the spouses are principally intellectual or social companions, financial partners, workmates, affectionate sibling figures, or several of these, an affair need not disrupt that bargain. Those ties are for some solely sufficient to hold them. Both spouses gain enough compensation from wedlock to live with the idea that the husband's extramarital affairs will continue.

The woman who feels that her identity comes wholly from her

husband is apt to cling to the marriage at any price. Historically, women who knew their economic and social options were limited were unwilling to challenge their husbands directly. Lack of skills and general economic dependence kept them quietly frustrated or surreptitiously vengeful. Today, women are less restricted.

The Indirect Approach

Trying to pique their husbands' interests again or to create new bonds or obligations for them, some wives react indirectly. I heard about the following patterns, and the results they typically engendered, from all three groups interviewed. The wives may have another child against a man's wishes, make changes in their appearance, or act more seductive or sexual. Extra weight gets shed, routine sex lives are infused with new techniques or attitudes, lovers taken, husbands' girlfriends befriended and attacked. I have heard about a number of telephone games played by wives trying to frighten or harass other women and vice versa. Minor improvements help minor infidelities or those based solely on a man's temporary personal or business problems. But it is not the cure for any significant attachment.

Advertising which subtly tells a woman, "You're inadequate, should be better, must watch out, make him happy," sells a lot of sexy clothes, vaginal deodorants, and makeup. But these things cover up, never reveal what troubles the couple has. The cementing factors between the spouses must be explored in depth with communication techniques. If not already practiced by husband and wife, these techniques are best learned with professional help.

No profound outside love affair is going to be permanently affected or relinquished because a wife gets thinner, learns to enjoy oral sex, or buys new clothes. And getting pregnant never improved a poor man-woman union. For instance, Christine's husband, who wanted her to travel with him, merely resumed seeing other women after she had her third child against his expressed desires. While such plans may keep the marriage intact, they do nothing to halt his interest in lovers.

Another response to a philandering husband is to take a lover of one's own. According to a recent *Cosmopolitan* poll,* 50 to 70 percent of married women surveyed have had lovers during their marriages. (The majority of these may well be independent actions on the women's parts rather than reactions to unfaithful husbands. The survey didn't distinguish.) Women, especially if they feel they have missed out on this during single days, now want the freedom to have a broader range of sexual experiences, up until now an exclusive male privilege. The vengeful affair often makes a wife feel desirable again or that she is getting even. Nonetheless, it does nothing to improve her difficulties with her husband.

All these generalities have exceptions. One wife who did turn to another man told her unfaithful husband, "I think this is working out fine. Why don't you just keep on with your thing and I'll do the same with mine." He immediately ended his other relationship and supposedly remained faithful. This solution is not necessarily going to work with any other man and woman, especially if the man is in love with someone else; nor does every woman have this wife's controlled behavior. An individual couple's method of interacting is the only factor determining what will work for them.

Occasionally, "indirect" wives find out the other woman's whereabouts and befriend them to satisfy curiosity, gain their loyalty or, in rare instances, take on their identities (the reverse of the girlfriend's seeking to fuse with a wife). Curiosity, and the wish to threaten them, are more common motives for seeking out girlfriends. A wife may want adultery evidence** in states without no-fault divorce. Otherwise, confronting the other woman can hurt the wife badly. If the girlfriend is much younger, more glamorous or accomplished, feelings of inferiority and jealousy may develop. On the other hand, when the wife finds the other woman unappealing, she is usually angry or hurt at the unworthy competition.

None of the knowledge gained in secret investigation is useful in

*Linda Wolfe, "The Sexual Profile of that *Cosmopolitan* Girl," *Cosmopolitan*, September 1980, p. 264.

**The justice system is peculiar. To get adultery evidence you must break and enter, which is illegal, but the evidence obtained is admissible in court.

improving the marriage, either. There are painful surprises, especially if the wife finds out her rival is a man. Detective Lerner informed me that a significant portion of the husbands he investigates are bisexual. Feeling she cannot compete with a man or cope with the fact of her husband's dual life, a wife's reaction is frequently violent.

There are rare exceptions when a woman can accommodate to this fact and continue having a workable relationship at home. One who did adjust expects her husband to go off for a week every few months or so to spend time with a man. For her, the rest of their life together is worth this sacrifice.

Compromise is part of the indirect approach. Many told me they felt it was more gratifying than doing nothing and less risky than confrontation. A wife willing to pay the price of her roundabout methods might decide they are the least harsh alternative. She probably senses that her husband uses the affair to keep some part of himself from her exactly as he uses her as an excuse not to commit himself to his lover. He may not even be aware of these factors; but if his wife is, she can determine the best means of handling her problem.

The Direct Approach

"Direct" doesn't mean hitting him over the head with a rolling pin and demanding the details of experiences in bed with his girlfriend. That is great for those ready for the divorce court. Women who believe their marriages have a chance, or realize they themselves have changed, perhaps become complacent, argumentative, and so on, or who know they cannot live with the duplicity that exists, or who plain want better than they have got, confront their men. Occasionally a wife imagining her husband's having deep or multiple relationships discovers a single superficial or brief interlude that he has forgotten or regretted.

The optimum result of a husband's extra love interest is to alert both concerned parties to conflicts in the marriage. Unaware of these, or unwilling to face them before now, husband and wife can initiate a new kind of dialogue between them. According to my survey, no matter how painful the information, examining conflicts usually leads to a resolution or more comfortable accommodation.

When a husband discloses the information himself, the chances for mending the marriage are considerably enhanced. It indicates his wife is still his confidante and that he believes in their relationship. Unless he is on his way out the door, the confessing husband obviously wants to improve things with his wife and considers himself partly or wholly responsible for the event. The other woman the husband tells the wife about may be unimportant, but her presence in his life can signal the beginning of a series of liaisons unless the couple works through the conflicts that have brought this situation about.

If a wife gets the man to talk about his girlfriend, they may be on the road to a solution. The only description of his lover that matters is his. It provides the clue as to what quality he needed from her. Looks are rarely the significant attribute. They attract, but they don't hold men (or women). Therefore, whether his description is literally accurate is less the issue than how he sees the other woman.

Assume the man doesn't come to his wife with any admission and she fails after several attempts to get him to discuss it. The best observations of professionals and wives indicate that the vital thing is to avoid panic. A wife's highly emotional or vengeful behavior ends up being destructive to her rather than her husband. Explosiveness continuing after the first shock or impact always makes her feel worse about herself when it is over.

The constructive approach, even if a wife decides to say nothing to her husband, is to focus on what is happening in their relationship. That is most easily done with a competent professional. He or she possesses more objectivity than family or friend, though the comfort of both is invaluable at this time. Even if the couple wants to divorce, it is best to discuss their problems with a marriage counselor, psychologist, or psychiatrist. He or she will have a better grasp of the focal issues involved after listening to the couple. If the wife must go alone, it can nonetheless help her to explore her feelings, her situation, needs, and goals before deciding on her best course of action. In the event of heightened emotions, an impartial expert can be of significant help.

Even if a husband is not willing to go for help, and psychotherapists tell me it is usually the husband who refuses, a wife being counseled can initiate changes in the relationship which may lead to the resolution of the crisis. Often the one on the couch is not the spouse most in need of help. People who refuse their partner's appeals to work on themselves are from the school of "Learn to lie to yourself and let your partner pay the shrink." A woman may ultimately have to choose between adjusting to her spouse's extramarital life or leaving the marriage.

That was Jo's dilemma. She was devastated when, at thirty, with two children, feeling like the perfect supportive wife and mother and helping her husband in the carpet business, Jason announced, "I'm in love with someone else but I love you too." Jo felt even worse after finding out that Jason's lover was a neighbor with a gorgeous figure. Jason then wanted to forget the whole thing and agreed to end the affair. He never understood when, after that, Jo was melancholy, sad, withdrawn, or nervous if he didn't come home on time. But he promised to be faithful.

> I always felt that a little of his heart and soul died with the relationship. But I didn't look like Karen or wear the bikinis and all. I used every fighting trick there was. He liked a sexually aggressive woman. I did what he liked, aggressively and more often.

Still, Jo felt destroyed and realized she could not trust or rely on Jason.

Her suggestion that they see a marriage counselor together was refused. Jo began noticing other negatives in their marriage. Even though Jason telephoned more often to let her know where he was, she began to think for the first time about what she wanted for herself.

Her best friend told her, "You can't depend on this character.

You'd better take care of yourself and find out what you can do." Though Jo had gone to college and studied English literature, she never thought of working full-time. She began considering journalism, studied the format of magazine articles, and tried to write a few herself.

In the year before she sold her first article, Jo went back to school to study journalism, continued playing sports with the kids, entertaining, taking care of the house, and helping Jason in business. "The anger churned and bubbled. I had all of it to propel me, to give me new energy, I could go nonstop forever."

Within a few years, several more of Jo's articles appeared in print and she thought this should have made her happier. When she began therapy, she learned that in her work she was as anxious as she was in her marriage. Beginning to write about the lighter side of politics and politicians was a thing she had never done before.

> As I became more successful professionally, my sexuality went down to nothing. I didn't even think about it, certainly not with Jason, because I was still too angry. The children were getting older and didn't want the parenting as much. I didn't understand that, but I still ran the household, did the shopping and laundry and cooking.

Jo found it difficult to believe that the newspaper job she was offered a few years later was real. She took it and perceived that Jason was growing more competitive. This conflict was even clearer when the children became teen-agers. Jo tried not to neglect her husband. She continued going out with him socially even when she was exhausted, and having sex though she didn't really want to. "You try to be that supportive person for your husband, but it doesn't work because you're either not treating yourself right or you're lying. I didn't know where my feet were planted. I was just like a lost lamb."

An unusually time-consuming assignment increased Jo's pressure: husband, children, work were all tearing her in different directions. She realized much of the pressure came from sacrifices made on behalf of an empty marriage. Finally she spoke to Jason.

> "We're certainly living different lives than we used to. We're not close anymore." He felt it was my lack of interest in sex, but I explained that sex was only part of the whole relationship which wasn't working. "We never talk to each other, even when there is time." He got very serious and said, "Did you know I tried as hard as I could to fuck your best friend but she wouldn't do it."

Jo asked Jason to go into therapy, but he refused again. She insisted he leave the house because she felt she couldn't trust him ever again. He talked and talked until he persuaded her to share their house and lead separate lives because he couldn't afford another place to live at the moment.

He wanted, after a few weeks, to talk to Jo about his new girlfriend. Jo refused. Jason kept asking Jo for advice on business and his new social problems until she realized he had always treated her like his mother—the one responsible for all his needs.

Jo continued working hard but still felt nothing inside, emotionally or sexually. Once, when Jason was particularly needy and kind, Jo went to bed with him but still felt nothing.

> I was enormously depressed. I thought that maybe I was being unfair to him, so I tried to give him pleasure but I felt nothing, not like a woman. I went back to my therapist, who said, "Why are you punishing yourself?" In a few weeks I was okay.

Suddenly everything changed for Jo. She was talking to a man at her newspaper office who told her, "You're very attractive."

> When he said that, it was the day I started to feel differently. It was like somebody put the key in the keyhole. There it was—myself. I felt like a woman, very turned on, very sexy, after a

man only looked at me and said a few words. From that moment on, I was a whole person.

Soon after that, Jo went away to a conference she was covering and met her first lover. She had been a nineteen-year-old virgin when she married Jason. There had never been another man.

I considered my husband creative in bed and we had an excellent sex life for a long time. But this was an entirely different kind of experience and I was surprised at the timing and choreography. He was very gentle. I felt like the most gorgeous Persian cat—the way he stroked me and all. It was totally easy.

Jo's newspaper work got better as she became interested in men and sex again. At forty-three, this whole woman almost didn't know the unhappy wife of ten years before.

I'm not recognizable. Part of me stands back and looks at the other part. I'm in awe of the person who gets up at press conferences and asks questions, who talks with senators, etc.

By listening in on Jo's phone conversation, Jason soon discovered his wife's sexual episode. Though he had had several affairs himself by this time, Jason was livid. "You ought to know something," he said. "I fucked your best friend on June eighth and I said I went over to take her to dinner."

I would have liked to kill him and her. She was my closest confidante. I have not seen her since. She is out of my life and I'm surviving nicely. I have almost a surgeon's ability to just cut off something that doesn't work. When I think of her, I quickly channel my thoughts away.

Jason and Jo are in the process of divorcing. Now financially independent and emotionally secure, Jo is her own creation. The nineteen-year-old passive virgin didn't get the happily-ever-after with the prince. She is learning the "happily" with herself and whoever will play equal partners.

Jo responded to the first danger signal in her marriage by trying to get Jason to a marriage counselor. When that failed, she decided to prepare herself for a future without him, understanding that his infidelity was symptomatic of problems in their marriage and not the issue itself.

Something in Jason's attitude warned Jo that there would be a repetition of this experience and that Jason's refusal to get help indicated his lack of interest in solving the difficulties between them. She developed herself instead, learning a satisfying profession and gaining insight about herself in therapy.

By the time the second painful jolt came, Jo, then forty-three, was able to handle it. She saw her loneliness within the marriage and tried to dissolve both those things. She could have accomplished that sooner and less agonizingly by insisting Jason move out earlier or only stay if he would go for professional help. The one very right thing Jo did was take control of her own life, face Jason and, more importantly, herself.

Like so many wives in the stories I listened to, who are frightened and seemingly dependent on their husbands, Jo fared well in her new life. Her change meant a willingness to give up the old image of Mrs. So-and-So in favor of a new, self-defined person. Dr. Paul Olsen observed to me that women who let go of the union voluntarily succeed far better than those who hang on to shattered marriages or the ones who never give up on them, even after the divorce is finalized. Most women, though, find unexpected strength within themselves during and after the divorce.

Of course, confrontation with a husband does not always lead to divorce. And when he admits his infidelity he is not necessarily asking for some kind of permission. It can be a request to rid himself of guilt and start things afresh.

That is how Lila saw it when Ronny told her about the affair he had had during his business trip to Hawaii. His fling had been over for several months and Lila felt that a sexual diversion was bound to occur at least once in a twenty-five-year marriage such as theirs. But Ronny didn't tell his wife about the next involvement, which was neither short nor a fling. Lila suspected something from the way he interacted with their accountant's assistant but, never a confronter, she said nothing. When the distance began to widen between them, Lila told Ronny, "You seem depressed. I get a feeling of animosity from you. Is it another woman?"

"Yes, and I must get out of our marriage."

Lila was astonished but had always had a strong self-image, much of which she had gotten from Ronny. After pausing, she said, "Go ahead." She explained to me,

> I had always thought our marriage couldn't be better than it was. In twenty-five years we had never had an argument. I felt that this crisis had nothing to do with me. Ronny and I had both gotten married young and he was probably having a mid-life crisis. If he felt being free was better for him, I would try.

Lila didn't push Ronny out the door or ask who the other woman was. She tried to talk to him about their problems, but he continued to be distant during the three months he was trying to decide when to leave. He finally did leave, none too eagerly. This married couple continued to date and speak daily. One night Lila asked Ronny if his other woman was the accountant's assistant. "I had something with her," he answered, "but my current woman is much more special. You don't know her." Ronny explained that this other woman brought out emotions in him that Lila never did.

> What a fool he is. He'll never do better than me, I thought. I wouldn't have had the guts to clear the air except I felt it was all his problem. I knew I'd been wonderful in bed and out. He was much more fragile than I. I had been the equilibrium between us, the equalizer. I knew that he had been emotionally

nourished by me. If I had to lose him, though, I decided I'd be okay.

I felt Ronny was looking in the wrong direction for what was missing and that the whole thing was one big sadness for him. I guess I thought, "He doesn't know what love is. He's searching." The only time I was really angry was when I realized later that I was out of town taking care of some business he asked me to do while he was home with her.

Two months later, when Ronny decided it was over with his special lady and wanted to come home, Lila insisted that he return only after he saw a therapist for a while. Ronny went for a short time, began cancelling appointments, and then stopped going altogether. Lila understood that the therapist must have been touching on delicate issues that Ronny could not cope with. She went into therapy herself, continued to see her husband, but would not allow him to come home unless he really worked on himself. Back to the therapist went Ronny. Lila remembers:

> I felt that if we didn't stay separated and get the truth out, we would waste more of our lives. I can't live any other way than with the truth now. I don't have the patience. I realize I've had tremendous needs of my own, like demonstrative love, I ignored. I got tired of living a phony reality. Ronny was content to go back to the way we were, but I wouldn't do it.
>
> I also knew that if he really loved the other lady, he would have divorced. It was an affair. I spoiled his fun by getting it all out in the open.

For nearly two years this couple stayed separated while Ronny was in therapy. They continued to date, and Lila, who had never worked, began working for a travel agency. After a year, she opened her own agency with a friend. Lila felt stronger every day. She had a short affair of her own, still continuing to see her husband.

Finally Ronny demonstrated to Lila that he had grown in therapy and come to understand his problems. Lila found out that the women Ronny was attracted to were all very dependent types He obviously liked taking care of them, which he had never had to do with his self-sufficient wife, even though it was he who had taught her self-sufficiency.

These two people have just moved back together. Their relationship is more open and passionate than it was before the rift. Lila has told Ronny about her own affair. He was far from happy with the news, but they both feel they have the truth between them at last.

Recently Lila telephoned me. Her voice sounded like that of a woman who had just taken a new lover. "Can you imagine what it's like to have an affair with your husband after twenty-five years?"

Lila believed in herself and Ronny. The way she confronted him— "You seem depressed. Is it another woman?"—demonstrated her concern with their own involvement and not the specifics of his outside sex life. Clearly, this couple shared a degree of intimacy before Ronny's detour, because he was able to discuss his most personal experiences with Lila.

Like many sensitive wives I met, this one didn't want to nag or act paranoid so she denied her first suspicions and smoothed things over. Any marriage without an argument in twenty-five years must have had two skilled "smoothers-over." Eventually, though, Lila faced matters squarely and was not afraid of the consequences. "If I lost him, I'd be okay." This from a woman who, at the time, had never slept with any man but her husband, was very much in love with him, and had never worked. She was willing to be a whole well-run island or learn to be one rather than remain part of an ailing empire.

The most productive move Lila made was insisting Ronny see a therapist. Though she continued to share things with him and maintained their sexual relationship, she stuck to her demand that he find out the underlying motive for his affairs. The closer the husband and wife are emotionally, the more willing they are to repair the damage. If Lila had been less secure, she would not have admitted that their seemingly perfect long life together had its unexpressed discords.

Her calm reaction may not necessarily be a reflection of what she was feeling, but it was a deliberate decision to do what was best for their relationship. Confronting Ronny angrily would have made him defensive. She realized that none of us can control our emotions but that we can control our behavior. Lila may not have even wanted to let Ronny move out, but she knew that asking him to stay would worsen matters.

Psychotherapists who deal with love triangles every day emphasized that women who do not panic handle these crises best. Many go for professional help and try, like Lila, to ascertain the focal issues connected with their husbands' infidelities. With or without their husbands, these women can handle their own fears more effectively once they are expressed and examined with someone else. The issues become less those of blame than of the couple's relationship. Wives who do confront their husbands calmly to explore their feelings about the marriage, affair, and each other, do learn much more about the situation than those who launch into the subject at the moment of those first charged emotions.

Dr. Rinzler noted that, "If a man admits an affair out of a true desire for openness in the marriage rather than sadism toward his wife or a desire for absolution from his 'sin,' he is likely to consent to marriage counseling or therapy. Whether the goal of therapy is to save the marriage or gain clarity about the outside relationship, these men may seek honesty in the affair more than those who remain furtive about it. Also, men who admit affairs may see their wives less as punitive, maternal, authority figures than those who do not. The men who are honest tend to see their wives as equals with whom a dialogue is possible."

Even when the wife goes for therapy alone she may find out a great deal about herself and her husband. The denying husband is naturally a more implacable problem. When a woman knows she has a philanderer on her hands and cannot get him to discuss or admit to his behavior, she needs to decide whether or not she can live with his infidelities. If she cannot, and decides to divorce, creating a network of support systems in her life will make the whole transition easier That means increasing her social circles, finding (dare I use the word?) *meaningful* work, and generally diversifying her sources of gratification so that she is not dependent solely on one experience or person for everything.

The consensus among wives, husbands, and therapists seems to be that outside affairs do not improve marriages although they can stabilize existing ones. A woman may stay married or not. If she understands the basis of her marriage she can better cope with the conflicts she faces. The solution for one is wrong for another. But knowing her options allows the wife to proceed with a sense of control over her life.

Luckily, today's women have real identities beyond those of their husbands. They are individuals, whether their self-images include jobs or some special interest or involvement. Middle-class divorced women, even those in their sixties, are far better off financially and emotionally than they were a generation ago. In fact, several therapists agreed with Dr. Rinzler that, "divorced women tend to guard their hard-won independence carefully, and are judicious about entering new relationships or marriages."

Some of the mothers leave children with husbands now to get their careers going, to test their independence, or because it is a better all-around decision for everyone concerned. (In fact, an increasing number of women who left their homes and children have formed groups to work through their common problems. One such group currently meets at U.C.L.A.)

No one can make an informed judgment about what is right or needs changing without knowing the reality of—the actual needs and possibilities of—his or her own life. The same complex factors of any interpersonal relationship may constitute a bad marriage for one person and an ideal one for another. Practical decisions can only be arrived at by grasping the related issues. The marriage partners are usually too close to them to judge these objectively, but consultations with experts seem generally to prove fruitful and emotionally economical. They will get to the truth faster.

The truth is heady stuff. It is not for everyone. But after a glimpse of it, illusion, for most, is a tedious landscape.

Conclusion

TODAY'S SHARP break with past customs means a difference in what marriage represents to women. It is coming closer to the same function it has always had for men—a structural reference instead of an exclusive, binding focal point in their lives. Likewise, the concept of extramarital relations is constantly evolving; right now it has a less serious connotation than it used to. Three-way attachments sometimes become stable and even open—where the wife knows of and accepts the situation, however reluctantly, rather than ending the marriage.

As divorce becomes commoner (could it get commoner?), there will not only remain the present willingness to sever relationships but also a greater caution toward marriage in general. More people are creating live-in arrangements,* marrying later in life or at a later stage of development, having fewer children and, before making the union legal, understanding the bases of their marriage contracts—the expectations and possibilities of fulfillment on both sides. Additionally, there is an emphasis on honesty and intimacy

---

*The number of unmarried couples living together has doubled since 1970. Susan Jacoby, "Couples Who Live Together," *McCall's*, June 1978, p. 82.

before marriage which should prevent a good deal of the agony later on.

It is a time when women are deriving pleasure from each other's friendships as never before. Maybe it is a matter of necessity, but together we are opening up intellectual and emotional vistas ignored in the past, forging business networks, and discussing money and politics in the same way men always have. These days, single women prefer an evening with another woman who is interesting to a date with a boring bachelor. That is a big change from the time when the single woman felt obligated to accept dates with men in order to fulfill the imperative to marry.

Listening to the three participants in different love triangles is a little like watching *Rashomon*. Each person's point of view sounds more or less valid.

To a lot of people, affection, whether emotional, physical, or both, is as vital as food. If they cannot get it where parents and books taught them to, they get it from where they can. For single women that may be, increasingly, married men. While two single Mr. Wrongs do not make a married man Mr. Right, it seems enough disappointments can lead a woman to someone else's husband, especially if he is attentive, appreciative, and enthusiastic. Also, a growing number of women who have no lesbian relationship do form strong connections with each other, sharing living quarters and expenses rather than living alone.

The majority of people in this world still want long-term partners. Most do marry. As women's economic independence becomes the norm, marriages and love relationships increasingly resemble real *alliances* that include the sharing of more roles. When fewer men bear the entire burden of a family's economic well-being, and more are willing to divide the privileges derived from that "burden," many will be able to develop the tenderer sides of their personalities. As they contact these tender feelings, it is hoped they will act out conflicts differently than they do now. Communication between the sexes should improve overall.

Obviously, married men now have more action than they can handle. Wives seem to have no trouble finding lovers. Gays have all sorts of places to meet each other. It is only single and divorced women who still complain there is no one to share insomnia and New Year's Eve with. I guess all the good ones . . . but then:

Barbara was excited about the week ahead. She had just been made a partner in her advertising agency. At thirty-eight, she had financial security and was considered one of the best art directors in the business. Best of all, Carl, the man she loved, would soon, it seemed, be hers. Nine years of waiting and he had finally gone back to the therapist who had told him seven years ago to divorce. His children were finally all in college, and life at his home was getting impossible, even for a martyr such as he. The dream that everyone called her a fool to pursue was coming true.

She had taken a week's vacation for Carl's visit. "Where would you like to go?" he asked.

"Let's stay home." "Home" would be theirs soon and Barbara was determined to make the week perfect. Carl didn't know she had redecorated her apartment since the last time he had visited her city. And in the midst of a very big campaign for a new client Barbara had spent every night making all the foods he loved and filling her freezer with them. She even got her friend's grandmother's recipe for strudel.

As she handled the impossibly delicate filo dough for the first time, Barbara thought how little men knew of these things women did for their pleasure. Her first strudel. It was good, but she had used too many layers of dough. It had to be perfect. The next day Barbara went back to the Middle Eastern bakery and bought new filo leaves, shopped for new ingredients, and repeated the whole process.

"So what if I haven't had children?" she thought. "I have a wonderful career, terrific friends, and will soon share the ongoing intimacy of a perfect, private love—the kind every woman dreams of."

Barbara cleaned with the cleaning lady to make sure she got every nook and cranny. Her dearest, married friends, who wanted to meet Carl, had delayed their trip to Europe by one day so they wouldn't miss him. Carl would come in on Friday afternoon. He could rest and lie in the sun while Barbara prepared dinner. She had also arranged the use of a friend's secluded country home for the two of them on Saturday and Sunday.

During her lunch hour on Thursday, Barbara went out and had her hair cut the way she knew Carl loved it. When she got back to the office, her private phone rang. He always seemed to know just when she walked in.

"Hello."

"Hi, darling. Just one small schedule change."

"Yes?"

"I'll be coming in on Sunday instead of Friday." Barbara couldn't believe her ears. "It's my daughter's birthday . . . I completely forgot."

"But what about dinner on Friday, my friends, the whole weekend?"

"What can I do? You know there'll be hell to pay if I leave before Sunday. You know how much I want to. . . ." After that, she heard nothing.

The screen of Barbara's mind was suddenly full of other birthdays, anniversaries, Mother's Days, children's graduations, his wife's skiing accident, his nephew's nervous breakdown, a cousin's wedding, and on and on. They were always her disappointments and ruined plans. She hung up the phone without saying a word. Barbara picked up her coat and told her secretary she would be out for the rest of the afternoon. Her private phone was ringing as she left her office.

Barbara walked out into the street where men and women with licit relationships hastened to homes, appointments, jobs. Only she moved slowly, without direction. "The king is dead," she thought. Carl had done it to her just one time too many. All the years of pain came back in one huge lump which she couldn't swallow. She looked into the faces of the men in the street—those men she had ignored for nine years. They looked friendlier, more sensitive, lonelier than she remembered.

After Barbara and I talked, I recalled that only two of my single women friends had married in a number of years. During the 1980 New York City transit strike, one was given a ride uptown by a fascinating, unmarried professor of Near Eastern studies who got nearer over the next six months. They have just wed. Another friend married the thoughtful neighbor who brought her an extra shovel while she was digging her house out of a Los Angeles landslide a couple of years ago. But strikes and landslides are simply not dependable.

And most people are not built for long-term aloneness. Getting married is one way to go which often doesn't work out. Someone to hug and kiss and share inner thoughts if not loving sex with is more important to lots of people than doing the "right" thing. How long to wait alone for Mr. Right is a question many women are confronting . . . and concluding it is not necessary to be lonely when so many apparently loving married men are around.

But Barbara said she would not go that route again. An attractive, accomplished woman, she was strict about her "bachelors only" rule for ten months. Last month, I saw her having a drink with a man who was wearing a wedding band. The next time we had lunch, I asked her about it.

"I thought you had new rules."

"I did."

"What happened?"

"We're only friends," she answered, in a mock naive tone.

"Isn't it always like that?"

"Yup." Barbara gathered her briefcase and handbag.

"Is he that much better than the single ones you've met?"

"Even better than that."

There was a sympathetic silence on my part as we walked out of the restaurant onto Third Avenue. Barbara was proud but knew her needs.

"I've missed being with a man who matters," she said softly, kissing me on the cheek. I watched her walk away.

"What happens after drinks, lunches, and the always-too short afternoons?" I called after her.

"I'll jump off that bridge when I get to it," she yelled back.

Barbara may not have to. Fortunately, bachelors still walk dogs, go to cleaners, supermarkets, and unisex hair salons. And everyone is acquainted with some modern matchmakers—they are a single woman's best married friends who know a marvelous guy who is just separating . . . "He's not ready yet, but when he meets you, it won't matter."

According to the last U.S. census, there are currently over seventeen million unmarried men over the age of twenty living in the United States. Presuming half of them are "eligible" (the other half are explained in Chapter 1), that still leaves three or four possible compatible bachelors any woman ought to be able to find. It is a competitive sport. But then there is no point worrying about *all* the good ones. Even if most of them are married, the cheery truth is that if he is really good, it still only takes one.